The World Needs Dialogue!

Six: Your Organization Needs Dialogue!

Dialogue
Publications

This edition first published in 2024

Dialogue Publications
The Firs, High Street, Chipping Campden Glos
GL55 6AL UK

Typeset by Ellipsis, Glasgow, Scotland

Ordering Information:

Quantity sales – Special discounts are available on quantity purchases by libraries, associations and others. For details, contact the Special Sales Department at the address above.

The World Needs Dialogue! / Six – 1st ed.

Classifications:
UK: BIC – Society (JFC): Cultural Studies and JFF: Social Issues)
US: BISAC – SOC000000 Social Science

ISBN Hardback: 978-1-7384072-2-4 ISBN
ISBN eBook: 978-1-7384072-1-7

Printed in Great Britain and the USA

On the Cover:

The cover graphic of a tree, including its roots, trunk, branches and leaves, is a metaphor for any organization. It depicts the complexity of organizational structures and processes that sometimes makes it hard to see how every part is connected and interrelated to every other part.

Contents

DAY ONE
What is Dialogue?
Why Does Your Organization Need Dialogue?

DAY TWO
What is Dialogic Leadership?
Why Does Your Organization Need Dialogic Leadership?

PART THREE   145
Plenary Conversation:

Hosts:
Harold Clarke (USA) – Academy of Professional Dialogue
William Isaacs APDP, APDPA (USA) – Dialogos

DAY THREE
What is Dialogic Decision-making?
Why Does Your Organization Need Dialogic Decision-Making?

PART ONE   163
Panel Conversation:

Hosts:
Peter Garrett APDP, APDPA (UK) – Dialogue Associates and Academy of Professional Dialogue
William Isaacs APDP, APDPA (USA) – Dialogos

Panel:
Mine Bolgil (UK) – Air bp
Laura May Brown (USA) – Virginia Department of Corrections
Marcus Reisle (Switzerland) – Swiss Agency for Development Cooperation
Efrain Jimenez (USA and Mexico) – National Network of Mexican Migrant Federations and Organizations in the United States.

DAY FOUR
What is a Dialogic Culture?
Why Does Your Organization Need a Dialogic Culture?

DAY FIVE
What are Multi-Stakeholder Dialogues?
Why Does Your Organization Need Multi-Stakeholder Dialogues?

Trustee's Foreword

The theme of the sixth conference of the International Academy of Professional Dialogue was *Your Organization Needs Dialogue!* This publication captures the collective thinking of over 200 participants from six continents in the five-day online conference.

What a bold theme and position to take, some may opine! There are leaders and members of organizations throughout the world who might disagree with the selected theme, even considering it a brazen and unsupported statement. I have had many conversations with leaders and their colleagues who do question the value that comes from introducing dialogue into their organizations. For them, it is something that they may consider when the time is right and there aren't pressing issues needing more attention. They seem to be so focused on operations and outcomes that they choose not to take the time to investigate dialogue and its potential benefits – not realizing that dialogue would help improve their operations and be instrumental to their success. People, including leaders, often simply do not know what they do not know, and they are not skilled at inquiring how to discover the unknown – the very outcome that dialogue would help them achieve.

I was impressed with the diversity of organizations that participated in the Academy's sixth conference, including national and local government, educational, commercial and non-profit organizations with varying missions. Experienced individuals (23 of them) with key roles in these organizations participated as panelists during the conference. Their contributions are included in this book, and their perspectives deepened the enquiry into the different aspects of dialogue considered each day. Many are members of organizations in which dialogue is routinely practiced. Others did not yet have regular organizational experience of dialogue but shared their positions on their perceived value of what dialogue could bring to their organizations, along with implementation challenges and concerns regarding sustainability. The overall view was that the introduction and sustained practice of dialogue in their organizations would certainly improve their culture.

Discussions on dialogic leadership and how dialogue helps to create the right culture to get desired results were among the many topics considered during the conference. In dialogic organizations the voices of all staff are welcome and encouraged, leading employees to feel valued and willing to share their opinions without feeling vulnerable. They choose to be empowered, significantly improving morale and the generative culture of the organization. Ultimately, in my view, the state of health of the culture will determine the degree to which that organization achieves its goals and objectives.

During the conference, much was said about the role of the head of an organization, and whether it is possible to have a dialogic organization if the leader is not fully committed to dialogue. You will see the variety of views expressed in the excerpts from the Participatory

Dialogues held each day that are included in this book. Organizations can be difficult to manage and operate in a seamless fashion that benefits the whole organization and its intended outcomes. By their very nature, these complex constructs are often fragmented, with interdependent activities disconnected from one another and adversely impacting the entire organization. Dialogue is a proven response to diagnosing and addressing organizational fragmentation.

In the 1990s, while serving as the Director of a state correctional agency, the Nebraska Department of Correctional Services, I was first introduced to dialogue. After attending a series of dialogue trainings over the course of a year, I became convinced that dialogue could help my department achieve the results I was seeking. I introduced dialogue into that system and secured dialogue training for all senior staff and those at headquarters. I subsequently moved several times to become director of three other state correctional systems, eventually retiring from the Virginia Department of Corrections late in 2023. Given my experience in Nebraska, I felt compelled to introduce dialogue into each of the three systems almost immediately upon my arrival. In Virginia, I went much further by extending the dialogue training from senior leaders through to every employee (over 11,000 people), and eventually the dialogue training was made available to inmates.

It was Bill Isaacs and Peter Garrett who first introduced me to dialogue. In introducing dialogue into all four correctional systems I led, I called on external input from current members of the Academy, Peter Garrett and Jane Ball, who are highly skilled and experienced in dialogue. They were instrumental in implementing dialogue in the Virginia Department of Corrections and helped to develop many practical applications that are now business practices. The external support I received to introduce dialogue was critical, and the International Academy of Professional Dialogue was formed in order to assist other organizations to introduce dialogue in a similar way. In 2022, the Virginia Department of Corrections received the distinction of being recognized by the Academy as a *Dialogic Organization*.

I had the privilege of leading four correctional agencies. Did they need dialogue? Yes! and each benefited significantly from introducing dialogue into their operations. Initially there was skepticism, then curiosity and ultimately wide acceptance was realized. I credit dialogue with helping to change the cultures of these state agencies and consequently improving the operations. They were able to realize outcomes not previously achieved, including leading the country in many areas of correctional performance. Highlighting this, it is on public record that the Virginia Department of Corrections (where I was Director from 2010 to 2023) has had the lowest or the second lowest rate of recidivism of all statewide systems in the USA for the past eight consecutive years.

I highly recommend that you read **The World Needs Dialogue! Six:** *Your Organization Needs Dialogue* if you want to see the potential benefits that dialogue can bring to your organization.

Harold Clarke
Trustee of the Academy of Professional Dialogue and
Former Director of Virginia Department of Corrections

Editor's Introduction

The Academy's annual international conference *The World Needs Dialogue!* provides an opportunity each year to take stock of the progress of the Academy. The non-profit charity held its first conference in 2018 under the theme *Gathering the Field*, deliberately basing its approach on David Bohm's Implicate Order ontology. At that conference, there were far more advocates for dialogue than there were experienced practitioners able to provide guidance. Indeed, many had rarely, if ever, convened a dialogue and they came for the opportunity to have a first-hand experience of dialogue for themselves. The experience of participating in dialogue is an important aspect of the annual conference, and in our sixth conference, we continued to incorporate Participatory Dialogues for everyone to deepen their experience of dialogue with people from different cultures across the globe.

The sequence of conference themes in subsequent years caption the developmental story of the Academy, purposefully progressing from *Setting the Bearings* to *Shaping the Profession* and *Putting Dialogue to Work*. With the 2022 conference, we broke new ground with *Dialogue as Story* by both simplifying David Bohm's notion of pervasive fragmentation in human consciousness and revealing how that fragmentation comes about in unnoticed ways as we make sense of things. By then the Academy had held a series of consultations to determine an educational curriculum for professional people to learn how to use dialogue, and the Academy was providing accreditation programmes and quietly growing a community of Accredited Professional Dialogue Practitioners (APDPs). This added a new function for the conference by providing a forum where experienced practitioners could present their work to have it reviewed by their peers and then published to affect society more widely.

In 2023 the Academy further defined its direction and purpose with the theme *Your Organization Needs Dialogue!* This theme acknowledged that we live in an era of organizations, where almost everything is determined in or by organizations – including our births, health, food, education, employment, transport, finances, clothing, government, safety, entertainment and funerals. To ignore organizations is to ignore the opportunity to influence the decision-making that affects us all. Yet many advocates of dialogue deliberately separate the practice of dialogue from any kind of decision, let alone organizational decision-making. In this regard, the Academy has distanced itself from the part-time philosophising kinds of dialogue and moved to an emphasis on the deliberate use of dialogue in people's working careers and professions.

The online conference *Your Organization Needs Dialogue* ran over five consecutive half-days with over 200 participants from six different continents – with only Antarctica lacking representation. Within the overarching consideration of dialogic organizations, each day had a different theme. Participants explored the nature of dialogic leadership; the kind of dialogic culture it aims to generate; how that facilitates the joined-up making of decisions; the wisdom, enjoyment and ease of working dialogically; how and why introducing dialogue into any organization helps to improve the flow of outcomes; and the impact of introducing dialogue at the interface between multiple organizations that are interdependent (such as in the criminal justice system) despite being led, resourced and measured separately. These considerations were rich in robust theory and examples of practical application.

The conference sessions were co-hosted by Jane Ball, Harold Clarke, Bill Isaacs and Peter Garrett. Each day they named the theme for the day and introduced a panel of four to six experienced practitioners who further primed the conference with first-hand stories of their work in settings like the United Nations, Mexican presidential politics, carbon-neutral aviation fuel, food co-operatives, university campuses, union negotiations, prisons and multi-stakeholder re-entry councils. There were plenary sessions, short breakouts to meet other participants and Participatory Dialogues with 10 to 20 participants in the middle of each day. These were co-facilitated by experienced practitioners, 26 of whom were Accredited Professional Dialogue Practitioners (APDPs).

Harold Clarke provided dialogic leadership for four large organizations during the past three decades, most recently in the Virginia Department of Corrections from which he retired as Director a month before the conference. His inspiring Foreword for this book is therefore of special note. He currently serves as a Trustee on the Board of the Academy of Professional Dialogue and chairs the Academy's Professional Standards and Accreditation Board.

Debi Lethem of Ellipsis designed the cover and did the typesetting, as she has for the previous five books. Finally, I would like to acknowledge Helena Wagener APDP who has helped me with the editing of this and the previous two books. We have found a quiet and effective way of working together, and we both appreciate the additional learning afforded to us by working closely with the written records from the conference. We try to respect the fine distinctions between written American English and British English, but given we so often have speakers of both tongues co-facilitating the same session, this is hardly possible.

Peter Garrett APDP, APDPA
Editor, Dialogue Publications

Hosts

Jane Ball: *(UK), Dialogue Associates and Academy of Professional Dialogue*

Acting as a consultant, intervenor and thinking partner, Jane has been bringing Professional Dialogue into commercial, government and not-for-profit organizations internationally since 1999. Almost imperceptibly she enables discordant groups to collaborate, whilst visibly helping people to learn new skills and leading them into new ways of working together. Her latest initiative takes dialogue into primary school class-rooms in Iran, South Africa, Argentina and the UK.

Harold Clarke: *(USA), Academy of Professional Dialogue*

In his 50+ years of experience working as Director or Commissioner in four different correctional systems in the United States, Harold Clarke has continuously committed himself to cultural change. On his appointment as Director of the Virginia Department of Corrections in 2010 he introduced staff training in dialogue for over 11,000 staff members by 300 internal Dialogue Practitioners, and saw the culture improve, performance levels rise and recidivism plummet.

Peter Garrett: *(UK), Dialogue Associates and Academy of Professional Dialogue*

Peter's new book *A New Kind of Dialogue* details how his work has shaped the development of Dialogue over the past 40 years, from the early conceptual insights with theoretical physicist David Bohm to the founding of the Academy of Professional Dialogue. During that time, as a pioneer, advocate, consultant, educator and patron, he has introduced dialogue into hundreds of teams, organizations and organizational systems.

Bill Isaacs: *(USA), Dialogos International*

For 30 years Dr William Isaacs has served as a leadership advisor, educator and architect of systems transformation for CEOs of start-up and global corporations, fund managers, development professionals, national policy and political leaders and prime ministers. By raising the level of collective leadership, he enables people to access their collective intelligence. His book *Dialogue: The Art of Thinking Together* is a classic in the field.

TWND! 6: Your Organization Needs Dialogue!

DAY ONE

What is Dialogue?
Why Does Your Organization Need Dialogue?

Just over 200 participants from six different continents gathered for the Academy of Professional Dialogue's sixth annual conference that was held in the Academy's online Conference Centre during the week of Oct 30th to Nov 3rd, 2023. The themes were different each day but interrelated. The first day was an enquiry into the questions: *What is Professional Dialogue?* and, *Why does your organization need Professional Dialogue?* The four conference hosts were Jane Ball, Harold Clarke, Peter Garrett and William Isaacs. They paired in different combinations to host each of the five days, with Peter and Jane hosting the first day.

The day had three parts each of 70 minutes:

PART ONE

The first was a plenary session. Everyone gathered in an online room with occasional small-group breakouts so that individuals could engage with other participants. The main activity was the spotlighting of a panel of four experienced dialogue practitioners to hear about their experiences with dialogue in different organizational contexts.

PART TWO

Primed by the panel presentations and plenary conversation, for the second part of the day, participants were divided into seven different rooms to give everyone the chance to talk and continue thinking about the theme of the day. People chose to join one of seven Participatory Dialogues, based on short descriptions of them in the Conference Centre and written by the co-facilitators prior to the conference. These sessions were co-facilitated by skilled dialogue practitioners, most of whom had been formally accredited by the Academy as Accredited Professional Dialogue Practitioners (APDPs). Each Participatory Dialogue had between 10 and 25 participants.

PART THREE

For the final part of the day, the entire conference reconvened for a plenary conversational session, co-hosted by Jane and Peter. The aim was to harvest some of the experiences and thinking that were emerging for participants and the members of the panel.

This pattern of activities was repeated throughout the conference, with each day having three parts as outlined above.

DAY ONE

What Is Dialogue?
Why Does Your Organization Need Dialogue?

PART ONE

Plenary session with a panel of four practitioners

HOSTS

Jane Ball APDP, APDPA, (UK) Director, Dialogue Associates and
Trustee, Academy of Professional Dialogue

Peter Garrett APDP, APDPA (UK) Director, Dialogue Associates and
Trustee, Academy of Professional Dialogue

PANEL

Parveen Daeipour APDP (Iran) – Endless Path of Dialogue Institute

Patty Hawk (USA) – Nebraska Wesleyan University

Jon Steinman APDP (Canada) – Heddlestone Village Cohousing

Carrie West-Bailie APDP (USA) – Virginia Department of Corrections

Jane Ball:

I welcome you to our Sixth Annual Conference, which has the title: *The World Needs Dialogue*. This year we're focusing on *Your Organization Needs Dialogue*, and we'll spend the next five half-days looking at that. I'm Jane Ball, and this is my colleague, Peter Garrett. I'm one of the Founders and Trustees of the Academy of Professional Dialogue, which is a non-profit educational charity set up to inspire, inform and upskill people to use Professional Dialogue in their work, and in their organizations and communities. So welcome! People are still gathering. We have over 200 people registered for this conference, so people will be dropping in over the next few minutes from their part of the world. Some of them will be waking up, and some of them will be winding down as their day moves towards evening and night.

I hope you all enjoyed the music we started with. It's from an organization called *Playing for Change* and they bring musicians together from across the world, people who use their skills and their passion to promote the use of music to make the world a better place, as the song says. I thought it offered a good beginning because it's very similar to the mission of the Academy. Whereas they think that the world needs more music, which I agree with, we really believe that the world needs more dialogue.

Peter Garrett:

Good morning, good afternoon or good evening, depending on where you are in the world. We are stretched right across the globe. as you will find out. I can see some familiar faces. Welcome back! Good to see you again from recent conferences, and from further back. Others of you I have not had the chance to meet before. I look forward to it. Welcome.

This year we're focusing on organizations and why organizations need dialogue. I should explain why we chose that theme. Why, organizations? You might not have noticed how dependent we are on organizations. With almost everything we do, from birth through to death, organizations of different kinds are involved. Our homes, our water and electricity, our clothing, our roads and transport, our education, our jobs and our money. All these ways involve organizations! In the UK where I live, there are over 3 million registered organizations. I don't know how many are not registered, but the number registered illustrates how much of the world is run by organizations. So that's one thing. Organizations are pervasively widespread. I think ubiquitous is the right word. They're everywhere. You can't do things without them.

The second point is that organizations are fragmented. In small organizations, you have 20 or 30 people and you can all meet in one room to talk about what you are doing and name the challenges that arise, and then you can think together about them and work out how you're going to do things differently. When you get a bit larger, it's no longer possible to stay aware of what everybody's doing. One reason for this is specialisation. Specialisation leads people from different parts of the same organization to think differently. In finance, they think differently from manufacturing, in sales from compliance, and so on. The second thing is location, and being on different floors in the same building, being in different parts of the same complex of buildings and being in different parts of the country, in different countries or even different continents. This makes it very hard to stay aware of what is happening and how people are affecting you, and you them. A third really big factor is hierarchy. People in more junior roles in an organization and people in more senior roles may live in very different worlds. They may not understand each other's needs and aspirations. We have to accept that although organizations are inherently fragmented, we are dependent on them, and they are very widespread.

What we therefore want to do over the next five days is to understand organizations and understand how Professional Dialogue makes a difference. We want to explore how organizations function, how joined up or fragmented they are and how they work. That's why we have this overall theme.

Jane:

Each day also has a theme about how your organization needs dialogue, and they are the five elements that we think are the most relevant to managing organizational life and the kind of experiences that we all have every day. We'll start today with the generic questions, *What is Dialogue?* and, *Why does your organization need Dialogue?* Rather than trying to sell you Professional Dialogue, we want to understand in more detail and learn from our own experiences of what organizations are like, and why Dialogue could make a difference. Tomorrow we'll go into leadership, asking, *Why do organizations need dialogic leadership?* and explore the question of what dialogic leadership looks like, as opposed to other kinds of leadership. On Wednesday we'll go into, *Why do organizations need dialogic decision-making?* I can see some of you sitting at your desks in your workplaces. I wonder how many decisions you make every day sitting at that desk, how many people you work with, and how many of those decisions are being made together. On Thursday we go into culture and ask, *Why do organizations need a dialogic culture?* and then finally, on Friday, we look at the need for *multi-stakeholder dialogues.* I think you'll find there are lots of interconnections, and that one day will build into the next.

Today we start with this question, *What is dialogue?* What does it look like and why would it make a difference where you are? The day itself has several parts. We're going to start with a process where you can meet a couple of other people by putting you into breakout rooms. Then we're going to have a panel where a few people will talk about their experience of dialogue and bringing dialogue into their organizations. After the panel, and following a break, the second part of the day is much more experiential. You'll be in a smaller group of around 15 people, and able to see everybody on one screen. You can talk and think together with them in a co-facilitated Participatory Dialogue guided by a theme.

You should already be booked into your Participatory Dialogue. The third and final part of the day is a plenary session when we all come back together. At that point, we're anticipating there will be 100 to 200 of us gathered to talk and think together about what we're discovering and learning – what's standing out for us about this thing called Dialogue.

We do have a little bit of etiquette about participating in this conference. We want you to be present and attentive. We all spend a lot of time, I'm sure, on audio-visual calls and it's very easy just to mute or turn the camera off and do a few emails when it gets boring or when you can't concentrate. However, we really want people to be **present and attentive** throughout. This creates a different kind of listening and a different sort of atmosphere together on Zoom. But also, importantly, we are going to use breakouts. If you put your video camera off and go to make a cup of coffee and whilst you are away, we put you into a breakout room, then the person that you're paired with will find that you're not there and they have nobody to talk with. So please keep your camera on. If you must be away because something happens, then actually leave the Zoom room and later just come back in. If you can't be **present and attentive**, then rather leave the Zoom room for a little while.

Peter:

Yes, we're encouraging everyone to behave like we would if we were all in the same physical room together. Your concentration will affect the room, and the atmosphere in the room online as well. We'll have a much richer experience this way.

Jane:

So, who is here in this room? We have just over 200 registered participants from 19 different countries, I believe, and six continents. As Peter said, we have people here that we've known for many years, and who are very experienced. We have some of the world's most famous authors on dialogue here with us at the conference, and many people who are just starting out on their journey using dialogue. That's a big range of experience. We also have our own Accredited Professional Dialogue Practitioners. You'll see some people have APDP after their name. That stands for Accredited Professional Dialogue Practitioner, and many of the Participatory Dialogues you go into will be led by our Accredited Professional Dialogue Practitioners, along with a few of our other very experienced members and associates. You will also come across Trustees of the Academy. As well as me and Peter, there are four other Trustees present here. Furthermore, we have what we call Associates of the Academy, people who have formal roles in different ways. Again, as you can see, we have a wide range of participants here. If you find the profile section in the online Conference Centre, you will be able to see photographs of everyone and you can find out more about who's here, and maybe identify some of the people you would like to meet.

Now we have the chance for you to meet a couple of other people. This is the moment to turn on your camera, if it is not already on, and to turn off your mute because everyone is going into a breakout room with two other people to introduce yourself to them. It will be down to the Zoom algorithm who you will end up with. When you get into your room, just introduce yourself. Perhaps your name, your physical location and the name of the organization you work for, and then maybe a comment about what led you to come to the conference. So, name, location, organization and what led you to come? You have 5 or 6 minutes for this.

Participants went to break-out rooms for 6 minutes and then returned.

Jane:

I'm hoping you enjoyed that chance to meet a couple of other people! Now we're going to move on to our panel on today's theme questions, *What is Dialogue?* and *Why does your organization need Dialogue?*

The four panellists joined Jane and Peter, and they were spotlighted so that everyone could see just six people.

Patty, Parvin, Carrie and Jon. Very good. Welcome. This is our first panel of the week.

Jane:

Maybe we could start the same way, *Who are you? Where are you? What's your organization?* Could we hear just that from each person? Why don't we start, Jon with you?

Jon Steinman:

Sure! Thank you, Jane and Peter. My name is Jon Steinman. I am located in Western Canada, specifically in the city of Nelson, British Columbia, and the organization that I'm most familiar with engaging in dialogue is the organization that I also live in. I live in a co-housing community. It's a model that we borrowed from Denmark, and I've now been living in this model of co-living for nine years, and I've been involved with the organization for 11 years. What's unique about our co-living development is that we manage the housing and the property together. We don't hire a company outside to do it for us. This involves the unique form of not only working with each other but also living with each other.

Jane:

Let me just bring the others in, so that we hear from everybody briefly – where they are, what their organization is – and then I'll come back to you with a more difficult question.

Patty Hawk:

Hi, I'm Patty Hawk, and I am located right in the middle of the United States, in Nebraska, where it's very cold and windy. Today I'm a professor of communication studies at Nebraska, Wesleyan University.

Parvin Daeipour:

I'm Parvin from Tehran in Iran, and I'm a clinical psychologist, and an Accredited Professional Dialogue Practitioner as well.

Carrie West-Bailey:

Good morning, everyone. My name is Carrie West-Bailey, and I am the Dialogue Co-ordinator for the Virginia Department of Corrections and an Accredited Professional Dialogue Practitioner. I'm excited to be here! I am looking forward to today's conference.

Peter:

I'm Peter Garrett, in the heart of England, in The Cotswolds, in the UK. I could choose several different organizations, but I'm going to choose my role as a consultant.

Jane:

What is dialogue? This is our first question, but I think it may be more useful to start with the second question, *Why does your organization need dialogue?* I've been working with Dialogue since the last century, since 1999, when I began my career with Dialogue. Over that time people have often said to me, *How do you sell Dialogue? How do you get people to do Dialogue?* That is advocacy. – explaining what dialogue is – and please do advocate that people do it!! But I think it's much more interesting to start by asking what organizations need, and why organizations may need Dialogue. Maybe we could hear from each of you. What's one thing that your organization needs, where you believe dialogue can make a difference? What's the organizational need where dialogue makes a difference? Let's hear from everyone.

Peter:

I'm thinking of a man I worked with who has been very successful. He now has 40,000 people reporting to him as the CEO of a very large organization. When I worked with him, he had a staff of less than 5,000 people. He brought together the national product distribution organizations into a single European organization within a global company. Every month, he brought together the leaders of each of the 11 countries involved to meet with him. The culture in that global organization was such that when any leadership team met, the expectation was that the CEO told them what was required and what things had to happen. As one of the leaders you expected, in the meeting, to get clear about what your part was, and what you had to do. You were expected to report on how well you were doing and to try to hide the things that weren't working so well, or at least to demonstrate that you had a plan to deal with them. That, in his view and mine, was not a high-level way of operating. It depended on the CEO making all the decisions and everybody else following.

We turned that around during the first six months. When they met, decisions were not relayed. Instead, decisions were made in the room with everybody present. They were made based on proposals put into the group, *I'm thinking we should do this. What do you think?* and the whole group talked about it. Long reporting sessions stopped, and, instead, reports were circulated beforehand, or handed out with the key points highlighted, but to be read at another time. The questions in the meeting were, *Why? What should we do, and when? How are we best to address these challenges and these needs?* The quality of thinking together, and the quality of decision-making went right up. They all knew exactly what was involved. They left fully informed and thinking about how to proceed. There was no attempt to get buy-in. They created the solutions together. Few decisions were remade. It took time. It took three days every month. That group of 11 national leaders plus the CEO and his assistant in one room around one table for three days every month. Actually, it really took them a week. The monthly meetings were hosted by a different country each time, and they would fly in on a Monday and leave on Friday. That leadership team was phenomenally successful. And they had great fun. They enjoyed being with each other. So, what's the one thing they needed? I think leadership needs dialogue for high-quality decision-making. Not depending on decisions coming from one CEO, not sitting in the room trying to work out what answer that CEO wants us to tell him or her, but actually thinking together, contributing to and helping to shape the best answers. It was not acceptable to sit in that room and say, *I agree with the CEO.* Other team members wanted to know why, *What's your view?* So, I believe it's collective leadership decision-making that is fundamental.

Jane:

I'm not going to go into that further right now. I'm going to bring in other perspectives first. I think we'll come to you now, Patty. You're in a different situation, in a university.

What's one thing needed there?

Patty:

As I've been preparing to discuss why our organization needs dialogue, I was reminded of a conversation that I had with our Director of Diversity, Equity, and Inclusion in 2019. We wanted to bring our campus together in dialogue. Three things motivated that.

First, like many university faculties, we had a tendency to fracture into resentful enclaves when there was a crisis, and we hoped regular dialogue would help the community build trust and relationships.

The second was about the system that we had to address bias incidents on our campus. At the time, what happened was that the community member reported the incident to the bias response team. The team then reached out to the accused and the accuser, but the broader community was not brought into that learning. Oftentimes members of the community had witnessed this sort of bias incident, but confidentiality made it impossible to talk about it. The effect was to inspire suspicion. We hoped that regular dialogues would offer a chance for the community to discuss issues outside those specific incidents and that we would talk about things like race and racism, gender fluidity and reproductive rights.

The third motivation was to have conversations between colleagues from communication studies and the other departments. This would limit the tendency of the administrators to reach out to have a Dialogue only when there was a crisis. So, we hoped to nurture a culture of dialogic engagement on our campus that could foster trust and build relationships across university boundaries.

We started our Civil Discourse project in the spring of 2021. We averaged about between 25 and 75 faculty staff administrators and students, and in these dialogues, we made several helpful decisions at the beginning. For example, we trained student facilitators and when students facilitate the dialogues, anxiety goes down and people become sort of more generous with what they're sharing. All faculty staff administrators and students were invited to participate, but no one was required to participate. That's been very important. We created a routine so that people get comfortable with this habit – one dialogue a month, same time, same place, same set-up. We have snacks, and we never go over time. After the dialogues, we sent a survey, an anonymous survey to everybody who participated to see if we were meeting the needs of the community, and what we almost always get is positive responses. We get a lot of people saying thank you. One of the staff members said that having such a large group join and demonstrate openness to the discussion helped them to feel comfortable. The last dialogue we had in October was on gender fluidity. I sent out an email reminder, and I received a response from one of our adjunct instructors, who's also a trans man. He thanked us for opening a space to have that kind of conversation, which is exactly what we were hoping would happen. We hope we are productively building a habit of turning toward the community rather than fracturing apart when we come into crisis.

Jane:

Again, I could go into an enquiry with you, but I'd like to bring in everybody first. Let's hear from, Parvin. You say you're an organizational psychologist and a Dialogue Practitioner. Could you choose one of your clients' organizations and tell us what they need?

Parvin:

Yes. One of the organizations that I work with is a private insurance company. They have about 2,000 employees. What I have found is that one of their main problems is the poor communication between the leadership and the body of the organization. When I'm talking about poor communication, I mean that when they work together, the leaders just think about the result of the work and how people should do the job. They don't think about the people. So, they don't have good communication. Because of this environment and culture, everybody thinks that they should just do their own job, and it doesn't matter what happens in other sections. This is a kind of fragmentation that we've seen in the organization. After I offered some Dialogue training to the body of the company some of the people could find their voice. They realised that they could say the things that they are thinking, their ideas and the things that they think about the organization. Before that, they did not have a voice. They couldn't speak their thoughts and because of that, their participation in the job was just a matter of, you know, just obeying instructions or orders. Finding their voice was very important, and I was so excited for them that they learnt how they could use their voice, with attention to the other practices. Now they can, and they can say whatever they think it is necessary to say in their work environment. That was a very great experience that I had there.

Jane Ball:

Very nice. Thank you. Carrie. What about you? Please bring your voice in.

Carrie:

Well, my story's a little different. Mine is about the history and the culture change in a large organization, the Virginia Department of Corrections. I started at the Department in 1996 and, obviously, many things changed over the years. But I think the biggest impact was when we had our Director come into the Department of Corrections. When he got here, he basically said that we're going to start with Dialogue. We're going to create a Healing Environment. That was not the culture at that time. Correctional officers believed they were in a small role, and they were to be seen and not heard. Orders were barked. It was a command-and-control environment. As we started hearing Director Clark's ideas, we all saw a really large change in the culture. Previously we never knew about anything that was happening. Creating a strategic plan was something that as a line staff you didn't know anything about. You just came in and did your job. You weren't engaged. You didn't ever see a Captain or a Lieutenant. If you did, you knew you were in trouble. You didn't ever see a Warden, and if you did see a warden, you were scared because you thought you were going to lose your job. The differences from the change? It was a culture change that impacted the whole department by first allowing people to find their voice. People listened to you. Being in rooms you were never invited into before. It just changed how we thought about our jobs. If you read Forbes Magazine, that's one of the things that keep a new generation of employees, they feel that they're valued, that their voice is heard and that they're a part of something purposeful. So, redefining our purpose, and really understanding how important it is to make people successful. Creating an environment where people can treat each other in a respectful, ethical way. Not being in an environment where you feel as though you're going to be treated unfairly. I think the culture is very important.

Jane:

Thank you, Carrie. Jon, we started with you. Can you say more about your situation?

Jon:

What's unique about the organization into which I bring dialogue is that we're voluntary. None of us are paid to do what we do, but at the same time, there is a requirement to keep our organization functioning. In order to hold each other accountable, ten years ago we developed what we called a Participation Agreement, that outlined what we expected of one another. My first experience with dialogue and bringing it into our community was just under three years ago, in 2020. We participated in a dialogue on Zoom, and it was quite effective, as I am sure we will find working with dialogue in this format over the course of this conference. What was unique is that we wanted to explore our relationship to participation. We posed a question to our group, which was, *What does participation mean to you, and what might it mean?* We started with a smaller group of people having a dialogue, that we all witnessed. That first question, I think, really spoke to the importance of dialogue, and why my organization needs it. The question that was posed to everyone was, *How do you feel when you read this question?* It gave us an opportunity to drop into something more than just what we think, and into what we were feeling. What emerged was a unanimous feeling among the first group of people speaking together that when they read that question, they felt a sense of guilt that had been there for all the years that we had been living and working with each other. Within this really important core agreement, there was a relationship everyone had to this idea of participation that was one of guilt. If we fast forward to just 45 minutes later, we could recognise through the contributions of everyone in the room, that the participation was different from what we had been experiencing for all those years. One person remarked that for them, participation isn't showing up and doing. XY and Z. It's simply being here and being present. To which everyone agreed. That led us to recognise that for all those years we hadn't been using the word participation in a way that we all believed and felt. We have since turned the name from the Participation Agreement into our Responsibilities Agreement. Participation is now something very different from what we had always done. It's important for us as an organization, and for any organization, I think, to be able to find the space to question the structures, the ideas and the beliefs that are already in place so that we can evolve and change.

Jane:

We've done a couple of rounds and heard from each person on our panel. Before opening it out, I want to say what I'm hearing. One thing is the variety of organizations. Between you, you are talking about two commercial organizations, a university, a governmental correctional organization and a voluntary community organization. All with quite different structures and intentions, I guess. Then the needs described are everything from leadership's ability to make good decisions; in the University making things discussable, that otherwise are not, yet deeply affect people; communication between different organizational silos, and between levels of hierarchy where more junior people can't speak openly to the levels above them, (and I notice that when you have military ranks like Lieutenant and Captain it makes it feel stronger somehow); and then about participation and what it actually means for people in your community, Jon.

I now want to open it up for you to raise whatever you choose. I was trying to draw out what each one of you was looking for, and what the things are that you have in common. I noticed something about routine. Everyone talked about some kind of routine with the dialogue that you're bringing, be it a monthly meeting on campus or a regular meeting for your client. Peter, for you it was not just a one-off event, it is something that was working on a continuous basis. But beyond that, I'm wondering what happens in this dialogue process. Patty, you bring people together on campus once a month. You have snacks. What goes on in that dialogue? How many people will be there?

Patty:

Well, we average around 30, but we've had as many as 75. We always start out with a short video clip or tutorial from a faculty member. We prefer a short video clip because tutorials from faculty members can go on a lot longer. So, we usually show about a four-minutes clip of a video. The whole idea is that there will be people who will join this conversation who literally have no idea about the topic. Take *gender fluidity*. We'll have people in the room who will say, *That means what?* So, we show a video that updates people so that they feel somewhat competent, and then we put them into small groups that are facilitated by students. That's for 20 or 25 minutes. Then we pull them into a big group for about ten minutes to see what came up. We don't ask questions like, *What did you learn in your small group?* because we don't want them reporting out. Rather we ask questions like, *What's still sticking with you that was talked about?* They might respond, *I was listening to Jon talk about participation* or *I was listening to Carrie talk about how the culture shifted and what it's done.* It's helped people relax into difficult conversations, which is what we're hoping – not just those conversations in the dialogue, but any conversation on campus so that they can take a breath and move into difficult conversations.

Peter:

What's interesting is that your groups are voluntary, and people choose to come for different reasons. Much of my work has been with people who don't want to be there. If they are in the leadership team, they can't say, *I'm not interested in being there.* They are obliged to be there. So, I found quite a big issue is, *How do you help people want to be there, even though they have to be there?* If they don't have to be there, it's hard to get the tough nuts, the people who really are not interested, and who are not going to shift if they never come into the dialogue.

Jane:

Interesting question. From Patty's comments, there was an openness about what you feel. what you think, the relaxing of things to be able to say it and not feeling like you would be wrong to say what you really think would feel.

Carrie:

That requires a level of trust to be built amongst your teams and creating a space where people can start to get acclimated to opening up. I think people know that container development is very important in organizations, especially when you have so many different stakeholders inside of your organization – let alone how you reach those who are outside of your organization. Bringing in those many stakeholders, including dialogues with inmates.

Peter:

So, are you saying you trust them all, including all the incarcerated people, and because they all trust you and you trust them, you are able to be in dialogue?

Carrie:

I believe that you can trust the process, and you can trust people to be themselves and have high expectations of themselves and others. I think that one of the things that we do with inmate dialogues is to try to build up their understanding of what the dialogue process is. A lot of people think of dialogue and the English language as a form of communication yet the work, the spirit of dialogue, is working on yourself. Working on yourself internally allows you to communicate with other people differently. So, giving input and information to individuals who are incarcerated, allows them to have a space. That is number one. I'm not seeing you as the inmate, I'm seeing you as an individual. I'm not the judge and jury. I can't go back and try you for whatever your charges were. I see you as a human being, allowing you the proper amount of respect – not just the Aretha Franklin version, but putting myself in your shoes. So that impact makes a difference when we're talking with inmates and teaching them dialogic skills. What has happened over the course of time, with offering Dialogue Skills Training to inmates, is that it changed the culture of the location.

Peter:

I know I was talking about voluntary, and I think participation has to be voluntary, but often it doesn't start that way. Are you going to get trust between different nations at war with each other? If you need trust before dialogue, you may never get it. Perhaps it's more about respect. Respect for the history and the background of everyone involved. Even though you may not trust them, you've got to talk together and work this out. I think a lot of dialogue is based on the idea that first, you must have trust, but then we can't get into the tough stuff. What do you think?

Jon:

Well, I appreciated what you what you shared earlier. In a lot of these spaces, it's a voluntary opportunity to dialogue, and of course that's the case with us. For us, it's been an interest group. When you mentioned the word, you know that there are tough nuts in the community who might be resistant to coming to our dialogues. What I've witnessed over the two-plus years we've been doing this is that there's a slow level of comfort in stepping into what we're doing, and that's been consistent from the folks that have now been doing it for years quite consistently. But those who are coming in always seem to leave our dialogues feeling better than when they came in. That stands out for people, because up until having this as a mode of communication, generally, we would leave meetings feeling exhausted, tired, spent or unfinished. I've always likened the experience of being in our dialogues to yoga. Everyone feels great after yoga. I know I usually do. And this is kind of like yoga for communication. Afterward, I feel lighter. I think part of what's happening is that through dialogue we're depersonalizing a lot of the communication and also putting equal emphasis, not just on what's being said, but on how things are being communicated. We slow down and spend time looking at how we're communicating with each other. For us, this is critical because so much of what we do is consensus and decision-making, and everything we decide affects everyone in more than just a professional way. It is in our homes as well.

Peter:

Parvin, organizations are often seen as efficient ways of getting stuff done, including selling insurance, processing insurance claims and so on. It sounded like your Dialogues are about humanising the organization. Is that relevant to what you're doing?

Parvin:

Yes, exactly. Exactly. I want to emphasise that. Dialogue is a new behaviour. You can't just have a short course and be sure that people have learnt how to do it. So, the follow-up sessions are very important. We have a monthly follow-up session to practice dialogue together, and to realise if we are ready to respect everybody, whomever they are, and whatever they have. *Am I ready to listen to people? Am I ready to be myself?* We need time to see the impact on the organization, to see the impact on the relationships and on the structure of the organization. One of the important things, as Carrie said, is developing the container. The container is very important, and the container is made by people. So, people come to understand that they are responsible for a safe and strong container. Dialogue needs time in the organization, you know, to change people's minds, to set the way that they work and to begin a new way of looking at other people and looking at themselves. I believe, as Jon suggested, that dialogue is a kind of meditation. You must be careful about the way that you use dialogue, and it needs time to be embedded into the organization.

Jane:

Let's keep our audience on its toes. Bobby, we've had the chat closed as part of our process to keep everybody present and attentive. Maybe now we could open the chat up, and just invite our audience to put any questions that they have into the chat. so that then we can share them.

Take a moment and think to yourself. *What are you hearing? Do you have a question, or a comment you'd like to make?* Then put the question to our panel, and maybe we could share a few of those. First, just be quiet for a moment and wait to see a few other people's questions and comments and read them.

A lot of your questions are about the container in different ways. Particularly about respect and trust. I've thought about trust. The difference between how much you trust people and how much you respect them. It's quite hard to keep track of reading the comments when more appear! Have you found one that you'd like to answer, Carrie?

Carrie:

I think that there was a question about trusting inmates, and I want to explain what I mean when I say trust in the inmates. I think that people don't recognise that it's not about

trusting them to keep you safe. Although I think that it's very important that there's trust, it's not trust that we need to have a dialogue. We could have a dialogue, as Peter mentioned, with difficult individuals, about how they aren't willing to participate in the dialogue or don't want to be there. But you, as a facilitator or practitioner have to trust. And start with a conversation about the process of what dialogue is, and how you can shift. This step requires that the person who's facilitating has a particular skill set. Then, you also need to trust that you will find some resolution, even if it's something small, even if it's something that gets other people interested enough to be engaged. That begins the trust. When we talk about the container part with most leaders we can ask, *Why do they have people that don't trust them?* One, it may be because they haven't ever shown any vulnerability. People change how they perceive you when you show them some vulnerability. I may be the person that's at the very top, but when I have a conversation with you and open up a platform for you to be able to speak – and for me to talk to you on a one-on-one engagement especially if it's in an area where you can ask me questions – showing vulnerability is a lot. So, trust has to be developed in the process.

Jane:

We're trying to open up the thinking, so, whether you put an idea or a question in the chat or not, take your thinking into the next session, which is participatory and where you can talk as well as listen.

My question is, *What are the preconditions?* If a precondition is trust, we have a lot of people who may not have it. If a precondition is that it is voluntary to attend dialogues in organizations some may choose not to go. It may not be so much that we need trust, but we need people who want to be there. The question is, *Are we held up by preconditions?*

Peter:

Sometimes people don't like each other and don't want to work together, but they are bound together in organizational situations. They are trying to get out of the mess. This is what, kind of provocatively, we've been opening up to go further into right through the day, and to talk about when we come back.

Patty:

I love the idea we're thinking about preconditions! *Are there preconditions for me?* What I think I'm hearing from all of you, is that it is the gift of time that allows people to be their authentic self. And that is what we value in a dialogue. You are bringing your whole self, and my job is to open a space big enough for you to find yourself so I don't think it's a precondition, I think what we're trying to do is build a culture where we can nurture.

Jon:

Let me say final comment, *I agree with Patty.*

Parvin:

I don't believe in preconditions always. Sometimes I invite people and tell them, *Just come to my circle and see what dialogue is, and if you don't like it, you can leave, okay?* But always I see that people find something that, for years, they have been looking for. So just by encouraging them to come to our dialogue circle, they can see what dialogue means. It's very difficult to explain. Please come and just see and observe what is dialogue.

Jon:

I would just add that the question of trust is unique and appropriate to our community because we explore the topic of trust through dialogue. Instead of talking about trust, we talked about what trust meant to us. We went into the meaning of the word, and by going into the meaning it evolved into another series of dialogues that were connected to what was underneath the surface of our experience with trust. And that is just another way to describe what dialogue is. It's an opportunity to go behind the meaning, behind the words and concepts that are as important as trust or the word respect. We get to explore what that means. We're not tiptoeing around what we think it means or what we think others are meaning by it.

Jane:

I am left with a big question, *What does this look like?* If we were invited to work with an insurance company in Tehran, I am wondering what happens in insurance companies in Tehran. It's so different in different cultures, in different places, isn't it? So, thank you all. I think, as Peter said, this is just the beginning. Luckily, we have the rest of the week to explore this more. If you don't bump into these guys in any other session, you can contact them. You can send them messages. We have an open lounge before and after, so there are many places in which we can carry on the conversation. We also have four and a half days left of this together. We are really just starting.

DAY ONE

What Is Dialogue?
Why Does Your Organization Need Dialogue?

PART TWO

Seven concurrent participatory dialogues

There was a fascinating range of considerations in the seven concurrent Participatory Dialogues. The sessions ran for 70 minutes and had between 10 and 25 participants who had chosen which session they preferred to attend. The co-facilitators welcomed people and opened with an introduction and a check-in round of comments from each person in the room, followed by an open dialogue for most of the session. Individuals were encouraged to offer their first-hand perspectives and stories, and not to quote things they had read from others. Towards the end of their time there was a check-out, or closing round of comments, that participants understood was being recorded for potential publication in this volume. Some weeks after the conference the co-facilitators were invited to reflect on their Participatory Dialogue and what they had learnt, in the form of a written Postscript. The intention is to show that learning is an ongoing process and that the description of the proposed Participatory Dialogue, followed by the experience on the day, and then the reflection some weeks later all contribute to what is learnt.

What follows is all three sections:

- The pre-conference description of each Participatory Dialogue written by the co-facilitators in advance of the conference and available to participants in the Conference Centre.
- The check-out round of comments made by the participants at the close of the session.
- The subsequent reflective Postscript written by the co-facilitators some weeks after the Participatory Dialogue.

By reading them, and following the transcript of the day's plenary sessions before and after them, it is possible to get a good sense of the depth and breadth that first day's enquiry into the theme: *What is Dialogue?* and *Why does your organization need dialogue?*

A similar pattern was followed for the Participatory Dialogues in the middle part of each day of the conference.

Thumbnail sketches

Thumbnail sketches to introduce the seven Participatory Dialogues that follow:

Thomas Köttner (Argentina) and Jon Steinman APDP (Canada) raised the curious question *What is a Community Without Dialogue?* By the close of the dialogue, this had become a rhetorical question since there was general agreement there cannot be a sense of community without some level of formal or informal dialogue. In the absence of any dialogue, there is a fragmented state, little acknowledgement of the whole and a sense of discomfort when individuals are asked to express their views. What a profound example of why your organization needs dialogue!

Meg Bower APDP (USA) and Tecora Davis APDP (USA) held an enquiry into *What Aspects of Dialogue Help Funnel Change into a Growth Mindset?* They explored how to shift from emotionally charged situations into productive ones, particularly in an organizational context. The focus moved from novel solutions like a *What's your headache?* exercise and recognising 'silent quitters', to meeting emotions with emotions – which requires starting at home with one's own emotional state and deepening one's own container to impact the collective container.

Loshnee Naidoo APDP (South Africa) and Shakita Bland APDP (USA) explored the question *What is Organizational Dialogue – and the Roadmap for a Successful Journey?* using a reflective enquiry into the success of the Virginia Department of Corrections (11,000 plus employees) that is recognised by the Academy as a Dialogic Organization. Emphasis was placed on the need for executive commitment, the involvement of relevant parts of the organization in determining policy and good practice and operational decision-making through the Working Dialogue business practice.

Eddie (Troy) Adams APDP (USA) and Susan Dandridge APDP (USA) offered a simple invitation *Let's Talk . . .* They observed that despite more and more talk through many forms of media, there seems to be less and less talking together. They explored listening to understand; refreshed people's thinking about a genuine *I-don't-already-know-what-you-are-saying* kind of enquiry; and noted the safe and contained atmosphere this generated. Their postscript gives an eloquent exposition of the core practice skills needed to cultivate professional dialogue in any organization.

Elisabeth Razesberger APDP (Belgium) and Qingmian Chen (China) considered *Dialogue Facilitation – Mindset and Practice.* They investigated how to help any grouping of people, within or beyond organizations, to get into dialogue so that people hear each other and have the experience of being heard. Notions of messiness, 'crunchiness', vulnerability, suspension, discovery, respect and authenticity give a sense of the territory they covered in exploring the mindset and practice experienced during dialogic facilitation.

Laura Little APDP (USA) and PJ Manning APDP (USA) asked the more immediate question, *What Does Dialogue Look Like in Our Personal Lives?* There was a remarkable openness and interest in learning from others as people described using dialogue in their personal lives. For example, some chose to reveal their struggles with ADHD, and there was an enquiry into different traumatic responses like fight, flight, freeze and fawn. One recommendation was the simple act of checking one's understanding of what another has said with what they meant.

Leo Hylton (USA) and Wendy Hendrickse (South Africa) advocated *Dialogue: A Pathway Towards Mutual Awareness and Exploring Connection.* By deliberately slowing down the pace of their session, they explored the first-hand experience of an enhanced quality of interpersonal connection. The consequently enriched space helped participants to co-author the dialogue. Some participants were from a command-and-control culture, and that led into an enquiry about the directive use of positional authority vs letting go to the flow of what is emerging.

What is a Community without Dialogue?

Thomas Köttner and Jon Steinman

PRE-CONFERENCE DESCRIPTION

Communities have been fundamental to human societies throughout history, as people naturally form groups to provide mutual support, share resources and create a sense of belonging. Dialogue is necessary in a community because it serves as the lifeblood of communication, understanding, problem-solving and collaboration within the group. To truly understand what Dialogue is, it is helpful to identify the default situation that occurs when Dialogue is not present within a group or community. Identifying these defaults is particularly valuable to a professional who needs to comprehensively scan an organizational environment to determine where Dialogue could be of greatest value. To explore this need we'll base our enquiry on Dialogue within the context of „community" which expresses itself in a myriad of ways, and uniquely so across cultures.

CHECK-OUT

Thomas Köttner:

I saw us all taking notes, and perhaps our check-out could be, *What are our takeaways, our food for thought or our reflections from our circle today?* (the ambiance and climate of which I appreciate very much). Let's take a minute of silence and after that, whoever feels like 'starting the check-out, please do so.

Speaker:

I want to say, we have a concept in our country, or at least in my province in the west of Iran, and it is that 'a day when you are in nature, with the mountains and with the fresh weather, does not count as a day where you age'. It is as if you are not all there on that day – you are not getting older! I want to say that this dialogue experience was like that for me. It had a very beautiful sense that it's me rather than the days or the hours of my age, and I'm not older because of it. Of course, I am more experienced, but not older. Thank you everyone for your participation in this taste of dialogue. Thank you. John and Thomas.

Speaker:

I think the conversation has been an interesting exploration of the challenges of dialogue in community, and it makes me think that there is probably always a form of dialogue within a community. I mean, we need there to always be a degree of dialogue otherwise, there is no community, I believe there are always challenges, and these challenges can be quite severe and quite diverse. There are many different types of challenges in having dialogues, and I think this has been a good exploration of that reality . . .

Speaker:

I follow what you said. That is where I think the focus has been, and not only regarding community because I was also thinking about my own family. We have seven siblings, and it is so hard to come to an agreement on seven different perspectives. So, I think the focus on an outcome, and how it relates to the audience we invite, can play a very positive role in getting the desired decision or outcome, or in reaching a solution that favours everybody. Differences are very important because they paint the full picture of a situation. One person cannot think through an issue on their own in a wholesome way, as there are so many different perspectives that make up that situation and the issue as a whole. Differences are therefore very constructive, and at the same time, when dealing with differences, there is the question of how to bring the problem-solving technique of convergent thinking to reach a decision. How do people converge to a single point, and how do the dialogue facilitators play a helpful role in getting to that point? Of course, it is important that we have the right information to reach a decision.

Speaker:

What I take away from our session is that if we come with an exploratory mindset it generates better results than if we don't come intending to share our views

Speaker:

We are commonly considering the idea of community. Thomas, you mentioned neighbourhoods and communities. Are they the same, or are they different, these areas and communities in each one of our lives? That's where we live, where we work, where we go to school and. where we might have faith-based stuff going on. I would proffer that all communities, no matter where you live, are diverse, at the very least, as each individual has different thoughts, feelings and views about the world. So, if I'm going to think about this down the road in my world, I will move along something that I've already been contemplating but now I might put it into action more. It is to provide training through the re-entry councils, civic groups or in libraries to anybody that's interested, and on a very small scale. We might then grow a core base to learn about dialogue, and we could encourage the development of dialogic practitioners in the community who are neutral, trained and able to lead community dialogues. I'm imagining that our future will always hold situations that are uncomfortable, sensitive, emotional, and thought-provoking. Our world always has such questions. *Should we build this new hospital right next to the baseball stadium?* The last thing that I will carry with me is that whatever happens in a community dialogue, you need to dialogue and there's no pressure to form a solution.

Speaker:

To be completely honest I was dreading the idea of spending my evenings on zoom after my long workdays – but now I'm feeling that this was actually a breathing space for me. It gave me confidence in dialogue. And in slowing things down when we are looking for hasty resolutions to our differences, such as dividing into two camps and fighting it out - or forcing a consensus or giving up on our own ideas because we think that we need consensus. Yeah, confidence is slowing down.

Speaker:

I realised that if a community doesn't have dialogue or a good breathing space, there are reasons that cause the community to stay without dialogue. It may be an unconscious defaulting pattern, or conflicting mindsets, misconceptions, tense attitudes or sticking only to your own information and lacking others'. This helps me to understand that before introducing dialogue to a group or community, I should become aware of some of these reasons and that I may have to do something about them before starting the dialogue.

Jon:

I am happy to check out, and I want to acknowledge and appreciate just how diverse all the takeaways are. There doesn't have to be just one final thread that emerges clearly. In that moment of silence we took to consider the question, *What is a community without dialogue?* what struck me was something someone shared at the beginning. A community without dialogue would be just a group of people hiding from each other. So, what I'm taking from this is a different view of what it means to hide from each other. There's the physical possibility of hiding from each other. But what I've noticed in my experience, and what I was hearing here, is that there's a possibility of hiding from each other by only identifying another as their thoughts rather than seeing the fullness of who they are, and all that they bring. Certainly, in the world before dialogue here where I live in my community, there was a very strong tendency to only recognize people for their thoughts and to identify them with those thoughts. For me, dialogue is a space to open us up, to see more of who we are. This dialogue, in whatever way it took, has led me to see that more clearly. I appreciate that.

Thomas:

I was taking notes. First, I offer gratefulness for this space and to all of you. I realised that when I'm really interested in something and the time to finish comes, it is great when people say, *Oh, no! Why? Why can't we go on?* I was also appreciating the richness that comes from our diversity of places, cultures and perspectives. I take many, many pieces of food for thought and reflection. This has been so interesting and so nice. I feel really good, and as a dream, I would love to continue this dialogue in the nice places I see on the screens behind different people.

POSTSCRIPT

Communities have been fundamental to human societies throughout history, as people naturally form groups to provide mutual support, share resources and create a sense of belonging. Within the context of the Academy of Professional Dialogue, the role of dialogue in communities is a relevant one. The Academy was formed, among other goals, to "inspire people to transform organizations and communities through Dialogue". In this articulation, communities are distinct from organizations.

This participatory dialogue inquired specifically into the default situation when dialogue is *not* present within a community. We used this enquiry as part of the wider enquiry of the theme of day one of the conference, *What is Dialogue?*

Within the dialogue, it was suggested that, regardless of the presence of formalized, intentional dialogic spaces, there are most likely always various forms of dialogue taking place in any community. A conversation among community members, for example, may alternate in and out of dialogue, discussion or debate. It would therefore be an incomplete enquiry into *what a community is without Dialogue* if we did not acknowledge that dialogue is indeed occurring casually. However, the purpose of our enquiry was specifically to consider what a community is without an *intentional* dialogic container. In retrospect, our question might have been worded to be more specific in this regard.

Participants enquired into the nature of community, with some acknowledging community as geographic and neighbourhood-oriented, while others pointed to the presence of community within workplaces, schools and places of worship. No matter the context, there was a strong sense that communities are composed of societal groupings either by choice or circumstance and, regardless of any unifying factors, communities are nevertheless made up of a diversity of individuals with different thoughts and beliefs. The role of dialogue in accommodating this diversity was frequently referenced.

Some suggestions for what a community is without dialogue included:

- Fragmented - individuals thinking independently from one another and therefore unable to fully acknowledge the full picture or the whole.
- Unacknowledged differences – a place lacking information.
- Patterned and tense - individuals hiding from each other.

That led us to enquire further into this notion of hiding from one another, particularly non-physical forms of hiding such as the tendency to avoid uncomfortable topics, and individuals feeling uncomfortable to express the fullness of who they are and how they feel.

We find particular interest in Merriam-Webster's definition of community as a *unified body of individuals*. Using our enquiry into what a community might be without dialogue – in other words. being unable to see the whole, tense, or hiding from one another – we consider the appreciable difficulty in forming or sustaining a community (a unified body of individuals) without a concerted effort to engage in Dialogue. Without adequate spaces where difference and diversity are welcomed, it seems rather insurmountable to establish and sustain unification. Rather, we propose that establishing and sustaining unity around a common interest or purpose requires the revealing of difference. As a contribution to the question, *What is dialogue?* we consider that dialogue is an essential ingredient in the forming, sustaining and evolution of any community.

What Aspects of Dialogue Help Funnel Change into a Growth Mindset?

Tecora Davis and Meg Bower

PRE-CONFERENCE DESCRIPTION

Change is inevitable, but it can be frightening. When people are frightened, they don't often interact constructively together. How can Dialogue provide a path to negotiate the fears associated with change so that there is room for it, but constructive progress can still occur?

CHECK-OUT

Tecora Davis:

Our check-out question is based on our session today. *What might you do differently to bring productivity to an emotionally charged situation?* This is free form so that's why we wanted to ensure that we gave enough time to open it up and have things bubble up within you. Someone was talking about being more solution-focused versus focusing on the buy-in. For my check-out, I agree with that. We still have a job to do, and that's not going to change. So how can we accommodate these changes and move forward? I like that.

Speaker:

Yeah, I agree. Sometimes you have to do a little handholding because different people learn at a different pace. I will attempt to do a little more of that. Keep with the smoothing aspect of reminding folks that it's not personal, but then getting right back to business, which is the ownership aspect. We all need to move forward. This is the directive. And what do you need? Get right to the point. What does this team need to get this done? So, I think reiterating that it is not personal, then honing in on ownership and asking what they need.

Speaker:

I think, I had better think about my own emotions and how to deal with them before I give an opinion or try to get anything done. Make sure I kind of check myself. That usually helps if we don't want a lot of process.

Speaker:

One thing I might do going forward is to make sure that I always understand the "why" when somebody's expressing their concern or their hesitation about a change, to understand really what their issue is about. It may be something that we can talk through and work out. The other thing is revisiting the issue later if it's not a decision they like. See how it's going, see what concerns they still have, and if we can do something to help them with it.

Speaker:

I follow that, I think it is very important to understand the 'why'. That's probably the one thing that I need to work on more.

Speaker:

I'm not a lot for emotions. Luckily the Lord gave me one daughter to help me be a little bit more emotional. I read in a book somewhere that allowing people to celebrate what was, helps them to accept what is to be. Oh, my gosh! You know I don't like listening to a lot of complaining. But I guess sometimes you have to allow people to get it out so that we can focus on what we need to do now. I need to try to do that more.

Speaker:

I was trying to figure out how to identify complaining gossip, when it turns into where it's not just venting but it's actually kind of making a negative impact on people. There is a difference between that and constructive complaint. I need to get away from the complaining and let the dialogue be constructive instead of just negative.

Speaker:

I'm going to listen more because I'm the type of personality that wants to find a solution and give an answer to whatever the problem is that is being brought to me. But sometimes you do have to find that line between letting them vent versus it becoming part of a bitching session where we've got to stop it right there. We can't let it that cross that line. So, I'm just going to say that I'm going to listen more because, just like my probationers, sometimes my staff just need to get it out.

Speaker:

One exercise that I like to do to avoid what you called a bitching session is an activity called What's your headache? Everybody writes on a piece of paper what their headache is. and then we exchange papers. Everybody gets each paper as they cycle around the entire room, and everybody writes a solution to the original person's headache. That way, we're solution focused. You've entered, you have your issue, whatever the issue is about, you have a headache, what's your headache? Everybody writes solutions to that headache, and then you get your paper back. And now you have a list of options to cope with your headache or to battle with that headache?

Speaker:

Oh, that's fantastic. I love that!

Speaker:

I do, too. What I'll probably take back is to my team is student mode. We're constantly learning. Think of it in terms of when you're in college, when you had this subject, that subject. We're constantly a learning organization and do your best to embrace it and own it. I like the ownership piece, too. Then, I'll do my best to meet people where they're at as they are trying to embrace the change.

Meg Bower:

I really like what you guys have been saying about taking a decision and saying, *You know, we don't have to stick with this forever, this can be short term and we can revisit in a few months.* I keep going back to that topic of time, and I keep thinking about something I used to tell my daughter when she was little. She would say, *I can't do it,* and I'd say, *Yet! You can't do it yet. Eventually you'll be able to do it if you keep trying, but don't quit.* I was thinking about that in this context, and about grieving the decision. People might not be on board yet, but if you can get them to give you a chance, maybe you can say, *Look, if you give me your best effort for the next 3 months, we'll revisit the decision. Then you can weigh in again, and we can talk about it again'.* I think that's what I would do and what I would take back based on this dialogue. There was also a thought I had related to trust. I think if you have a really solid container, and you have really good trust, it's easier to get people to buy into a decision that they weren't part of. If you just say, *Trust me this time. Have I done right by you before? Come with me this time. I promise you it'll be okay if there's good trust.* I think they're more likely to come along. So, I think there's something in there about that. You can learn about your group and your team and the trust if they're not willing to come along . . .

Speaker:

Correct me if I'm wrong. What you just said would factor back into the handholding about that person's perspective of what the change is? Would that be correct?

Meg:

I think it goes to the practices, but that could just be because I was thinking about those when I was reminding you guys of them at the very beginning of this session. I think it goes to listening, respect, voice and suspension, which leads to a better understanding of someone's motives.

Speaker:

One thing that I took from this is definitely being solution oriented. I think the best thing I can do is just keep open communication. I've been with the Department of Corrections since March and like in previous jobs I just felt like I wasn't being heard. So, then I stopped communicating, and I turned into a silent quitter. So, I would like to do things differently this time around. How I can do that? Just by being open with my communication and giving everything a fair chance.

Speaker:

I would say that I will just remain the same as I am. I got an award for remaining calm when everything is in chaos. I'm the one who stays calm and everybody kind of gravitates to that. They look to see, well if she's calm then there's really no need for us not to be also. So, I think I will remain doing that. Just remain in calm when there are situations that are emotionally charged.

Tecora:

We do still have a few minutes left. Let's open the floor for comments.

Speaker:

I just wanted to say to you to Tecora and Meg. I think you guys did a wonderful job facilitating this topic. I really did enjoy it, I learned a lot and got to meet some new people. Thank you so much.

Meg:

Since we have a few more minutes, a question for you guys, about the whole idea of change in your organization. If you think back to the original question and how you felt coming into the session, I'm just curious to know if people have a different feeling about change at the end of this dialogue. Maybe you came into this discussion feeling some anxiety and wanting to funnel the energy. Now it feels like this group is very calm, and it feels like this group is settled. I'm wondering if people feel differently than they did when they came in?

Speaker:

Yes, about my anxiety. We did alright and got everybody on board. And I just heard so many good pearls of wisdom to kind of regulate my excitement and pull in people who are frustrated. To redirect. This has been a fantastic opportunity to gain some insight, and I just thank everybody for speaking up.

Speaker:

I don't think my view of change has changed but I do appreciate hearing the insights from other people on how to deal with change, and the methods they use to handle it in their own work.

Tecora:

Yes, I also thank you so much for your important contributions. I was helpfully reminded of how important it is to hear different perspectives.

Speaker:

I have a question, if I may, *What is a quiet quitter? Where did that come from?*

Speaker:

It's been around. I think quiet quitting is that quiet resignation thing that people do. They just sort of fly under the radar until they can change their situation. They call it quiet resignation. People just do what they need to daily but they don't go the extra mile. They don't want to be noticed, either. It's just kind of going along.

Meg:

Yeah, I think it can be used to refer to someone who just does their 40 hours. They just put in their time, and then they leave. It's not necessarily something to fault someone on, because it could be anything from just having proper work/life balance boundaries, to someone who just scoots by, doing the bare minimum.

Tecora:

For us it's been different with different individuals. One could be that they are preparing to leave. Maybe they are burnt out, preparing to retire or just know that they are ready to change their position or path, or perhaps leaving the agency altogether. It normally occurs before their quitting date. What you see is that the person has already concluded that this probably really isn't for me. Right now, I'm over it. I'm done. They still show up to work, but you will see a decline in quality of work and the completion of the task. Sometimes they'll do the bare minimum, sometimes they won't, but they still show up. Those are some of the things you'll see sometimes. Not all the time. Some people work super hard before they leave, so they don't leave a mess as they're transitioning position.

Speaker:

When I transition from one role to the other, as I just did, I make sure I did everything because I don't want to leave a battle for the next person, and I want to stay with the organization. But if you're leaving for good, it may be different and some people won't do anything at all, like she said. They just show up. They'll do just the bare minimum, so they don't get noticed.

Speaker:

I'm in HR and there are studies that classify employees into different groups. Everybody's described by some of the categories, except those silent quitters. They still work for you. They have just silently checked out. So, there is a question of, *How do we get people to stop resigning?* How do we keep people at the Department of Corrections? That's been something that they've been looking at. What kind of employees do we have? And how can we address these issues? But I also wanted to point out how, interestingly, the person who brought this to our attention has only been here at DOC a very short time. And she brought that up. We're finding that with younger employers and new employees in the workplace. They not going to deal with employment like an old head like myself would, who might put up with some things. Younger employees are demanding a certain quality of work-life balance, and if they don't get it they will silently depart. They will depart. They'll take actions that maybe we wouldn't have taken back in our day. So, I think it's important to hear those younger workers so that we can understand their mindset. It is not the same as ours. Her comment was loud for me and because it came from a new employee.

Speaker:

I like that work-life balance has come into question. I think it's a good idea, and I think that's what the younger people are fighting for. It's not a bad idea. I think that in this country, and some other countries, the work side is too much. Then you have countries where there is that balance, and people get the compensation as well as the time off. and they're more productive. The numbers in the studies give evidence that it is better. Germany and some other countries have implemented a better style, and it is more productive. People are getting their results. I know in Germany they measure work by productivity, and they respect downtime and things like that. Now there is evidence as to what works. I think that younger people are coming up with this, and for years the American worker has been a little bit on the other side of that balance.

Tecora:

> Well, that was pretty amazing! We need to finish now. I so appreciate everyone for your participation and engagement.

POSTSCRIPT

This session intended to explore ways in which Dialogue can negotiate fears associated with change within an organization. Our session acknowledged that fear is a heightened emotion commonly paired with change, but that big emotions like fear are not usually perceived as constructive. The discussion moved into ways the Dialogic leader can guide interactions to open a space for emotions around change to be expressed, but also navigate back to productive interactions that encourage growth.

The group accepted that, while emotions in general can have a powerful impact on groups, they are frequently disregarded or ignored in the professional setting. Negative emotions (such as complaining or venting) are perceived as distracting from the mission. Those who express big emotions, even good ones, are seen less favourably, even negatively, in professional settings.

For a dialogic leader, it is important to look behind any big emotions right away by asking good questions to determine the cause. Emotions typically indicate a legitimate concern that needs to be addressed. Some people need to process their emotions before they can be productive, so letting emotional responses into the workplace can allow those individuals to participate at a higher level. The concerns that generate big emotions can sometimes be resolved immediately. If immediate resolution isn't possible, the dialogic leader can schedule a separate time to have a focused dialogue around the cause of those particular emotions.

Whether resolved immediately or not, it is healthier to keep any big emotions in the room, where they can be addressed openly using a dialogic framework. Disallowing emotional expression can lead to complaining, negative gossip, or similar destructive outlets. Team members may quit or "quiet quit" if their feelings are not met, which doesn't benefit the team. Finally, allowing emotional responses (including fear) to be explored openly can make people feel accepted as they are, with big emotions or without them.

Emotion speaks to emotion, so a dialogic leader must be able to engage emotionally, while maintaining control over his or her own emotions. A calm dialogic leader is one who can receive powerful emotions without being provoked into an emotional response.

Dialogic exercises can help elicit and resolve issues that can include emotions. One exercise to keep people solution-oriented is called "What's your headache." In it, group members write their biggest problem on a paper and swap papers. Each person reads their colleagues' "headache" and provides written support on solving the issue. This exercise creates a better understanding of the problems of others, plus group support and ownership of individual problems.

A leader must sometimes make decisions that do not please everyone. The group recognized that not having one's ideas chosen can create feelings like grief. Big emotions directed at the leader are the inevitable outcome of leadership decisions. To mitigate the disruption of big emotions related to unpopular decisions, the dialogic leader may implement the policy on a 'trial basis', leaving the door open for revisiting the decision later to fine-tune or modify aspects of the policy that haven't turned out optimally.

Reinforcing the container to strengthen the sense of trust, or to build a higher sense of trust, will allow the group to be willing to tolerate a greater magnitude of change.

The group concluded that emotions are a constant human condition, with emotional responses to almost everything that happens. People may mask their emotions, but emotions often govern how people respond to change. By reinforcing a safe container and softening the boundaries around policies the dialogic leader can welcome emotions, create a group that is resilient and accepting of change, and render change less frightening.

What is Organizational Dialogue and the Roadmap for a Successful Journey?

Loshnee Naidoo, Shakita Bland

PRE-CONFERENCE DESCRIPTION

The driving force behind this enquiry is to look at a large organization, such as the Virginia Department of Corrections, and be reminded that despite its size, positive change and adaptation can happen. This session thereby hopes to define organizational Dialogue and identify key principles and how they can be implemented on a large-scale basis - to combine ideas, thoughts, exercises and actions for the betterment of the work environment. This is a way of thinking that can and should include everyone within the organization and lead to cohesive behaviors and actions to ensure the vision of the organization is realized. During our session, we hope to go in-depth by further unlocking the gems of organizational Dialogue and the success of an organization. We seek to allow for the emergence of new thinking as it relates to organizational Dialogue and explore how we can use it to thrive within our own companies. This enquiry matters because if large organizations can use Dialogue as a tool to change for the better, this could have a ripple effect on the world.

CHECK-OUT

Loshnee Naidoo:

> When you constantly ask a question, you go to deeper levels that you hadn't thought about, and I think we were just about getting there . . . but we are running out of time, and we now want to head into a check-out, which is a key part of the dialogue. I'm going to hand it over to Shakita for the check-out.

Shakita Bland:

> Thank you so much. We would like to hear everyone's voice in the check-out, and it's a specific check-out: *What is one takeaway from today's session that you will implement or continue to think about as it pertains to organizational dialogue?*

Speaker:

> In this dialogue, I think we are from very different cultures, but we've been able

to listen to each other. I've been able to learn a lot about different perspectives from all your contributions. Thank you for this good conversation.

Speaker:

For me, it is valuing the small wins, and I do like the recommendation that someone shared, to highlight what is happening so that other people can see it. Also, working on getting leadership, the executive team, on board with dialogue.

Speaker:

I would say dialogue should function as built-in instead of as an add-on. Start to introduce it as a part of the organization at the very front end. It's not something to add on later. It's an essential part of the culture.

Speaker:

I would like to continue to think about something . . . Virginia Department of Corrections is a very hierarchical organization. We have lots of voices, and we need to include inmate voices. I meet with inmates, I train them, and they dialogue amongst themselves. But the reality is that 90% plus of the decisions I make don't include the inmate voice. And what happens? I don't know what the answer to that is, but it's an interesting thing to continue to think about.

Speaker:

Let me just mention something that was not specifically said, but it is an implication. It's what I would call the threshold of authenticity in terms of the embracing of the concept of dialogue. In practice, and in organization life, we can follow top-down directives. We'll walk through the motions, versus really taking it in, embracing it and demonstrating it. How do we identify what is working and embrace it? The authenticity needs to show up.

Speaker:

I go with that. Authenticity involves creating a self-container, and that comes back to oneself. The other people that are there, the environment that you are creating, the reason why you're doing it, the vision that you've got and the outcomes that you're trying to achieve. I think we use self-container too quickly to understand what it means for us in the dialogue.

Speaker:

I must think more about how to involve different levels in decision making and how to make the management structure flatter. I think it can help everyone to take part in decision-making. I should think about that.

Speaker:

My takeaway is that as a Dialogue Practitioner in my agency, and there are several of us on this call, it is time for us to reinvigorate. That's what I'm gaining. My takeaway is just reinvigorating what we need to do to continue growing dialogue in the agency.

Speaker:

I'd like to follow what was said a moment ago about looking at practice, how things develop and who all is involved in making decisions. A really key takeaway for me is letting the practice that we do shape the ultimate policy. There are probably a lot of things that we continue to do in the Department of Corrections that, if we listen to each other and together think through what that could be, could tweak the policies and make those policies even stronger and more beneficial for all the folks involved. It takes time, I acknowledge that, but it is what really resonated with me.

Speaker:

I want to follow the idea that it takes time. I think a radical and cultural shift needs time and patience, dialogue and a change in our consciousness. I really like it.

Speaker: I think that our organization is currently in a very interesting spot where we will be tested. How we have implemented dialogue is going to be tested as a new director came into the role - and the director that brought dialogue to us and really modelled it has left. Now we will know. Will it truly stick? Well, what do we have to do? Continue to be effective and continue to be valued. I'm thinking about the outcomes that were mentioned early in the dialogue, and the measurements. It's great that we have data about retention and employee attrition, but what I'm keeping in mind is that there must be more. There must be a clear connection that dialogue, the practice of dialogue, is what resulted in and created those outcomes, and not some other practice that we have implemented. We had many of them happening in parallel and concurrently to one another. So how do we make the connection that it's dialogue that is making the difference?

Speaker:

I'm loving how my brain and my whole sensing is sitting with this uniqueness of cultures. I'm thinking about talking and working with a financial services organization, and I'm working in manufacturing organization. From the outside, I'm thinking about how dialogue starts in each of those organizations. It is really powerful. And I'm even thinking about the idea of coming in with that open mind as an executive coach, as consultant, as a team coach - and thinking about how I could have a dialogue with my client, with my client's contacts. How do I involve them in a dialogue to think about what's good? What's appropriate for this particular organization, and if dialogue is even appropriate for the organization at this time. I think there's a lot that we can apply in terms of change management principles as well as how we approach conversations, in whatever group or organization we're working. So, I'm letting go and holding lightly of this idea that I have the answers. I certainly don't.

Speaker:

I take away a lot from this very nice conversation. I have learned a lot. First, I am now even more clear that, in order for us to be more effective in our networks, we need to promote a more meaningful dialogue. Dialogue that is open enough, that promotes understanding. And that once we are more aware of the situation, we understand more clearly what it is that we need to improve. Then we will find new ways of collaboration. So, that is something that I am glad to realize. I'm learning a lot.

Speaker:

The concept of a Working Dialogue is what I am thinking about. Getting the different ongoing parts incorporated into the schematic of things, whether it's a different agency or a client, or even the Department of Corrections. Getting the different parts needed to make a change, coming together and doing a collective thing, a Generative Dialogue. Getting a bunch of different ideas, and then maybe narrowing it down to a Working Dialogue is what we're all tiptoeing around. It seems like it's the one word that we haven't actually used a lot, and I think it is the key. My takeaway is getting better with our Working Dialogues, as well as dialogue in general with our employees.

Speaker:

May I speak now? I'm starting with this question because this is my first experience of getting involved in a Zoom dialogue. I can call it the Zoom Dialogue. Actually, it was really a bit difficult for me to keep myself involved and engaged with the conversation. It was a bit hard, but really all the fellows here were so lovely and kind, and the conversation was really informative for me. I want to mention my takeaway. I like the part when you spoke about the metrics. Highlighting the metrics, such as turnover and insurance claims, to make some convincing data. This was my take-away from the session here. Thank you.

Speaker:

I will add the re-energizing that needs to happen. There are several people here from our agency and I think that we need to be reminded that this works, and how much we enjoyed it when we learned it. What is the value that it will provide the agency as a whole? We just need to re-energize ourselves.

Loshnee:

One of my takeaways is not to go too quickly into the policy space, because then it becomes more of a tick box, almost a measuring exercise as opposed to a lived reality that embodies it. I think that was very important for me. To understand first. You've got to live it before you can put together a policy. And I would love to see a case study, to know what you all actually did in the process to know whether dialogue is embodied strongly enough in the organization to continue even with the change in leadership. That'd be a great case study to do. And finally, for me to take into the organization that I'm working with as well. So yes, thank you for that.

Shakita:

My takeaway was just how wonderful this session has been with you all participating and allowing the conversation and dialogue to just flow. Covid, wonderful Covid, I thank you for helping us to be a part of this Zoom video, and to have this level of in-depth conversation, short as it was, but still it was very good. I take away a plethora of knowledge, and I'll continue to utilise what I've learned here to further our growth and development. Thank you all for your time and participation. We greatly appreciate it.

POSTSCRIPT

Our Participatory Dialogic on 'Organizational Dialogue and the Roadmap for a Successful Journey' proved very successful as evidenced by the maximum attendance of 25 participants from various parts of the globe. The session commenced with the sharing of experiences from Virginia Department of Corrections (VADOC), a large and successful dialogic organization, which formed the basis for further dialogic exploration. VADOC was used as a case study to unpack lessons and for the group to explore their individual roles in taking their organizations on the dialogic journey.

The evolution of communication within VADOC, using dialogue, continued to spark thought- provoking questions and creative ideas about how to address challenges within entities. The importance of creating space for all voices within companies was brought forward, and how the Dialogic Practices may enable these safe spaces. The concept of inclusion within organizations has become more profound as the work environment blossoms with the assurance of voices being heard.

This reflective dialogue flowed effortlessly throughout. A large component of the dialogue revolved around how to start the journey of becoming a dialogic organization and the more challenging aspect of convincing decision-makers of the merit of dialogue in enhancing the value of the company. Further ideas that were explored included the use of dialogue to create a more productive work environment, and the challenge of measuring the benefits of a dialogic organization.

As offered during the check-out, the group found the use of VADOC as a case study valuable in identifying key principles and success factors that they could implement within their organizations. The dialogue did allow people from different backgrounds to engage and reflect together, as proposed in the initial rationale for this enquiry.

Let's talk . . .

Troy Adams, Susan Williams

PRE-CONFERENCE DESCRIPTION

In this session, we will examine the concept of Dialogue, that is both an art and a science. If you ask any random person what it means to dialogue, they might say, *To talk or to have a conversation*. Yet, those who truly understand Dialogue know that it's so much more. In today's world, we spend lots of time talking to one another – via email, in meetings both virtually and in-person, on the telephone or via text, across social media, and so on. We spend more time talking than ever before, but are we really communicating effectively with each other? Let's talk. Better still, let's explore and dialogue together. *What is this thing called Dialogue? What is the point? What is required to do it well? What's in it for me?*

CHECK-OUT

Susan Williams:

> We want to tag the check-out. For those who are not familiar with that process, one person speaks, and when they have spoken, they select the next person to go. That will be efficient for us. We do wish that everyone contributes to the check-out. This is the question for our Check-out, *How might you be able to use the information from the dialogue that we had today, going forward? What will you be able to use or take from this for the future?* Eddie, while people are still reflecting, did you have anything that you wanted to share with the group?

Eddie Adams:

> I think it was a really great experience. It was a good dialogue, and I appreciate everybody that shared. We talked about a lot of things with the practices, voice, suspension, and what dialogue is all about, how everybody comes together, including everybody's voice and our coming together to create a common meaning. We are looking to inquire and trying to learn. So that's a lot of what I gained today.

Speaker:

I really need to be conscientious as I respond to the question. Am I coming into the Dialogue thinking I already know, as opposed to coming in here with some excitement and some curiosity?

Speaker:

I took from this dialogue that I have to continue to practice my skills and continue to have my voice heard when I'm at the table, regardless of how uncomfortable that might make me feel. To have my voice heard and to be genuine.

Speaker:

Today is like a refresher. I'm looking and focusing on my conscious awareness, and that brings inclusivity. If I can hold on to that, then I know that I will have quality conversations and dialogues, and I will include every voice that needs to be heard. Today is a reinforcement or an enhancement of that notion.

Speaker:

Noticing how people speak, how they absorb information, and how they listen is really helpful to me. It'll help me to understand better how I can use my communication skills in my work and in my personal life, day to day. If I keep on doing that, I think I'll get a lot better.

Speaker:

The aspect that I brought away was the importance of creating a safe container in the work environment, and what I can do to create the safe container in my role where I am involved in a lot of informal dialogue to accomplish goals. We've got to have a safe container. So it's, *What is my role in creating a safe container?*

Speaker:

The most interesting thing that was said was about curiosity and speaking up. It gave me a new perspective of what dialogue is. I will investigate more to find what other people might understand by the word dialogue. Thank you very much for sharing your perspectives.

Speaker:

Dialogue is something that happens within and without. It's happening within you as a person, as you're engaging, and it's happening outside of you. But first it must happen within. Because if you don't let it happen within before you add your voice, then what you're voicing may not be adding value.

Speaker:

I am very grateful for someone sharing that they can't talk, listen, and process at the same time. I'm very slow at processing and listening and creating a response at the same time. So that gives me more confidence to kind of sit in silence and absorb and reflect. It's nice to know that I'm not in that space alone and I feel like I can be more comfortable in the quiet now, and that feels so much less pressured.

Speaker:

It is amazing that you picked me to come next, because you said what I was thinking about as well. My takeaway, too, is a thank you for opening that space for someone to share their struggles because I, too, sometimes have to stop, slow down and let things process. If you give me too much too fast, I will shut down. It is like my memory goes out the window. For the longest time I thought I was flawed in some way. So, thank you for that space. Anyone who's ever done a dialogue with me knows that sometimes I just like to slow it down. Just let people talk things out. In reality, that's just for me to catch up. So, thank you for that, and I'm encouraged like the previous speaker I feel better about my space now.

Speaker:

Yeah, this morning is valuable to me. I'd say, as facilitator, I now understand how important it is to establish safe space so that I can hear someone's authentic voice. And personally, I realized I need time to develop my own authentic voice, not just speak up with the first thing that comes to my mind, but to really think about it, to give myself time to make sure what I really want to say.

Speaker:

I have to follow what you were saying about slowing down and not just regurgitating what you've heard prior to a response. I think many times we have already planned in our head what we're going to say prior to anyone speaking because we have an agenda. So just learning to slow down. Silence is a good thing. We are all uncomfortable with the silence and think we must fill that void, but I'm learning. We must learn how to take in what we're thinking, and not say anything. I'm still working on that. I'm new and I have something to learn. I going to say it right.

Speaker:

You said it absolutely right! Thank you so much for that. What I got from this is more of a refresher, but it also reminded me that I need to slow down when it comes to listening. I didn't really listen to understand. I think I listened to kind of fill that void. So, this is a good reminder for me, that I need to slow down and listen to understand better since I've created the safe space to do so.

Speaker:

I'm confident that dialogue can occur within smaller groups, where individuals are not overly concerned about the size, but I appreciate that we might not have sufficient inputs from all the perspectives present in a larger group.

Speaker:

I've been away from dialogue a little, although I used to use it all the time. Suspension was at the forefront for me, listening to everyone, and the speed of engagement. I tend to go fast, so I know I need to slow down and make sure that we have all the voices in the room. And I think vulnerability plays a big part as well.

Speaker:

So nice to be with you all again. What I'm sitting with today is the importance of the container, the space. Allowing the space and the awareness that there are barriers. There are language barriers and cultural barriers, so the importance of creating that space to find the time for the voices to join in the conversation.

Speaker:

Yes, I'm more of a bystander than anything. I have to work on giving and receiving, which for me is my voice and active listening. That way I can relay dialogue to others, as I understand it, through active listening.

Speaker:

My takeaway is listening for understanding, as opposed to listening to respond. Having that pause so that I can actually hear opposing or other views. Giving myself that moment so I can hear what's going on inside my head as well as everybody else's words.

Speaker:

My biggest takeaway is the lower-case *d*, and the upper-case *D* of dialogue. Actually listening to everyone's perspective. It just shows that I'm on the right path. I was brought up in a family that came from a space of because I said so. It kind of opened me up in here to listen and change my way of thinking about and understanding dialogue.

Speaker:

> I liked the different meanings of dialogue. And not to be overly concerned about the words but attend more to the content of what people are saying. I actually had to write this down so I could remember it. I think what really stood out for me is that when I want to argue or defend, it will be really helpful for me to see if I am feeling excluded and to ask to be included rather than get defensive at that moment. To do this comes from a whole new level of vulnerability than it does to come in with what I think is wrong with a conversation or a dialogue.

Speaker:

> For me, today was a good reminder about being intentional, not only with listening but with what it is you're saying. Not just speaking to be heard, or speaking to speak, but to contribute.

Susan:

> For me? It was value-added, and I felt like all of you had value-added, and this was a very worthwhile dialogue today. I appreciate you coming to our session.

POSTSCRIPT

Quality conversations begin with the Dialogic practices. There are four Dialogue practices that enrich communications. Firstly, **voice** – speaking authentically, secondly, **listening** – attentively listening, thirdly, **respect** – seeking to understand, and, fourthly, **suspension** – revealing your thinking and exploring thinking together. These practices provide the foundation of the process for quality interactions.

In professional dialogue it is important that everyone involved becomes intentional in the process, in order to speak, hear, and understand. Sometimes it may feel scary to speak to others with a genuine authentic voice. For this reason, it is important that respect is present, and suspension is utilized along with the practice of not only listening to hear but rather listening to understand. This combination of skills will help create a safe container where everyone is included and afforded the opportunity to speak with their authentic voice and express their genuine thoughts and ideas.

Inclusion is an essential part of dialogue. Should one feel left out, then ask oneself what do I need to do to be included. The answer to this question must come from within, which in turn may derive from curiosity. This may bring about inquiry which is another important element of dialogue. Inquiry may be expressed in the form of a question or may simply be a spoken statement said with curiosity.

The practice of suspension, and the taking of time out to listen for understanding, both provide space for the common understanding to blossom. Often, people come into the dialogue with the thought: 'I already know'. This limits possibilities and shuts down growth. Conversely, revealing one's own thinking and keeping an open mind to another's thinking also contribute to the development of the safe container – that is an atmosphere where people are comfortable, curious and excited to exchange ideas with one another.

Space is needed in dialogue for many reasons, such as time to process one's thoughts which may be exaggerated by cultural or language barriers. In dialogue, everyone involved should become comfortable with momentary quietness. When a conversation is slowed and silence is embraced, everyone is afforded the time to think and process their thoughts for a better understanding and not feel pressured to speak. When the dialogue begins to slow down, and participants are not just speaking to push personal agendas, a deeper understanding may be achieved – and this is the goal of dialogue.

How to communicate more effectively? Be intentional with the practices. Not speaking just to speak, but to contribute, and to truly hear what others are contributing.

Dialogue Facilitation – Mindset and Practice

Elisabeth Razesberger, Qingmian Chen

PRE-CONFERENCE DESCRIPTION

What kind of mindset do you need to get into Dialogue and where do you start? Two facilitators will share impulses that have emerged on their path of learning to bring dialogue into conversations and professional contexts. Where can you start and how do you keep up during a dialogue? In this Participatory Dialogue, we will together investigate the ways in which we approach facilitating conversations that allow people to hear each other and be heard. This means observing your own approach and stimulating the practice of critical thinking amongst the participants.

CHECK-OUT

Qingming Chen:

I was thinking, in a way, if there is an established relationship already, it is much easier to have a Dialogue. But often when we are in a dialogue where there is no established relationship the question is, *How do we carry on?* We observe what is happening, see people and what they are talking about, and we carry on from there. I recall the first time I failed. We were not really in dialogue. In the group of people, everyone was saying something. We were not in Dialogue, but the moment people disclose themselves or show their vulnerabilities, at that moment it all becomes connected. You feel like you want to show your vulnerability too. I think that's the moment I feel I'm in a real dialogue. I feel the dialogue is more about feeling and experiencing the melody or speed of shifting. It's the experiencing part. You can't force people. As was said, it's not necessarily an existing connection but when it happens the connection will be there. That's my feeling about dialogue.

Elisabeth Razesberger:

I would now like to invite the rest of you to share a few thoughts. *What you are taking away from this session. Have you learned something? Was there anything that surprised you?*

Speaker:

For me, it was really helpful hearing stories from the Department of Corrections colleagues and being able to empathize with their context, what they're going through and how dialogue skills can be used in in many ways to support a culture that's got some very difficult challenges. It helped me draw parallels to what I'm trying to do in my own project.

Speaker:

I've learned that having a proper mindset and the practices go hand in hand when you're dealing with a dialogue. To execute the practices, your mindset has to be on the right path.

Speaker:

I'm thinking a bit about the relationship between facilitation and dialogue, and how it's easy to confuse the one with the other or to be pretty good at organizing a conversation without actually having the conversation. It's a tricky thing and I think it can often come out of performance anxiety. We want it to go well. If we talk about dialogue and open up something with no boundaries, some people might not talk (we think to ourselves), certain voices might not be included, or things could go wrong, depending on your definition of what right and wrong is. But I think this could be okay because it reveals what's there. Then maybe you can point out what's there without making trouble. Possibly because I'm keen to have some sort of experience, I may have the feeling of the rug getting pulled out from under me. Often, I find that when I'm in dialogue I have no idea what's going to happen next, and probably no one does. Then it's like, okay, whatever I thought I was doing (and I thought I had it all well-organized) something will show up to ruin that. Then I realize that this is the point because then something different can happen. I say this because I think it takes some courage to do it. It's a bit counter counterculture.

Speaker:

When you said, *Rug being pulled out from under you*, I thought that even in that instance it requires being authentic to respond correctly in that part of a dialogue, and I think that's where the crunchiness come in. I will suspend my consciousness going forward, utilize the tools of changing my mindset and put in practice the proper communication. When the rug is pulled out, I will be able to respond appropriately using the dialogic practices that we have discussed.

Elisabeth:

I really like this concept of crunchiness, which is new to me. Especially in the circles where we are now, where we try to always talk about the beauty of dialogue, but being in dialogue can be extremely painful and can also create a lot of suffering while it's happening. I think this is one of the reasons why people feel they want to get into dialogue but then prefer not to go there because they don't know where it will lead them. They ask themselves how painful might it be, and will they get out of it in one piece, or with injuries that they will have to tend to? Of course, it is worth doing it.

Speaker:

I was reflecting on the potential messiness of it all, and also on holding trust in the process. I recognize that it can be messy and could be uncomfortable for me and for other people. How then do I bring my presence and my attention in that moment of messiness? And what am I learning in that moment as I am sitting with the messiness of it?

Speaker:

What helps me with that is that when I suspend, I can respect what other people are saying. Listening, respect and using suspension, these three help me more than anything else. I don't have to change my beliefs and values because of what somebody else says or believes, their values or whatever, but I can listen and respect what they have to say. When I do this, I don't have a problem sitting in any dialogue, being uncomfortable or being concerned it could be painful for me. I use those skills. I enter the dialogue with that mindset. For me, it was about changing the way I went into situations or went into dialogue with individuals. I don't have to go along with everything you say, or believe what you say. I may not even like what you say, but I can listen to you and respect what you have to say and suspend. When I do this, I don't have a problem entering into dialogue. That's when I know I'm in dialogue, when I do those things.

Speaker:

Elizabeth, you said something that I've been sitting with for a while – that you don't have to be naked to be vulnerable or to be authentic. They're not the same thing. I have a strong affect-based willingness to share that.

Speaker:

I am appreciating the work that's been done in Virginia, and many of you are from there. Sometimes people are critical and say, you've learnt many skills but don't do so much dialogue, but perhaps you can't let things get out of control in an incarcerated situation even though you do want things to shift and change at depth. I think you're right to be looking back to facilitation skills, managing the time, checking in and out, and so on. It does take time, doesn't it? It's been ten years since we began in Virginia and now it's kind of maturing, and I'm impressed with what you're all doing. I say that from my perspective outside that system and living in Europe.

Speaker:

In the UK we have this really stereotypical view of the US correctional process, and I think we are quite guilty as a nation of feeling like we're so much better. But we don't have anything like this going on in the UK, as far as I'm aware.

Elisabeth:

We probably must stop there. We start again in 20 minutes time with the plenary session.

Speaker:

Thank you, Martin and Elizabeth. See you later.

People leave the Participatory Dialogue, apart from Peter who can see that another participant has managed to reconnect on Wi-Fi having been temporarily offline.

Peter:

Did you have a check-out comment you wanted to make before you go? What were you thinking?

Speaker:

Sorry, I had some connectivity issues . . .

It does require a level of vulnerability for people to open up and have conversations with you – but there also has to be a level of comfort with the person they engage with in the conversation. The dialogue will be somewhat forced if a person doesn't feel comfortable and psychologically safe, particularly if they don't have any familiarity with them and they may never have met before. I think those things are important to the depth of the dialogue. When a person doesn't feel psychologically safe and respected in a dialogue, they will hold back and be a little bit apprehensive about being transparent.

Peter:

Very good, thank you!

Speaker:

Thank you!

POSTSCRIPT

When facilitating dialogue, a dialogic mindset and a dialogue practice go hand in hand. In this participatory dialogue, the participants talked about what it takes to bring dialogue into practice.

Many of us know the feeling of frustration when we realise that we are not in dialogue. But what does it take to make dialogue happen? With many experienced dialogue facilitators present in the room, the opening question, *When do you know that you ARE in dialogue?* was intended to put the focus on the personal experience of dialogue as lived and perceived by practitioners.

To bring dialogue into conversations, meetings and situations, you need to create conditions where people can have a genuine enquiry, allowing AND inviting the probing of information, permitting questions like, *Why do you do that?* It is about discovering something together.

Problem-solving needs am unobstructed view of a situation. Dialogue involves the understanding of all the different perspectives to see a situation in its entirety. A participant described the process as, *unpacking something and making meaning together.* Another participant suggested being real and being true to oneself and one's own role, whilst also recognising the integrity of the other person and their role.

Dialogue facilitation means enabling a genuine conversation. How authentic can you be? Authenticity shows in speaking openly. In dialogue it also means being heard. This means deep listening on the receiving end of the story. How people perceive and rate open communication appears to be a reliable indicator of the atmosphere in an organization. It reveals the extent to which employees can contribute, and how committed the management is to cooperation. In this respect, authenticity is a key enabler for dialogue to happen.

Once you have the full picture of a situation you can go a step further and move out of your habitual way of thinking and shift something together.

Overall, the session examined what dialogue is, and what dialogue does, from the perspective of the practitioner. The opening question went directly to the core of what is needed to bring dialogue into practice. This question can be asked reliably again and again to identify clues and practices for successful dialogue facilitation.

What does Dialogue look like in our personal lives?

Laura Little and PJ Manning

PRE-CONFERENCE DESCRIPTION

It is amazing how we learn skills and yet we may only use those skills when we are in an environment where it is the expectation that we use them. How are we holding ourselves accountable to use dialogue skills when it is no longer an expectation? One way to enhance our skills is to practice them. The more we practice our skills the more they become a way of life. In this session, we will focus on how we hold ourselves accountable for and committed to using our skills; and the challenges we face using Dialogue in our personal lives.

CHECK-OUT

PJ Manning:

Alright! We have had a great dialogue so far. Now we want to have a check-out. We're going to use the same process as we did when we checked in, and we would like everyone to react by raising their hands when they have spoken to make sure everyone is able to check-out.

Laura Little:

Thank everyone for participating. When we do the check-out question, try to answer very briefly, just one word or two words. Could you do that? We want to hear a short reflection of something that was meaningful to you today, and make it short. The check-out question is, *What was really meaningful for you today?*

Speaker:

I'm going to use background and feelings, and I am going to feature the model for as much dialogue as possible because I think having a set format is helpful to everyone.

Speaker:

I would say, also the 4 Fs. I thought that was really interesting, and something that I think I can use at home as well. I appreciate that.

Speaker:

Honestly, everything. But to pick one thing specifically, it is knowing about the dysphoria that I have. I had no idea. So, knowing that I have it, that's going to help me operate accordingly and to have more meaningful and effective conversations and communications across the board.

Speaker:

I'm definitely going to look up the Four Fs, and can you all please tell me what they stand for because I will be doing some research. (*Fight, Flight, Freeze, and Fawn*) I think more people haven't been diagnosed, and we come across it a lot. That fills in some of the gaps.

Speaker:

The 4 Fs. I'm definitely going to use it and try to put it into practice. And yeah, I'm going to look into this more. It is going to be very helpful.

Speaker:

I would have to say the Cobs model (*for feedback*) as to what thoughts led to that behaviour.

Speaker:

I'll follow with the Four Halves Cobs Model, but I think the most meaningful to me today is rejection sensitivity dysphoria. I know I must do some research on that.

Speaker:

That is my like too. Today I was a little tired, but hearing the experience of people in other cultures was so exciting for me, and I feel so thankful.

Speaker:

Probably just listening to people's experiences and highlighting the fact that dialogic engagement is not necessarily a magic fix. There are still challenges within that. It's nice to hear the shared experiences. Perhaps I'm not doing everything wrong, just not adapting as well as I could to some people, anyway.

Speaker:

I would say the 4 F's, but what also keeps coming into mind is meeting people where they are.

Speaker:

Oh, I'm just so excited - and noticing that we have so many of you on this call that are from VADOC, whatever VADOC is. But you're a wonderful group, and you seem to be doing unbelievable jobs. My daughter is in the Ministry of Justice in the UK. She specifically wants to work on mental health in prisons, and we're very passionate about it. I've actually been on mental health leave for 5 years. I've not been well, and I'm very pleased if you found any of the little tools that I introduced are useful. I'm just grateful for that. Thank you.

Speaker:

VADOC stands for Virginia Department of Corrections, and we all work in different facilities. I work in the kitchen where there are 30 guys. We have all sorts of personalities and all sorts of levels of capability in handling things. For me, like you said, it's more about meeting somebody at their level. And for those who don't know, ADHD is attention deficit hyperactivity disorder. I had it and I was considered anti-social, but that's very common for women. Most of us don't have the hyperactivity part, but many of us definitely have the distractibility part.

Speaker:

My two are 'pause' and 'open-ended questions'.

Speaker:

Mine would definitely be the Four Fs. In addition to looking more into ADHD – and how to interact with it as my son has been diagnosed with it.

Speaker:

Mine would probably be 'defensiveness', because we can understand all of this but if other people are defensive, it's really hard to get through to them. So, we have to work on that.

Speaker:

I'm going to take away being really aware of your intentions – particularly the part where you said maybe somebody stepped on your values, and that's why you had to interrupt them. I'm a 'meet people where they're at' person, and I'm also going to place extra emphasis on what my intentions are, with any conversation at the outset.

Speaker:

I wrote down, remembering that emotions play into things in our personal lives. I think that's sometimes what gets me.

Laura:

I will say that we must be able to pause for a minute to see what's missing in the conversation, and then come back in.

PJ:

This concludes our session. We really enjoyed you all being here, and this was definitely something that I wish we had more time on because we really got to some areas that we wanted to elaborate more and learn more about from each other. I definitely appreciate what you all have given and how you contributed to this dialogue today.

POSTSCRIPT

As we thought about our title and description for the session, we reflected on the Dialogue experiences we've had since being introduced to Dialogue. Fragmentation is most often found within conversations when participants are not aware of the fundamentals of Dialogue. Therefore, we are likely to decrease the use of these skills when confronted with this issue. We also challenged ourselves to use the skills when we were not expected to do so. We thought it would be a good idea to hear from the guests at the conference. The question we posed was, *How often do you use Dialogue in your personal life?*

The participants brought a wonderful energy. They didn't take too much time to think about the question. It was as if they were waiting for someone to ask. We learned together, and the content was important for everyone. We learned that in communication barriers exist that could prevent a person from communicating effectively. Most of the participants admitted that they found it difficult to communicate effectively at home as their family was not familiar with the fundamentals of Dialogue. We learned together that we should take notice of some signs and approach the conversation in such a way that the message is understood as well as the intentions.

Everyone in the group frequently expressed themselves emotionally (in the language of affect) and what they said was meaningful. We became sympathetic to those who talked about struggling with a disorder that prevents them from receiving a message or communicating as effectively as they would like. We had a few participants who were transparent and shared their personal experiences of this experience with the group. A lot of information about

ADHD (attention deficit hyperactivity disorder) was shared as well as an associated anxiety that could complicate conversation. Some of the participants said they were interested to learn more about communicating with people who may have this disorder and were keen to know the signs to identify its presence.

Someone also talked about different traumatic responses and spoke about the 4 F's of Fight, Flight, Freeze, and Fawn. Those who tend towards the fight response believe that if they establish power over the threat it will result in security and control. Flight response is to protect oneself from threat through escape (for example, by leaving the conversation). The freeze response is the protection of oneself through dissociation (for example: spacing out mid-conversation), whilst the fawn response is the avoidance of conflict by pleasing people (for example, by agreeing with everything despite one's authentic beliefs and thoughts being otherwise).

My takeaway from the session was to examine fragmentation on a deeper level. For someone to receive what is being said, it has to be provided in a way that is acceptable to them. In addition, the way we communicate with someone should not only be respectful and authentic, and it should also be easily comprehended by people. I learned that we must be patient and check to see if we are being understood, or if we have the correct understanding of what another is saying. Are we following the conversation well? Asking open-ended questions, giving affirmations, reflecting on what was said, and sharing a summary of your understanding with others can all help to reduce fragmentation.

The energy of this session was so engaging that the participants were invited into a break-out room after the day's conference session to continue to dialogue on the matters being explored. I hope that we can expand on the information that was gathered to introduce an understanding of fragmentation at a deeper level.

Dialogue: a Pathway Toward Mutual Awareness and Exploring Connection

Leo Hylton and Wendy Hendrickse

PRE-CONFERENCE DESCRIPTION

We live in a "microwave society" where everything happens at speed, yet we have no time for the things we value or could prove of value to us. So why the rush to the finish line?

Wendy and Leo feel something is missing because of the absence of Dialogue. They feel we need to slow down and relearn how to just be with each other, remove unnecessary pressure production and free ourselves from the false sense of urgency with which we have been conditioned to impregnate our every interaction. Dialogue offers the opportunity to facilitate such meaningful connections without harmful assumptions that we must be in agreement in order to experience connection. Rather, there is mutual empowerment in freeing ourselves from our constrictions and co-creating spaces of shared meaning without the expectation of changing minds or seeking agreement. Participants are invited to join us to co-create a space like this together.

CHECK-OUT

Leo Hylton:

Thank you for showing up and engaging, for slowing down, for hearing each other. We still have 19 minutes, but I'd like to transition into another round of collective, sharing. No pressure but a very open invitation. A lot has been shared so far. There was the opening panel, and Patty thank you for lending your wisdom and experience to that. Then here in this room, there was so much experience, so much wisdom, so much learning shared. So, what from this dialogue are you going to carry with you into your life, practice or organization? We've talked about power, the creation of space, the co-creation of knowledge, the slowing down, and the being with each other . . .

I'd like to invite Patty to start us off. And then, you can tag the next person.

Patty Hawk:

What is going to stick with me is what I learned about the importance of stepping back as a facilitator, once the space was set up, to allow the group to find their own voices. By this time the students were in charge, and if they hadn't been in charge I wouldn't have stepped back. There's something about recognizing how power plays a role, understanding your own power and deciding what you want out of the process. Do you want people to co-construct the process, or do you want them (as my husband would say) to leave thinking, *She's really smart?* Part of the enquiry is recognizing your power and not trying to force people into what makes you comfortable.

Speaker:

Yeah, I like what you said, and I really appreciate overall just getting to learn about this. When people are comfortable, they are willing to share more.

Speaker:

What I try to do is to bring a catch of dialogue to my dear country, which is France. In France, there are more and more voices coming from different networks, with social media pushing for Dialogue - not conversation, not debate, but a really authentic Dialogue! The question I have, and that I share with others, is how to bring this into our society, how to bring a kind of prototype to address climate change. Climate changes are happening on a huge scale in our country. There is a need to address it, but the topic is becoming so fragmented that bringing this topic it into any room is really becoming violent. Violence is where the conversation is now. There are pros and cons, and we need to go faster. The government is doing nothing. It's really it's becoming a burning topic. What can we do to bring this dialogue process to address climate change in our society? Co-creation is really important. I have heard about co-creation before, and some of you mentioned co-creation today. For me this is the hub. this is the centre of dialogue. Responsibility, co-ownership and co-creation all go together. That's what I want. I share this with you because it's really in my heart and in my mind. I'm writing articles about this right now!

Leo Hylton:

That's good. Thank you.

Speaker:

Honestly, I'm not sure what to say. I think that Working Dialogue is important for any facility, or in any situation. In general, just to be able to understand the other person's stance, not just person-to-person, but for all of us to be able to understand, as a whole, whatever you are trying to get through. Honestly, I have kind of lost what the question was that was asked in the first place. Could someone reiterate it for me?

Leo Hylton:

That's quite alright. The question is, what are you going to carry from this dialogue into your life practice and or organization?

Speaker:

As far as my organization is concerned, dialogue is difficult and that is why I am trying to learn more about it. I do carry on conversations daily with multiple people from different backgrounds and different situations. I try to give my full attention, listening and taking in what they have to say, and being able to help them through whatever they need. But in my position that tends to teeter on the edge of fraternization, and we can't do that. We never can. It's not a feasible thing in my line of work. But I do always try to let whomever I'm speaking with have an open voice to get whatever it is they need to say out, and I try to understand it on a day-to-day basis. Outside of that, it's just a working process and a learning process. I've been in the corrections field for four years, and with VADOC for two. Prior to the VADOC, dialogue was not a thing I had come across, so it's been a learning process. I'm hoping to be able to walk away with a better understanding of how to be able to carry on a conversation and listen. I need to know all the working aspects of it, to be able to carry out my work from day to day without teetering over that line and being able to help and show others how to do it as well. To be able to better help other people. I think that's all I really have to say.

Speaker:

The conversations have been great. I've enjoyed listening to some of the points, and to the confusion. Going back to a couple of the comments, it's like people feel as though they're put on the spot, and they have to have a response, whether they have one or not. It's almost as if, when you don't have a response, you're not participating or you're not paying attention. But sometimes you just don't have a response, or a response isn't needed at the time. So that's where I am, still battling with the process - and whether the focus is on dialogue the noun or dialogue the verb.

Speaker:

I know I had some issues earlier, but the main thing that I am taking away from this session today is that in dialogue it is so important to say what needs to be said, instead of saying what you think you want others to hear. Because that provides a true and meaningful dialogue. So often we are trying to get something done and to do that we need to make sure that everyone is being truthful both to themselves and the issue at hand. I really appreciate listening to everyone's responses today and I think that there's been a lot of valuable insight gained.

Speaker:

I think this morning I've got a new idea about what happened with the way I introduced the dialogue I talked about. I did a lot of things that you talked about here, like getting the group together and creating a nice atmosphere. But it was about mixing two different formats. I was giving a little speech on how dialogue works, and then trying to do it. I think that was the problem because then we had different layers or different levels of conversing. I think we just left the dialogue part of it, and then we came back again. The whole process was interrupted. I'm not going to go into that any further now, but I think I've got a good idea about what happened. That makes me happy. I take that. Apart from that, I think it was a good process and there was a lot of learning.

Speaker:

Well, I feel quite reassured because we all seem to have very similar ideas about dialogue.

This is not self-evident, because there are many different dialogues in the world. It makes me feel comfortable that there are more people around the world who follow similar trains of thought, and there are many people calling for dialogue and don't know that there's a concept that already exists. Like you said concerning climate change, keeping the planet together is something that is really important, and I think dialogue is one of the tools that can help to bring this about.

Wendy Hendrickse:

Slowing down has been a big message for me because I've always been a doer. I want to get things done. I thought I was listening to people but now I'm not quite sure. I loved hearing what I learned - that taking time saves you time. Just taking that moment will give you so much more that you can achieve in other ways, things that you really want to achieve. If you're not really engaging, then there's no relationship, and there's no relational action happening. I think for me, it's really about that relational action happening. Relational action says that I was heard, and I heard. And that is what we need.

Speaker:

I think for me it's reigniting my curiosity about the interplay between dialogue, power, spaces and relationships. I leave thinking about that. The other thing it has reminded me to do is to go and practice more doing. I don't do enough. So, more practice.

Speaker:

I want to talk about what I learned. I don't really have a lot of past experience. The connection part of being all together, and the power. They are important. The power part, not so much, because I feel it should be a collective dialogue, and the community should come together. You should hear all the voices, because that's how it should be. You shouldn't let anybody be left out and feel like you left them out, because then they probably won't speak at all. We deal with that a lot in the institution where I work. They don't want to talk to anybody and that's why a lot of them turn to drugs. The drug problem in our institution is extremely high. If we had the right programs and used dialogue to see what is actually going on with them, I feel like the issues could lessen. We probably can't stop it but it would shrink. Some of them have deeper issues that we can't get to, but people could learn how to use dialogue. It's definitely worth it. Communicate with everyone. I'm also trying to get to the root of their rowdiness. So, I'm just taking in everything that everybody's said, and I appreciate everybody sharing their thoughts. I write stuff down, too, so I can share it with my group when we get back to our meeting in December. I want to say thank you, everybody.

Leo Hylton:

Yes. Thanks each of you. I'm carrying gratitude for the fact that this space existed today and that each of you were part of co-creating it. And I really appreciate what has been brought into this space, in particular around the need to honour people's power to pass, or not speak. Sometimes a person needs space. It is so powerful to give an open space for people to pass and be silent and say nothing. And in saying nothing, say everything. The collective wisdom in this room is something that I'm going to carry with me with a whole lot of gratitude.

POSTSCRIPT

What is missing with regards to mutual awareness and connection when dialogue is absent? The best way to explore this question is to engage in dialogue itself. In all manner of organizations, people have forgotten how to just be with each other. So focused are we on what needs to be done and on the latest deliverable required that we forget to really see and hear each other. Living in a time where everything is rushed, dialogue can help us slow down and find meaning. Together, on Day One of the conference, we invited participants to join us in this intentional slowing down.

The facilitators' intention can have a massive impact on the way a space is held. Together, we explored the ways that intention screams louder than words. Together, people can hear intention regardless of what words we use to mask it. Whether for good or bad, people in positions of power may hold an intention of, *Let me tick this box and move on.* As facilitators, our duty is to resist this temptation. A warm welcome, the framing of the space with a thoughtful quote or poem. These are moments that can either be sacred or performative.

Throughout the dialogue, we held the space within the intention of a welcoming openness, authenticity, and slowness. Additionally, with an intention to co-create a space that supports reflection, we invited the unique lived experience of each participant in all its wisdom.

Some learning that we have carried beyond this interactive dialogue includes the following. When you engage purposefully to make space for people to 'be', the intention with which you show up is vital. It is also important to attune to those present. Some people can be easily manipulated by words, due to a desire to believe what is being said. Alternatively, others test the waters with guarded and probing responses, gauging their safety by the reactions they elicit.

The interplay of people's responses is affected by the ways facilitators engage. Participants will measure the authenticity of facilitators, and this measurement will affect how the process flows. For example, the 'rocks and boulders' can form natural formations that are easily navigated or they can compact and dam the flow.

It is a powerful thing when dialogue facilitators enter a room, and their only agenda is to truly hear and connect with people. As with any meaningful dialogue, this one left us with many questions to ponder. What is the value of an agenda that has been set without incorporating the voices of those in attendance? How do we currently measure effectiveness in organizations that may be functioning in relationally harmful ways? How might we collectively become more relationally effective once we let go of the performative nature of agendas (and how these manipulate people to conform)? How can dialogue support a shift that allows for organizations to embrace the complexity and nuance of humanity while remaining 'productive' in the traditional sense of the word?

DAY ONE

What Is Dialogue?
Why Does Your Organization Need Dialogue?

PART THREE

Co-hosted plenary session

CO-HOSTS

Jane Ball APDP, APDPA, (UK) Dialogue Associates and Academy of Professional Dialogue.
Peter Garrett APDP, APDPA (UK) Dialogue Associates and Academy of Professional Dialogue.

Jane:

Let's make a start with everyone who has arrived so far. This is our plenary session. What we'd like to do is to put everyone into groups of three, where I'm hoping you'll end up with people who weren't in the same session as you last time, and you can reflect together. We're going to give you ten minutes to reflect together about what you are thinking from the last session, the Participatory Dialogue. You might want to first tell your two colleagues what session you were in and what questions you were considering. Then maybe just say a little bit about what you're thinking now.

Peter:

When we come back together, we can hear what people are thinking. We are not looking for a report back from the sessions as much as a live engagement.

Jane:

This break-out gives you a chance to chew it over with a couple of other people. Let them know what session you were in, and then what you were thinking as you left. We'll see you back here in ten minutes.

Participants went into break-out rooms for ten minutes, then returned to the plenary session.

Jane:

Because you're spread over several screens, please use the hand-raising reaction so that we know who's trying to come in to speak. It's in the bottom toolbar, where it says, 'raise hand', and that brings you to the top left of the first screen. We'd like to invite our panellists back up if they would all be willing to do that as well so that we can maybe hear a little from them about what's been percolating during those sessions. Patty, Jon, Carrie, and Parvin raise your hands and come on up.

Those who have something that they'd like to raise, please leave your hand up. This is not just for the panellists, it's for anybody. We would like to hear what you're what you're thinking and what's been coming up for you.

Yes lieutenant, you need to unmute yourself.

Speaker:

Alright, thank you. In the breakout session that I was in, we talked a lot about what dialogue looks like in our own personal lives. It was very, very interesting how open everybody was when talking about their own lives, giving information about their personal lives, and how communication and dialogue have affected them in so many different ways. I was surprised by how much dialogue affects your personal life.

Jane:

Good. Let's just hear a few more voices and see where we go.

Speaker:

I've done a lot of work for 30 years, and I have been really lucky in my commercial career to do some fabulous early training in dialogue, which Peter and Jane may just remember. I've been lucky enough to have a lot of practice in designing and running large-scale meeting events and in training. I'm always willing to talk about that, but during the last five years I've been off on mental health leave with severe ADHD (Attention Deficit Hyperactivity Disorder). It's been an interesting time. What I am so excited about is this; most things that I've gone into that are slightly work-related immediately bring back my stress. This dialogue work does not. I'm just filled with enthusiasm! I am so excited about what I think the VADOC group is doing, and I hope at some point we hear the story about how on earth you got so many people strategically interested in this. That must be an amazing story. But I honestly just want to end by saying that I think dialogue and the skills of dialogue that I learnt early on massively helped me.

Peter:

Great, thank you. On Thursday, on the day on dialogic culture, we will hear a lot more about the Virginia story, but no doubt it will come up through the whole week.

Speaker:

Me, too. I'm like you, and I was only diagnosed this year. I have literally never heard someone mention ADHD in an event such as this, and it's the most exciting thing ever. Just how many people in our present population are undiagnosed with ADHD? My psychiatrist was like, *My God, how are you even functioning?* And I've survived it for 42 years. It's so exciting because of the recognition of neurodivergence, and how different our experiences of the world are. So, the fact that all of you are beginning to talk about and recognise that makes me really happy.

Speaker:

I think like autism, there is a spectrum of functionality with ADHD. People deal with it. People can kind of get by under the radar and not know that they're dealing with it until later in adulthood when they can't deal with it anymore. Basically, it comes to a head at some point in their lives, but they have grown up conditioned trying to manage it.

Jane:

Hmm. I'm sure the two of you will bump into each other again. You can find each other by sending a message in the profile area. Okay? Good. Who's next? You have been waiting patiently.

Speaker:

Yes, I was in the Participatory Dialogue room with the two of them, and I loved all of it. My only complaint is that the session was not long enough. I feel like these topics need eight hours for me to be satisfied. But anyway, lots of jewels were dropped. and I am so looking forward to the sessions in these upcoming days, especially if they are anything like what I've experienced thus far. I mean, I'm just overwhelmed with excitement and joy. And it's just all positive and uplifting things. If anyone's come into this conference empty, they are going to be overflowing by the end. I truly feel like that. I'm so happy it caught my eye, and I joined the conference. I just love everything up to this point. Love it, love it, love it!

Jane:

Good. Now maybe one of our panellists. Maybe, Patty? Anything that you would like to add, either in response to what you're hearing or from the session you were in?

Patty Hawk:

One of the things that came up in the session I was in that was so powerful was, in fact, this notion of power when you're in dialogue. Do you recognise your power? Does everybody in the room understand that they have a power role and need to be sensitive about that? As somebody who does a lot of facilitating, the way that it was framed was important as it recognised that sometimes people aren't ready to talk. If you have a very organised dialogue where you start by saying we'd like you're from you, and yet a person may not be ready to talk when they are invited to do so. So, to really respect that, respect when people are really just needing to listen. That's what struck me a lot in my breakout.

Peter:

Jon. What came up for you?

Jon Steinman:

Well, I am reflecting on the theme of the day, *What is dialogue?* There's a part of me that's curious. I do feel like through the day – through the panel, and the Participatory Dialogue and some of the breakouts – I've come to a little more clarity around what it is. Part of what I've noticed is that it's an opportunity to engage with the separation between people. It's an opportunity to not just engage with it, but potentially to dissolve it. That's what came up in our Participatory Dialogue about the absence of dialogue. The title of our Participatory Dialogue was *What is a community without dialogue?* We were exploring what are the defaults when we're not in dialogue? And one of the defaults I started to hear through everyone's experience, including my own, was that we create separation in order to make sense of what's happening. It might be that we design camps, being on one side of a fence, or being on one side of a coin. In the absence of dialogue, it appears that we find a way to compartmentalise our experience. When we are in dialogue, we start to break down the lines of separation between each other. Or at the very least we get curious about what is separating us. Also, I want to add that in our last little breakout with just the three of us, I really appreciated a question that was posed, *How do you know when you're in dialogue?* I thought that was a great question for a future dialogue.

Jane:

Parvin, would you like to come in, and others are then welcome to follow you.

Parvin Daeipour:

Thank you. When I was in the last breakout with three other people, I noticed something. Although this is the first day of the conference, I somehow felt that the container is kind of busy because everyone was having a great experience, there was a great spirit. They were so happy, they were so interested and they gained lots of things from the conversation that they had in the Participatory Dialogues and the smaller break-out groups. It reminds me of something, Peter, that Patrick de Maré told you about Koinonia. He said, that when we are in a safe container, we can have good conversation and dialogue. The atmosphere is what he called 'impersonal fellowship', and I could feel it, even though we were in a virtual situation. Even though we are not all in one building together. That's one of the things that I felt in the break-out room, and I could feel it in other rooms as well.

Speaker:

I want to piggyback off of what was said earlier. The sessions are not long enough! There is so much information, and in the breakouts that you want to share your thoughts and experiences with others. One of the things that I wanted to say is that to me, dialogue is the greatest gift we have. It's an opportunity for us to establish relationships, not just to connect with others or gather information. We're getting an opportunity to connect with somebody and get to know their perspective and their experiences.

Also, when we are talking about dialogue, we often don't consider the psychological safety aspect and the emotional intelligence aspect needs to be given a lot of credence as well because we can connect emotionally through the tonality of the conversations. We have to be self-aware, and that kind of speaks to the power dynamic that you mentioned Patty, the social awareness, self-management and relationship management aspect. We're establishing relationships through conversation. I want to suggest people take a look at Travis Bradberry who writes about emotional intelligence. He helped me to understand the parameters when I am facilitating groups and people are reluctant to be transparent in the conversations. One of the things I try to do as a facilitator is to open up and create a space where people are comfortable enough to share. I want to be welcoming, in order for people to be forthcoming with their information. This is a fabulous and amazing conference, and I really appreciate being a part of it!

Jane:

The real enquiry is, *How do we create what we're creating now here together in your organization? In your boardroom, where there is a hierarchical difference, where there are different roles, responsibilities, accountabilities, decisions to be made, and so on?*

Speaker:

With what you are asking, Miss Jane, when it comes to having those higher-ups come into the room and try to bridge that gap, it is really the respect and the tone that matters, the tone of your words. It's the way you're saying it. Rather than coming out as angry or judgmental, it's about coming out with respect in your voice, showing through your voice that you don't mind hearing what anyone has to say. If you have that kind of tone, then you will have people open up and tell their stories. You will have people feeling comfortable with expressing their ideas. If you don't have the correct tone, then you're not going to have people express those ideas to the full extent by using their authentic voice. What I was saying with my group is that the Working Dialogues are really helpful, too. I get passionate about some of them. I believe the Working Dialogues are helpful because they help build a generative tone – leading into the dialogue that you actually need to have.

Speaker:

I just wanted to come in and say that the group I was in was awesome. It was an 'aha' moment for me to understand and realise that it's okay to slow down, to allow the process to happen. Because we have different people in the room and people think differently, people learn differently, people have different values. It's okay to slow down. The 'aha' moment for me was realising that I thought I was doing something wrong, missing something, that I was processing stuff too fast, or that I missed something, and then I beat myself up because I felt like I didn't focus enough, or whatever. But now, I realise that it is OK to just slow down, slow the process down so that everyone is comfortable. Then everyone feels safe. It's about the process and not how fast you can get things done.

Speaker:

Okay, I just wanted to share something. What we have done today is nice for me. Regardless of what we have been talking about, I can see that different people from different countries, different cultures and different time zones can talk and speak to each other and share ideas and thoughts. Everything is very safe, it is a very calm place and I feel so excited here. Everyone listened to me when I tried to share my ideas. I have been trying to understand what other people say. This is very nice and a very good experience for me today. Thank you.

Peter:

I was still thinking about the comment that Jon made earlier. He said that when you hear things or see things, perhaps read them sometimes, you need to make sense of them. You might assume other people are not being that helpful. Perhaps they don't want to be helpful. You may think they are just like that. Then that interpretation of the situation becomes a little bit embedded. And organizations are not good places for open communication. We're not encouraged to talk openly with some groupings or some levels of hierarchy, and so on. This is a common challenge in any organization. We assume that some group of people is not being very helpful and that they don't want to be. That might not be quite what Jon was saying, but I am developing the thinking. I learnt a new word today, which is 'crunchy'. Something 'crunchy' happens. Somebody is being a little bit sarcastic or talking a little sideways, and you can feel in the room that there's something not right in the rapport between people. At that point, you have a choice. You can ignore it or, with a bit of courage, you can take on the situation and find out how to go a bit deeper to sort it out. That is not necessarily a very welcome or pleasant thing to do. But if you don't do it, of course, you confirm the situation you started with. So, I think in dialogue courage is needed to name what you see and hear and to find out why it's like that. The courage to go into the difficult stuff and inquire openly about it, to help something happen. What are other people thinking? The crunch may be a silence which sticks with people, or having the rug pulled from under you, and you are not quite sure how this is going to work out.

Speaker:

I kind of resonate with that. Do they feel some way about something that was said, and they want to get it off their chest? They must talk through it. They want to talk through it, and it helps them get through that.

Speaker:

What have I heard up to now, and what stays with me? Well, I'm in Argentina. Our national music is tango. Yes, and we all know that it takes two to tango. When one doesn't want to tango, there is no tango. It really takes at least two to want to be in dialogue, right? And of course, when wanting to be in dialogue, it is so much about a dialogic attitude, a dialogic way of living. This is something so relevant that is underlying every approach to dialogue. It has come up on many occasions today for me.

Harold Clarke:

A quick comment, if I may. I was in the breakout group on the topic, *Let's talk*. We talked a lot, and we had a focus on voicing. Voicing is key, because voices fuel the dialogue. Often, however, people sit back and voice in a manner that is not constructive, in a manner that I think takes away potentially from the dialogue. People think that voicing means saying exactly what's on your mind. Well, you can say exactly what's on your mind, but you can say it in a responsible manner that does not injure the dialogue. So, I think that while voicing is key, voicing is also very tricky because you could derail a conversation by the way you use your voice. You should have a conversation first internally, and then play it externally. Your struggle ought to be to figure out how to be genuine, but not to voice in a manner that's conclusionary because you don't have the total truth. Even when you feel potentially troubled or offended, you have to voice. It's a major responsibility. And you must voice in such a manner that you're not arriving at conclusions, but you're leaving the door open for others to build upon what you have shared. But I think a lot of people hold back, and when they can't take it anymore, they voice in a manner that can be injurious to the dialogue.

Speaker:

Well, Harold, you've really put the pressure on with that comment! I now feel that I have to retool my thoughts. So, I've been thinking about dimensions. I work in space planning and I'm always thinking in multiple dimensions – and that comment has thrown another dimension in there. This is what happened. We started out in the first session talking about time as a dimension (good morning, good afternoon and good evening), and we carried that on through our break-out room with time as a dimension of pace, with people needing different times to understand, and wanting to talk at different times. They are ready to go at different times, and the dialogue helps to get everybody coalesced on the time axis. Then someone talked about the willingness to participate. There's got to be a willingness to be in the room and to have the conversation. That forms a different dimension to me, the dimension of participation. Now this comment about voicing. Those are just a couple of thoughts. I'm pretty visual and what is bubbling around for me are the dimensions of time and dimensions of engagement.

Jane:

Hmm! I'd throw into that what's been coming up for me repeatedly along with time is structure. We tend to think of the flow of dialogue, but the structure enables that flow. It provides a kind of framework within which the flow can happen. I don't know if that can be added as a further dimension? Let's see.

Speaker:

I want to share that this is my first time in attendance, and I'm excited about all of the information that is being shared here. I've heard a lot of that, different people are in different areas of processing. At this point, I'm trying to bridge that gap in a situation when you're dealing with individuals that may not be in the headspace to be ready to dialogue, and they are not processing what you're putting out there, yet we need to come to a resolution. I'm excited about what I can learn from the wealth of information that is here in this group. It's quite a bit! I'm just excited and pleased to be a part of it. I would like to extend thanks to everyone for that.

Speaker:

I know others had their hands up before me, but I will go ahead and speak really quickly, I'll be brief. In our dialogue session, it was about promoting change. I picked up the dialogue practices of voice, respect, listening and suspension. When she said suspend, she was able to look at whatever's being spoken about from a different perspective. I think that's something that a lot of us don't always do – to look at a different person's perspective, and to meet that person where they are, as well as going back to help them to understand why this needs to happen in some timeframe. What I really latched on to was the perspective, because if the person doesn't have a good perspective of what needs to happen it can slow down the whole process. Then you don't move forward and the timing of it is out as well. I really learned a lot in this session, and I'm really glad to be here.

Speaker:

Hello! We may not always get people who want to tango with us, but we could at least provide that structure. Let's turn on the music until the person wants to engage in that dance with us. Right? So, like, Jane was saying, we provide that framework, that structure. That's what dialogue is about. We start somewhere with us knowing what dialogue is and how we can have effective conversations, and that is how we start to build something. The dialogue allows for that tango to start, right? Dialogue allows that person to feel comfortable. They may not feel comfortable to tango with us initially, but if we continue the process and meet them where they're at, then eventually we could probably start dancing. As far as our clientele is concerned, you know, they never want to talk to us. They never want to have a conversation with us. I don't know what inmate or probationer actually wants to come and talk to us. It never is the case, right? But if we meet them where they're at and provide structure we'll hopefully get somewhere a lot quicker than if we are not providing it. Oh, and one other thing I wanted to add that I wrote down on my notes. I love the fact that two ladies touched on ADHD in our Participatory Dialogue. As an adult I was also diagnosed with ADHD. I want to say that when I got diagnosed, and when I started here with dialogue it was actually aligned. Dialogue gave me my voice that ADHD had shut down. So being here in dialogue has been huge for me. I speak to you guys right now. Had it been a couple of years back, I would never have raised my hand. However, being in this environment, being with like-minded people and knowing and understanding the structure of dialogue. That has given me a voice to be able to share with others. I like that, and I want to be part of that conversation, ladies.

Jane:

Yes! So that you know, we have about five or six minutes left, and we have a sequence of waiting speakers we can see on the screen.

Speaker:

I will be brief. Patty spoke earlier about power and there's another aspect of that I started to think about. There's power in letting go of control when we honour and acknowledge a process that we are co-creating in a space together, a space of engagement. Our Participatory Dialogue was about pathways for mutual awareness and exploring connection. It seems in this world we have forgotten how to just be with each other. Dialogue gives us a way to co-create that space of meaningfully engaging with each other. When we let go of feeling we need to control a space, and we just breathe into it and allow people to be with each other, , there's real power in that. Especially for folks who are occupying positions of power. There is real relational power in being intentional about suspending your positional power when you step into engagement with someone who is in a position of inferior power within the hierarchy where you operate. By being intentional about suspending that power differential, naming it and suspending it, it creates a connection that otherwise would not be possible, and is something that can't be unexperienced. That carries and spreads wherever both parties go after that. That for me is a big piece of the power of dialogue.

Speaker:

I appreciate Harold speaking about the skill of voicing, the practice of voicing. Frankly, I feel that it may be the most difficult of the of the skill sets or practices, to really understand the nuance of what voicing means. It's challenging both for extroverts who want to talk all the time, and for introverts who are holding back. Rather than coming from what we think needs to be said, which often is where extroverts come from, how do we experience what has been called forth? How do we resist feeling the need to continue to replicate something that doesn't need to be re-said but find something that is coming from the internal heart space as opposed to the headspace. Once you begin to open your mouth without having prepared what you're going to say, what is called forth in you? I think it's a subtle skill that needs to be understood and practiced. Thank you for opening that up.

Speaker:

I will make it as short as possible. Good afternoon and good evening, everyone! We discussed how you can have an Institution in Dialogue. At the human level and the individual level, we have conversation. We then expand the conversation toward the leadership circle, and leadership decision making. Please note that change is a top-down process. If you want to use a dialogue to push for change, we need to reach out to the leadership circle. Actually, we need institutional conversation for that mindset change. I would like to write it in bold and put it in quotation marks, that **'mindset change'**. We need to get into the leadership circle with the notion of institutional conversation and dialogue. We need to actually implant this so that it's embedded into the organizational leadership circle. It's not an add-on, it's not a check box. We must have conversations about that. This is a very important message in any organization, regardless of whether it is government, non-profit or for-profit. We need to get this message closer into the leadership circle. That change of mindset is the first and basic step towards actually expanding the dialogue and getting it into the decision-making process. Then the institution is part of the conversation

Peter Garrett:

Thank you. I just want to ask, *Are you in Tehran?*

Speaker:

No, I am not in Tehran. I live in United States, an hour outside DC, in northern Virginia, and I am practicing coaching, leadership coaching, and also agile enterprise coaching.

Peter:

Good! Well, welcome, nice to meet you. I think tomorrow will pick up on the theme of dialogic leadership. I have one comment I want to make before we close off. There is a distinction I think that is helpful to make. There is one level of dialogue, which I would call more operational. When we began this work with David Bohm, we broke down the word dialogue. 'Dia' means 'through' and 'Logos' is 'the word' or 'the meaning'. So, dialogue refers to a common meaning through a group of people. Now, typically the people in a group do not have a common meaning because they have different information, different experiences, different knowledge, different opportunities, and so on. They are without a common understanding. Sometimes the organization doesn't work because people have a different idea about what they are trying to do and how to do it, and they keep tripping each other up. So, there is one level of dialogue that is needed in an organization so that we have a common understanding of the situation and what we're trying to do. Therefore, we support each other in doing it. There is another level of dialogue which is more about opportunity and potential. What could emerge? There's an opportunity for something more to happen has been happening. An example would be the Virginia story, with Harold Clarke arriving at the Department of Corrections and saying they could create a healing environment. It is about an opportunity that he saw. In any situation, with any group of people there are possibilities and opportunities, they're here. These two levels of dialogue are related. We call the first one dialogue, and the second one Generative Dialogue. I want to name that because it does affect the way we work in organizations in particular.

Bill Isaacs, if you are there, could you raise your electronic hand to bring you to the front? We want to introduce our hosts for tomorrow, Harold Clarke and Bill Isaacs. Maybe you'd like to say a few words about tomorrow when we'll be moving into a consideration of dialogic leadership.

Harold:

What you all may not know is that in 1990 I had my first dialogue experience with Bill Isaacs, who was teaching dialogue to a group of folks at the Royal Dutch Shell headquarters down in Woodlands, Texas. That is where I first met Bill and Peter. And my dialogue experience took off from there! Well, as Peter was saying, we'll be looking at dialogic leadership tomorrow, which is all about the stance you take in yourself and the impact you have to catalyse the world around you. We'll talk more about that tomorrow. There are a lot of connections between what was being addressed today and what we consider tomorrow. The challenge, I think, is going to be keeping them separate as much as we possibly can.

Jane:

It should flow easily from one day into the next. Thank you. I look forward to tomorrow. We're going to close off now with a piece of music to finish the day. It was chosen by Xingmian who may have gone to bed by now because he's in China, so it's the middle of the night for him. He's part of our accredited practitioner community and he offered this piece of music.

TWND! 6: Your Organization Needs Dialogue!

DAY TWO

What is Dialogic Leadership?
Why Does Your Organization Need Dialogic Leadership?

The first day of the conference explored the general understanding of dialogue and why it is needed in any organization. During the subsequent four days, the aim was to be more specific by differentiating the various aspects of organizational dialogue. On the second day, the inquiry was into dialogic leadership, and why it is needed in organizations. The co-hosts were Harold Clarke, ex-Director of the Virginia Department of Corrections, and Bill Issacs, CEO of Dialogos, both of whom have considerable experience of providing and encouraging dialogic leadership.

Initially, there was a tendency amongst participants to talk about good leadership, but the interest of the conference was to go beyond that and to distinguish between dialogic leadership and other forms of leadership. It was an opportunity to articulate something that may not have been clearly stated before and to deepen the collective understanding of why organizations need dialogic leadership.

DAY TWO

What is Dialogic Leadership?
Why Does Your Organization Need Dialogic Leadership?

PART ONE

Plenary session with a panel of five practitioners

HOSTS

Harold Clarke (USA)—Trustee, Academy of Professional Dialogue

William Isaacs APDP, APDPA (USA)—Dialogos

PANEL

June Boyle (UK)—Edinburgh Napier University and Skye Change Practice

Ali English APDP (UK)—Ignitus Coaching

Scott Frakes (US)—S R Frakes Consulting

Bernhard Holtrop (Sweden)—WithNature

Thomas Kottner (Argentina)—CoachReady

Harold Clarke:

Good morning, everyone. Good morning to all of you. The two of us who are spotlighted, Bill Isaacs and I, will serve as your hosts for today. Bill, before I say more, why don't you tell folks just a little bit about yourself, so they know who you are.

Bill Isaacs:

Alright. I am living in a place called Concord, Massachusetts, which is just outside Boston. and I've been here for quite a few years now. I've been involved in thinking about dialogue with my colleagues here, Harold, Jane and Peter, and others, for many decades now, and it started with our experience with David Bohm a long time ago. Actually, even before that I worked with a very famous environmentalist named Danella Meadows, Dana Meadows, and we were talking about cross-paradigm conversations even before I met David Bohm. We started in that cycle of considering, *How do we get human beings to talk together in contexts where it looks difficult, or where difficult is an understatement?* It turns out, of course, that over the last few decades that problem has not gone away. It seems to keep repeating itself. I've worked in all kinds of contexts, from union management to global institutions and governments. I've met a lot of people, some of whom are on the line now, through the leadership programs that I've run. I'm happy to be here.

Harold:

Very good, thank you, Bill. My name is Harold Clarke, and I just recently retired as the Director of the Virginia Department of Corrections, a position that I held for the last 13 years. Altogether, for the last 33 years, I have served as a director of corrections in four different states here in the United States, in Washington State, Nebraska, Massachusetts and now Virginia, where I currently reside in Richmond. I was introduced to dialogue by Bill Isaacs and Peter Garrett in the mid-1990s, and I was taken by it immediately. I attended the Leadership for Collective Intelligence program that Bill offered in Maine. I've had the privilege of introducing dialogue into four different departments of corrections in the United States and I would share with you that as we moved from one state jurisdiction to another, we seemed to learn more about how to go about doing this work. That's what we are experiencing currently in Virginia, where the work is way more advanced than we experienced in any of the previous States that we were in. This just tells me that life learning is quite dynamic. It's something that I really have enjoyed doing for the past many years, starting back in the late 1990s.

Bill and I are going to serve as your co-hosts today. Yesterday our focus was, *What is dialogue?* and, *Why does your organization need dialogue?* Well, I am sure that conversation is going to continue right through this conference, and after this conference. We get into different topics today and on Wednesday, Thursday and Friday. We'll be talking more every day about dialogue. Why is it needed? What is this thing called dialogue all about? I went back to look at the chat from yesterday and some things there helped to set the stage for the conversation today. The focus today is on dialogic leadership. What is dialogic leadership? And does your organization need dialogic leadership?

I want to share a couple of things from the chat with you. One of the first comments introduced the idea that dialogue has pros and cons. I had to stop and think about that one for a while. I can certainly see the pros—but I'd like to hear some more from the person who wrote that about what the cons are, as we go along in this conference. I can certainly believe that there are challenges, if that's what is meant by cons. There are challenges in introducing dialogue into organizations and elsewhere. It begs the following questions, *Who is introducing dialogue? Who takes on that role? Is that dialogic leadership? And where does that leadership come from? What does it look like?* That is what we will really be exploring in more detail today.

A second comment that I saw in the chat yesterday was, *How can we introduce dialogue to tough nuts?* I put that together with the first question. The tough nuts probably equate to the cons part of introducing dialogue, which I just consider to be a challenge. And then one last chat statement, actually a question, *How does dialogue help move an organization towards purpose?* As a person who was in a leadership position, when I think about that question, well, the reason that I got involved and the reason why I thought it was so important is that I felt dialogue could move us as an organization together toward a common purpose. Hopefully, as we have our discussions today, more will come out about that issue. How do we move towards a common purpose?

Bill:

We want to give you a chance to reflect on the topic of the day and to get your minds and hearts around what we're going to talk about. We'll come back to this in a minute, but one thing that is evident is that there are dialogic leaders among us—Harold being a very clear example. The question for the day is, *What is dialogic leadership?* and *Does your organization need dialogic leadership?* Well, Harold has done some things in this regard, and many people who've been touched by that are here. It raises the following questions, *What is that dialogic leadership that allows something to happen inside the Virginia Department of*

Corrections, and in other places? What does dialogic leadership do? What do you do? What does it take? And what does it take from you? From me?

We'd like to give you the chance right now to go into breakout rooms for about six minutes in groups of three. As a general rule of thumb, it's really easy to get theoretical about these topics. You describe what you know other people have said. It is much better to talk about your own experience. *What is your experience of what you at least think dialogic leadership might be?* You may have the question that you are not sure even what dialogue is. Well, that'd be a good conversation to have amongst you. But start with your own experience, whatever that is for you. What was your experience? You may point to observations of other people, and what you have seen other people do. Take a few minutes to talk about that and then we'll come back and hear from you.

Participants split into Breakout Rooms for 6 minutes

Bill:

All right. Everyone's back.

Harold:

Please do highlight the panelists, Bobby (Frazier), but while you're doing that, we'd like to get a few comments from participants about the conversation in your breakout session. Just a few. Speak up when you are ready.

Bill:

Yeah, all through today we're going to encourage you to do what could seem impossible, but really isn't, which is to act like we're all in a big room together. To speak, you don't need to raise your hand, just go for it! If it gets a bit chaotic, we will guide things.

Speaker:

I'm going to jump in to say that I think there's a Harold Clarke fan club!

Harold:

I've got a fan club of one.

Speaker:

Oh, no, I know there are others. That's what came up in our conversations. Let's just hear a few comments while we gather

Speaker:

So, I'll speak. I am a Harold Clarke fan. I worked at the VADOC (Virginia Department of Corrections) for about a year and a half, and I can honestly say that I think the dialogic practices worked. The dialogue worked because of Director Clarke and the leadership. The dialogic leadership started with Director Clarke, and if we hadn't had his support, and his belief and commitment to that program, I don't know that it would have flowed down to the ranks for us to even have the opportunity to embrace it. That was the conversation I had with the other person in my room, Scott Frakes, and he had the experience of working with Director Clarke in another state. I think he's a Director Clarke fan as well.

Bill:

How about others? A couple of other quick comments. What was your experience? What came up? Listen to see if it's your turn—that's the trick.

Speaker:

We were talking about definitions, like, *Have you defined leadership?* and then we talked about defining dialogue. We also talked about organizations that employ certain styles of leadership for a certain purpose, and how effective they might be. Then we discussed leadership style, such as a democratic style and how effective is it. Also, those who are directive, where dialogue is obviously absent. We talked about this yesterday, too. What is the outcome? What are the metrics associated with that? That's my afterthought of our conversation.

Speaker:

They must know who they can depend on, and who can do this, and they must know their people. They should be able to walk in a way that their people will want to follow their leadership. They should be able to have open conversations with their people. It brought back to my memory that he did the work, he led with those energies, and everybody did want to follow. It was a great thing to follow!

Bill:

Excellent. We'd like to hear from the panel that we have gathered today, and we're really excited to have everyone with us. We're going to hear from them in two ways. First, we're just going to ask each of you to introduce yourself very briefly, like in less than a minute. Just give your name and your physical location. Then after that, we'll hear a bit more from you about the themes of the day. Maybe June, could we start with you?

June Boyle:

Good Bill. Great to see everyone. I'm June Boyle. I practice human resources and organization development, so for me, it's very topical to be talking about organizations and leadership. That's been a big part of my life for a very long time. I'm based in Scotland, and I live in Edinburgh.

Bill:

Bernhard. How about you?

Bernhard Holtrop:

Thanks, Bill. My name is Bernhard, and I am currently based in Sweden. I moved from The Netherlands to Sweden recently. I'm looking now out of the window and see a landscape with 20 cm of snow here, fresh snow. I have been practicing dialogue in societal development for over 20 years now, facilitating dialogues and dialogue programs in troubled neighbourhoods but also in boardrooms and organizations. So, I have been introducing dialogic leadership in both boardrooms and in society. Preferably, I take people out into nature. That's why I am in Sweden, because in nature it's easier to come to your own nature and to come into connection with each other. I prefer to do leadership trials in nature! That says a bit about me.

Bill:

Excellent. Ali!

Ali English:

Hi! Everybody lovely to see you. My name is Ali English. I'm in the UK. If you think about the British Isles, I'm about halfway down on the left-hand side. Originally, I lived very close to where June lives now, so there's a lot of Scottish in my blood. I spent 25 years in pharmaceuticals, and we can maybe talk a little bit about that later. With the curiosity that I had, I worked in all sorts of different places, like marketing and R&D. Latterly, before I moved into my own business, I worked in late-stage clinical development. Ten years ago, almost to the month, I left my corporate career and set up a business on my own as an executive coach, a leadership development specialist, and more recently, as a team coach. Team coaching is what got me into dialogue. I met Jane and Peter at a team coaching retreat and recognized how beneficial that kind of approach could be in coaching senior teams, to have them talk and think differently together. So yeah, a first career and a new second career, and one that I love to do every day. As a team coach, every day is a great day.

Bill:

Wonderful, Thomas.

Thomas Köttner:

Thank you, Bill. Well, I'm based in Buenos Aires, Argentina, and I've spent my life in business environments. I'm passionate about human behavior and seeing what we can do in our business environments. Having been an executive and going to the high ranks, I then went into consulting and for the last 18 years, I've been an executive coach. Being at the end of the world in Argentina, I chose not to spend my life on planes. In 2010 we started what was the first online Executive Coaching company. Since then, I have been running that company and coaching senior executives, working on leadership with them, helping them to generate dialogic attitudes and bring those ways into their teams and companies.

Bill:

Wonderful.

Scott Frakes:

Morning Bill. I have 40+ years as a practitioner in the business of corrections. I spent 32 years in Washington State, and then in 2015 I went to Nebraska as the director of that system for eight years, from which I just retired. I had the good fortune to meet and work with Harold when he was in Washington State. One of the amazing things Harold did was decide that we were going to use dialogue practices in our work. He brought Peter and Jane to Washington State, where I had the opportunity to work directly with them for a couple of years. So, over the last 18 years I have, what I would call "dabbled" in the world of dialogue. I have tried to use it in many different situations, including an opportunity to work with a group of lifers when I was a warden in a prison, and that was probably one of the most enjoyable and rewarding experiences that I had with dialogue. I value probably more than anything the idea of "seeking to understand rather than to be understood" and trying to create those level playing fields and open conversations with executive teams, mid-level managers and line-level staff. Seeing if we could just sit together and talk, and learn, and take advantage of all the things that a good dialogue could bring. I live in Connell, in Washington State, which is a long way from nowhere, and you can almost see the edge of the world, but not quite. It's currently 27 degrees. But there's no reception for cell phones . . .

Bill:

Great. Welcome, each of you. Each of you has your own unique angle on this theme of dialogic leadership, which itself possibly could seem a contradiction.

Dialogue is all about working together. What about leadership? People's image of leadership is of one sole individual and lots of other people following them. We're talking, I think, about something slightly different from that. But perhaps not so. I think it would be quite valuable to hear from each of you, and the illustrations and the stories that you have about it. I'm wondering, Harold, if you want to add anything as you as we start.

Harold:

Thanks, Bill. I've had, as was mentioned, the privilege and opportunities of working in a number of jurisdictions, using dialogue. I really believe that as some indicated, it takes a commitment, a major commitment. To do things differently, you cannot continue to be who you have always been. If you intend to be successful in dialogue, you must make some major changes, and it may lead to vulnerabilities. It may lead to you being uncomfortable because it's all about transformation, which begins with you. But I'll tell you it's worth the while. The individual who is committing to this new exploration is aiming for the benefit of all.

Bill:

I think that's excellent. When I think of the theme of dialogic leadership, I think of a few people, Harold being one. There are others. What I think about is the condition that they evoke around them. They're doing something in action, in words and also something inside themselves that is producing a condition around them. For example, I think of a Jesuit priest in Colombia. He's now actually the chairman or the head of the Truth and Reconciliation Commission in Colombia. A fellow named Francisco de Roux lived for years in the jungles of Colombia, experiencing the conflicts that were and are running there. It is a 50-year war with lots of different fragmented groups. Pacho, as he's known, and his team lived in these places and created peace zones. Pacho's a very unusual character. When he was experiencing very intense violence with people being murdered, he would go to visit the families of the people who were victims. An unusual context. Many would go to visit with the people who did the killing. His attitude was profound. This is a word we found coming up yesterday, *profound* respect for the dignity of human beings. He would make it clear that he didn't approve necessarily of how people were operating, but he listened for and held their dignity very closely. They completely responded to him. That was unusual in that context, to say the least—Pacho's very intense character yet very mild-mannered way. He is an example of someone who said, *We can create a different kind of environment here.* I think Harold's done that, and I think each of you on our panel has experienced or observed elements of this. So, I think it'd be terrific to hear from you. Perhaps we'll start again with June.

June:

Okay. Well, I think the story I will share is related to BP oil and gas. Some 25 years ago it was predominantly trading fossil fuel, but the CEO John Browne, now Lord Browne, who was constantly looking at how the organization needed to evolve into the future, took himself off around the world to really engage with external voices to understand what BP could be in the future. And those voices hugely influenced him. But he also had them think about the question, *How do you design an organization with that context in mind?* Actually, *How do you build an organization where learning and knowledge travel across the organization between leaders and between the systems?* His view became that you did it peer to peer. Now, those peers also have teams within their teams and that was key to how it all evolved. It was this idea that you've got a very technical organization that was going to have to wake up to a very different context at some point. The way we were putting retail stations together needed us to think about solar panels. All the leaders were thinking of at the time was the cost, not the impact it would have on the planet. One thing that we realized was that we needed to be a learning organization. The way that we went about that was to say that we were going to invest in leaders as peers. And through that peer-to-peer mechanism, give them the opportunity to experience things like dialogue. A number of years ago Bill was instrumental in helping these learning partners to really shift the conversation of the organization. Some individuals embraced it more than others, and that created disturbance within their teams and within the organization. But as we began to build the peer-to-peer process, it became more or less an accepted practice that we could create these conversational containers. Bill mentioned unions and management. We ended up being able to have dialogues that we never imagined between unions and management. Dialogues that were unheard of. Some of these contexts and conditions created an environment where dialogue became part of, amongst other things, the organization becoming a learning organization where we shared knowledge, knowing that we couldn't do it without beginning to think and act differently together.

Bill:

Really good! Let's keep going, Bernhard. How about you?

Bernhard:

I would like to share a short story that I experienced last year with a man whom I respect very deeply but who, when I met him for the first time was far from dialogic. I happen to be very close to him and I happen to be able to serve him a little bit, and the organization he works for. To become more of a dialogic leader, I can share a short anecdote. He is an entrepreneur and the CEO of a highly successful small consulting boutique with 40 consultants flying all over the world. He's some years younger than I am, so mid-50s, and he's about to say goodbye to the firm and to hand it over in a careful way. I've been working with them doing outings in nature with his team, building trust and things like that, and making new appointments, agreements and other things. I always noticed in the years before that something was missing. He had been trying to hand this over. He hired a new managing director but that became a flop and talent was walking away. He's a brilliant man, very inspiring and tremendously charming, but he also has a short fuse. He used to lash out at people when things didn't go his way, and it took away a lot of the self-trust we had built in the people around him. I could see that happening. People were afraid to fail and people were afraid to stick their necks out. They didn't show the best of themselves.

And then he called me. He said, Bernhard, *Are you willing to help again?* He told me about the failure of the new managing director. He said, *Are you willing to help*? and I said, *Yes, I am.* Then I asked him if he was willing to step back into the board of directors himself, and he said, *Yes, I am.* So, we each stepped in, and we went through the process. We were in the mountains last year and we had a beautiful meeting with 40 people. They were all sharing in small groups and then we rounded up in a big circle around the fire. Five of the six smaller groups reported back that the biggest hiccup was a lack of trust. They wanted the board of directors to trust them.

They could see that the CEO was really triggered, so I said, *Okay, let's have a coffee break.* We had to talk because he was really, really triggered. He said, *They can buy my shares.* He was triggered, so we decided not to talk about trust and lack of trust. Instead, I said, *Let's have a dialogue, and then trust will grow.* We started to have a dialogue with the top 11 of the 40 people. At first, he said, *They don't have the capacity since they had never led a company*, and then things really caught fire. After this dialogue, it was around midnight when he came to me, and he was shining all over. He said, *Wow! Did you hear that? What a quality! What a quality of people I've got around me.* I complimented him for giving it the space he did. He made the transfer, and at the end of those four days in the mountains, he confessed to the group. He said, *There had been a lot happening during the last half year in our company*, and he said, *Things have also been happening in me, myself, more than I ever expected.* There was a sigh of relief from the rest of the organization, and from there on we were able to build on this dialogic leadership that had emerged.

So, I pick up on exactly what Harold is saying. It is calling for a big step for the leader who is working dialogically. I have great respect for this man. I got to know where his trigger comes from and where his unrest comes from, and he dared to let go of that. So that is personal development first, and then organizational development follows. That's the challenge of dialogic leadership.

Bill:

Hmm. A very good colleague. Ali?

Ali:

The interesting thing, as I turned my mind to think about what I would talk about in this part of the day was that there were many, many stories of things that I've seen. This one story kept coming into my head, and I kept thinking, I can't tell that story to all these people. But the story would not go away and so I have decided to tell it. It's not a big story about dialogic leadership in a huge company. It's about late in the summer this year when my family got together to celebrate my brother and sister-in-law's wedding. They had married in Singapore during lockdown, and we weren't able, any of us, to be there. Later we managed to get five generations of my family around a table—a very big table, because it's a very big family. It is an occupational hazard of team coaching that you spend a lot of your time just watching the dynamics of what's going on around a table. You can't stop yourself. And what really stood out to me was how differently all those generations see the world. Very, very differently. I sat there with my fairly new understanding of dialogue. Scott was telling us that he's been doing dialogue for many, many years. I'm relatively new to it. But I looked at all that fragmentation around the table where the people are my family. They love one another. Yeah, we're a very close family. And in another way, we don't love one another.

That got me to thinking about leadership and what leadership has looked like during my lifetime. When I started in corporate all those years ago, gosh! nearly 35 years ago, we simply did what our bosses asked us to do. If they said, *Go and do this,* that's what you went and did. It wasn't all about what you think about it, and how you feel about it and what meaning we might give. But when I looked around that table, I thought to myself, *I can't sit with my nieces and nephews and my sons and daughters, and just say, you have to do this.* They want to know the meaning of it. How different that kind of leadership is from, say, the command-and-control style? It is a more meaning-based leadership that is now prevalent and will become even more prevalent. If I think about the people around that table, from the late 1930s to the early 2000s, it is just such a large span. In our workplace at the moment, we have some spaces that have those five generations. So, the leadership, to my mind, has to be really different. It needs to be a leadership that connects rather than a leadership that directs. For me, that is the dialogic part of dialogic leadership. Part of that is all about how to bring people with all those disparate views together. Allowing them to share and allowing them to find a common meaning.

The interesting thing is, you know, that sometimes the universe talks to you. Today I'm in somebody else's house, because we're having work done in our house, and I'm sitting in front of a bay window. It's autumn here in the UK and there's a great big tree outside that has five different colors. I've sat and looked at it for a while now and it just reminds me that all these colours can fit together because they're all leaves. They are really different colours all sitting together! For me, getting that to happen is what dialogic leadership is all about.

Bill:

Hmm, hmm, hmm! So beautiful. Next Scott.

Scott:

You know, the later you go in these panels the more difficult it becomes to focus because all these great things are being said, and all these great ideas are shared. I think I learned relatively early in my leadership career that I didn't have all the answers and that I was frequently not the smartest guy in the room. That is probably most of the time. If nothing else, the collective wisdom of the group was far smarter than me. That's one of the things that I love about dialogue. It instills a need, a desire, to really want to hear what everyone in the room has to say. To try to create spaces where people are willing to say it. I'm always looking for somebody on my team who will name that the emperor has no clothes because I don't need a team working with me who's always telling me how great I am, how smart my decisions are or how great my ideas are. But when they walk out of the room, they are telling each other, *Oh, man, I think it's muck.* It's not that that never happens, yeah, it does, unfortunately.

I think I'll wrap this up with my experience in Nebraska. Because I didn't have any resources, there were all kinds of excuses for why we didn't formally invest in dialogue. But I was doing it informally, working with my executive team and then working with the next layer of the organization, the top 25 of the organization. One of the places where it was valuable, incredibly valuable in that organization, was when we got into the conversations around inclusion and diversity. I had people coming to me to tell me that we were talking about things that they'd wanted to talk about for years and never felt that it was safe to do so. They never felt that there was an audience that wanted to hear it. Of course, I had others who sat in the room quietly and said nothing and then they would tell me afterward that they really didn't understand why we needed to have that conversation because to them there were no issues. That, of course, reinforced why we needed to have the conversation. I think that creating safe places to have conversations that encourage people to talk and giving people room to do so, is key. As a leader, Harold would use the word transformation. I've been trying to figure out, *What does it mean to be a transformational leader?* I've been working on that journey for a good ten years. There is no question that the world of dialogue and transformational leadership go hand in hand. Dialogue is one of the best tool sets you could have if you really want to be effective, to be a transformational leader.

Bill:

Hmm. very good, thanks. Finally, Thomas, let's hear from you.

Thomas:

Well, as Scott says, many things are being heard so a lot is going on in my mind. But I am thinking, *What's the angle to this?* What I've realized over the years is that the fundamental struggle leaders in organizations are having is the breach between what they would like to do with and for their people and what they have to do to deliver results under the pressure of shareholder value. Lately, that is more so with the much higher pressure of equity funds who want to squeeze results so fast and strong. It really puts a lot of pressure. So, you ask, *Okay, how do you help teams here to become dialogic?* What I've realized is that it's not about what a leader has to do but about who a leader needs to be, and what their attitudes need to be. But how? What are the things that constitute the person, that can be put on the table to generate a dialogic environment?

You were calling for stories. I remember working with a board of directors in South Africa in a company that was a leader in vaccine development. I was supposed to be there to help them with a two-day workshop on strategy. After listening a little bit as they started, their whole interaction, I placed a question which made the CEO stop and stay silent. He asked for a 15-minute break. He went to his office, came back, and said that everything that was planned for the day was now in the garbage bin. Instead, it was to be two days of questioning. He realized through my question that everything that they said needed to be reviewed and inquired into. Sometimes there are such fundamental things in an organization, or even in a team, so fundamental that you realize that if you don't consider them, you are building your structure on an unstable base.

So those two days, to me, were a journey of dialogue. It was all about inquiry, exploration and really thinking together. When it finished, they said this was the most wonderful experience they had had as a team to that day. It turned out that way, and this made me think that everybody has a book inside but very few sit down and write it. Do we all have a dialogist inside, but one that is not yet ready to practice?

Bill:

Excellent. I think you can hear that although the words were different from each different person, the music behind the words is actually very similar. It's evocative of a flow. Now the word dialogue, has the root words *dia* and *logos*, right? The flow between, a flow among, a flow through. Well, a dialogic leader creates a flow. Sometimes people walk into a circumstance and there isn't a flow. It's full of static, right? But the opportunity and skill to create something different in attitudes change the experience of people all around them. I think we've heard that in each of these stories. I want to suggest that this is an opportunity in this conference, in this conversation with all of us. We're not just hearing about something—we're having an opportunity to experience something together right now, all across the world. I'm curious about your experience and we have some time to have a conversation among us. We'll also open the chat now, so you can put some questions in there if you like. No promises about actually answering any of them, but I think it'd be quite useful for everybody to know what people are thinking. You will have a chance to raise a few things in a minute. But first I'm just wondering, as you guys on the panel all listen to each other, what your reaction is to what you've just heard.

June:

I think one of the things that I'm noticing is either our own resistance or the resistance of the organization. What's the resistance in us to step in, and to be able to make that first leap forward? I think there is something that holds us back and it's useful to know that for ourselves because we are as much an instrument for dialogic leadership as anybody else. I think we need to think about inquiring a little bit about where the resistance is that we meet as we step into this.

Harold:

You know, I think that after listening to all your stories, as was indicated, there is a flow. There's something flowing through different situations, different places. There's a flow taking place that makes it all happen. So, what is that? The panelists have spoken about dialogic leadership, but what is it really? What is dialogic leadership? How do you go about achieving it? Do you have to do something different? Of course, the answer is, yes. So, what do you have to do differently, especially with yourself as the leader? We can hear the panelist's reactions and then, as Bill said, we'll entertain the chats as well. So, what is this dialogic leadership? How is it achieved and what needs to be done differently by the leader within him or herself? These are great questions to focus on.

Bernhard:

Based upon what I've heard from my colleague panelists, I have heard some quite poetic words describing flow and a safe container space where one can say that the emperor has no clothes. Then I come back to how to create a safe place as a dialogic leader. I think a very important ingredient is to have a safe place in yourself. That sounds a little bit poetic, too. but it is about facing who you are yourself and facing your inner fierceness. And being at peace enough with yourself that you don't act out these interferences. That's a daily challenge for all of us in our day-to-day lives. I think you create, and you contribute to creating this safe space—a safe container where people dare to speak up in the moment. You, as a leader, have paid attention to that part in yourself. That's what I heard from Ali, Scott, Thomas and June.

Ali:

Bernhard, I really agree with a lot of what you just said. The word that popped up for me when Harold and Bill started talking was awareness. Self-awareness of what's going on all around. Other people may have this all figured out but for me, that's a lifetime's work. Whenever you get to one bit of awareness, there's another bit that needs to come up and be talked about and learned about. There's something about lifelong learning. Dialogic Leadership is not that I've been on the course and I'm now doing dialogic leadership. It's more like layers of an onion, I think. Then there is intentionality. Intentionally building psychological safety, inviting people in and leaving space to intentionally have curiosity. I think there's real importance in intentionality.

Thomas:

I have a permanent question. Are we treating dialogue as a noun or are we try treating dialogue as a verb so that dialogue is the flow? I see a river in dialogue and to navigate the awareness that Ali is mentioning, I think there are certain things that a dialogic leader needs to cultivate. Yes, awareness. Being someone who wants to give of him or herself. A giver's perspective is way more open than a taker's perspective, right? A taker's perspective will say, *Okay, how do I get to where I need to be?* Yes, I will use dialogue to get there. Okay, I just need to arrive where I need to arrive and get my part of what I need. A giver will be more generous in letting the dialogue flow in and in paying attention to people. What do they need to keep this flow going? What do they need to get inspired? How do we really get to that purpose together? And this, which seemingly takes more time, is the best investment that can be made because when those things are clear everybody knows what to do, how to move, and in what direction to go. That's the beauty of this thinking together. Thinking together openly needs a safe space, and fostering that is the responsibility of the leader, fostering the free flow of conversation and exploration.

Bill:

I think there's an interesting point here. The contextual expansion of awareness, as several of you put it, meets up against the fragmentation of resistances and difficulties. These challenges are in ourselves, in our organizations and in our teams. There's a threshold to cross here, to initiate something different. The interesting question is, *What does that require? What is required to open up something else?* Opening something else up and producing something different. We're describing a state, and the evoking of it. Even as we're speaking about it, there is a different quality of understanding, of feeling. One can get it by listening. The question is, *How do you produce that?* How do you produce that in a situation where people don't appear to want it? Or really don't want it? Or are really very suspicious of it? That raises the question, How do you deal with those factors in yourself? What do you do about the factors of fear, mistrust, resistance, whatever it is, the reactions being triggered in me? I'm sure each of the panelists would have something to say about this. It's only as you bring something to an internal reality that you have something to offer in an external sense. There are all kinds of techniques like leaning forward or looking interested that are not really that helpful right? We're talking about qualities of engagement that we must activate in ourselves. I'm curious. I think dialogic leadership is leading from who one really is, and that is collective as well as individual. It is in everybody.

We've got a range of different comments moving in the chat—a kind of parallel dialogue going on in the chat, which is great. Harold, what do you think? Maybe we should just hear a couple of voices from there? We probably have one or two minutes. Maybe one or two voices from the wider group? I saw some very interesting questions in the chat.

Harold:

I agree. Let's open it up, take a couple of those and address them openly. Maybe people who are making comments in the chat could also make an observation and contribute to this conversation.

Speaker:

I read a quote where someone said that the success of an intervention depends on the interior condition of the intervener. If you want to introduce something this powerful into a wider organization, people connect with the heart. We know when you've faked the funk, and we know when you're being truly genuine. I love that quote. It's spot on.

Harold:

I will add that it depends on the intentions.

Bill:

And they make all the difference. Hmm! Maybe one more? What got stirred in you as you listened to this so far?

Speaker:

I had something that started yesterday that made me do a little reflection and go into that space containing all the different colored leaves and the different generations. And now I have work to do. One of the conference participants got really excited about collaborating. They had a neurological condition, ADHD, and Jane created a space for them with a breakout session. We reconvened after we ended the Participatory Dialogue. I was looking at the breakouts and I saw one with that title. I wanted to learn more but I also didn't want to impose on them. So, I was struggling. That's my internal struggle that we're talking about. You know I have to search to find out why, I struggle with that.

Bill:

Alright. Well, one of the things that tends to happen when we talk about a topic like this is that things you need to do become more apparent. There's the overt agenda, and there is what is moving in you, that is not disconnected from the topic. That's the insight about dialogue. It shows up in us. I want to talk about this interesting idea over there, but it is inside too. They're the same thing. They're exactly the same thing. Having some compassion for whatever comes up in you is the starting point, as opposed to getting irritated about it, or ashamed of it. That opens the space. So, I think with that, Harold, we should probably let people go into the break, and then shortly after that into their Participatory Dialogues.

Harold:

I think as a leader, and you are all leaders, we need to begin by acknowledging that there is fragmentation. People are broken, organizations are broken. Then, if you sincerely want to do something about it, you will seek out and apply a number of different approaches. You will do different things. It may be dialogue, which I recommend, but you're seeking wholeness. You're seeking wholeness. You want to help people. In our case, it's both inmates and staff. It's not one or the other—and you begin with that premise. And then you go into it sincerely. That's when you begin to see outcomes. But you also must go through some changes in yourself. Amen.

DAY TWO

What is Dialogic Leadership?

Why Does Your Organization Need Dialogic Leadership?

PART TWO

Seven concurrent participatory dialogues

Thumbnail sketches

Thumbnail sketches to introduce the seven Participatory Dialogues that follow:

Loshnee Naidoo APDP (South Africa) and Jane Ball APDP, APDPA (UK) introduced an African leadership approach called Ubuntu, embodied by Nelson Mandela and others, that is inherently dialogic in contrast to the dominant leadership styles in other cultures. Participants engaged the new concept willingly, translating it into the behaviors of their existing dialogic practices where they found strong resonances. Beyond a shared purpose and vision, the core Ubuntu tenet *'I am what I am because of who we are'* reveals a shared destiny. That identity perhaps seemed a step too far for many.

Timo Nevalainen (Finland) and Ismo Huusko (Finland) proposed that traditional leadership styles deal poorly with tensions in groups of people. Instead, they proposed that the collaboration and mutual respect of dialogue are needed to manage those tensions effectively. The dialogic consideration centred on the reframing of tension as a positive phenomenon that called for clarity not resolution. People agreed that tension can raise awareness, and that leaders who reveal their vulnerability help to deepen the potential learning, rather than revealing weakness.

Leon Hylton (USA) and Tzofnat Peleg-Baker (Israel) proposed exploring a deliberate move from individual leaders to collective leadership. The participants, however, did not follow their lead. Instead, they collectively chose to consider the potential of dialogue within organizations. Notions of collaboration, inclusivity and shared power were superseded by the realisation that anyone can be a leader, not just the person with that title, as in the African proverb, *If you think you are too small to make a difference, you have not spent the night with a mosquito!*

Meg Bower APDP (USA) and Shaketta Thomas APDP (USA) asked how dialogic leadership can provide the stability to maintain a creative edge in managing massive change. People took this more locally, with one leader asking, *How can I create a space in my team for the authentic exploration of ideas?* Leaders were seen as the greatest potential beneficiaries of dialogic leadership, particularly if they can trust the dialogic process and enable opposing. One junior staff member said *Man, I wish some of our leadership was on this call to learn that all conflict is not negative!*

Joseph Walters APDP (USA) and Laura Little APDP USA invited an exploration of the opportunities and challenges of dialogic leadership. People particularly liked Joe's observation that leadership is more of a behavior than a role. Participants noted how staff seem to be getting younger every day, and they look to the older ones as leaders they want to emulate. Many of those present felt that dialogic leaders provide an 'intentional space' for generative inquiry, and that dialogic leaders choose deliberately to incorporate ideas from the team to achieve the organization's goals.

PJ Manning APDP (USA) facilitated this session on her own. She accepts that in her organization "leaders are leaders" and "supervisors are supervisors". Whilst staff members sometimes have the needed "missing" link, they tend to respond in a generally positive way rather than providing specific and genuine thoughts that can be used by leadership. In resonance, one speaker said she believed we are all leaders when it comes to dialogue. Another lamented the lack of dialogic leadership in his workplace, believing we should *talk with* people as adults, not *tell* them what to do.

Peter Garrett APDP, APDPA (UK) and Jennie Amison APDP (USA) questioned the effectiveness of one leader making all the decisions and the many followers carrying them out. That seems a poor use of collective intelligence. Perhaps dialogic leaders do not gather followers, but instead create more leaders. The formally appointed leader ensures that others participate in the decision-making that they will then confirm, given it is their accountability. It is not just that everyone has a voice—everyone contributes to understanding the challenge and finding the best way forward.

Ubuntu: 'I Am Because You Are' – a Dialogic Leadership Mantra . . .

Loshnee Naidoo and Jane Ball

PRE-CONFERENCE DESCRIPTION

There are many types of leadership styles but the western version, which embodies traits of individualism, hierarchy, dominance and control, has become normative. With current challenges and changes in the world architecture, such as globalisation and polarisation, is it time to embrace and embed new models of leadership. Could the African philosophy of Ubuntu offer what is needed? Ubuntu, *I am because you are,* is rooted in principles of dialogue, community, interdependence, inclusivity, equity, empathy, respect, dignity, reciprocity and a sense of shared destiny. The definition offers so much that we aspire to, yet it sounds like an unrealistic fantasy for many organizations and communities. These, however, are the principles on which many Southern African communities and societies are built and thrive. These were the traits embodied in President Nelson Mandela and Archbishop Desmond and Leah Tutu. Can we find ways to incorporate these reflective and transformative modes of being to provide truly Dialogic Leadership? What stops us?

CHECK-OUT

Loshnee Naidoo:

> The check-out. What do we do next? What do you do? What is one thing, one action that you could implement to encourage dialogic leadership using the Ubuntu principles or traits? Let's take it to a place where we can make it actionable. That's our check-out. We have about eight minutes to do the check-out, and we can tag each other.

Speaker:

> I'm going to say, just be conscious, and actively use the dialogue techniques in all your communication, at home, at work, at the grocery store . . .

Speaker:

> Always be present and be ready to give an account of yourself first.

Speaker:

When every one of us accepts that we are all travellers, that we are on the same boat, and we have a common destination.

Speaker:

The thing that has stuck with me, and that I want and need to do for myself, is the idea that people don't need to be fixed. How am I going to invite people into conversations without feeling that I already have all the answers.

Speaker:

The thing that keeps resonating with me is conscious awareness. It's like getting a full understanding of what's going on in the moment and how you're impacting the atmosphere. It leads for me and will help me to continue to practice inclusivity.

Speaker:

For me it's the issue of modelling. I think leadership is modelling. How do we show up? How do we use Bohm's notion of proprioception or thinking and feeling actively and showing it so people can see it. They say, *Wow! I'm seeing something different in you!*

Speaker:

Listening to understand, not to respond. And I will keep on doing that.

Speaker:

Being present and self-aware.

Speaker:

For me? Honestly, when I think of the question, *What could you do next?* I feel like I'm still in the now, and I'm not at the next level. This is my first dialogue. I feel like I'm still in a beginner level of learning what dialogue is and how it works. I do relate to a lot of what everyone's saying but I found it to be a little overwhelming just trying to figure out where to jump in, where to share. I like it so far and I do hope to be there one day. But I'm kind of still in the beginner level.

Speaker:

I will say it is to continue building, you might not see everything right now, but you'll see a progression with time. So, patience, I guess.

Speaker:

The question about the correlation between dialogue and empathy. I had to look it up and it says they both accentuate effective communication acts, such as listening and understanding other people's perspectives. So not fixing is what stuck with me as well. Not fixing, but intentionally planting seeds that I may not be there to see harvested.

Speaker:

I've been doing this for 15 years or more, and I might inquire around consent. I continue exploring what does that mean in a dialogic context? How do we consent together? Or how do I consent? How does he consent? How does she consent? Consent is a really important area for me that is completely neglected and ignored in the way we communicate in daily life. I'm looking to find out. Yeah, that's where I'm going. I'm going to continue to focus on that right now.

Speaker:

My action is to insist, wherever we are, that there is more than one perspective.

Speaker:

Keep it short. Keep it simple. I'm more familiar with the term 'genuine positive regard'. I've heard the 'unconditional positive regard'. The genuine always sticks with me, especially in thinking about leadership because who wants a leader that's not genuine? If I am genuine, I can't go wrong.

Speaker:

I would like to understand more about how Ubuntu is different from other dialogic approaches. I would like to learn more about the deeper aspects.

Speaker:

My action is going to be to double down on listening with my head, with my heart and with my intuition.

Speaker:

I can't help but follow that. I've been sitting here and continue to be fully present to work with what emerges. And to trust my gut.

Speaker:

I'm in training to become a dialogue practitioner. I've been in some dialogues and some things that I've seen I didn't like. It's not what I want to replicate. So, I'm just learning how to lead dialogue with good intentions.

Jane:

Everybody else has spoken so I'll come in and then come to you Loshnee to finish off. I can just encourage you to look around the room. I don't know if you can see the five, ten or 20 of us. I am thinking that I am because you are. Of course, that is what's been happening. Now, we know we are here together. We've had the dialogue that we've had because of who is here. And I thought what I thought and learned what I've learned because of you. That's one thing I'm going to do more of—that. Somehow, Zoom makes it more difficult but actually look and see. I see you all, and I hear you all and I appreciate what we're doing and thinking of together. I'm going to do more of that. And I want to think more about Ubuntu. I think this long-term thinking and shared destiny sounds so different from lots of organizations. They have a common purpose and vision statement. But to have a shared destiny feels like what the world really needs now. I want to take that forward in my thinking.

Loshnee:

Thank you, Jane. The thing that I take away is being fully present to how my words and my actions impact everybody else. You know, self-realization through others. I want to say thank you to everyone because it was really beautiful to engage on the concept of Ubuntu and how we can make this a reality. It has been a while since Mandela was around, but the ethos and the lessons still resonate for all of us. Thank you for engaging with that. What I'd like to do is to close with reading what Ubuntu is. *Ubuntu denotes both the state of being, and one of becoming. A process of self-realization through others, and the enhancement of the self-realization of others.* Thank you.

POSTSCRIPT

We are aware that Ubuntu has become a guiding principle for leadership, promoted by management schools, and included in leadership development programmes. This Dialogue provided an opportunity to start with our personal experiences, which differ, rather than books.

To illustrate, Jane's experience of leadership in English organizational, social, and political culture is typical of the western version we described in our introduction. She pushes against this paradigm, resisting the *great man* models of leadership and the professional expert models of leadership, and advocates ideas such as leading from where you are, distributing power and authority, succeeding and thriving together.

Having worked in large corporate organizations, Loshnee also experienced this norm. She experienced a different paradigm, though, in the indigenous culture of her home, South Africa. She grew up as the child of someone deeply involved in the anti-apartheid movement, of which she was also a part, where embodying the spirit of Ubuntu was critical and where self-realisation was achieved through the success of others.

Loshnee set the context with stories of the history of South Africa seen through the lens of Ubuntu. The Dialogue itself primarily explored the behaviour that would be associated with Ubuntu, summarised by participants in their check-out comments. One participant Laura Brown wrote an acrostic poem to capture these qualities . . .

UNIVERSAL
Is not accepting of living in silos

BEHAVIOR
Is not unhealthy actions or negative attitudes

UNITED
Is not being greedy, selfish or egotistical

NEGOTIATION
Is not compromise

TOLERANCE
Is not casting a blind eye or denying consequences

UNDERSTANDING
Is not complacency or indifference

These seem to be skills that can be, and are, taught. Many of them – listening, awareness of self and other and respect – are the skills associated with Dialogue. Everyone valued these skills and could see what a difference they made to others around them.

Another aspect of the philosophy of Ubuntu, beyond the observable behaviour, is a disposition to yourself, others and the world around you, which naturally leads to these ways of relating to others. Experiencing yourself as a part of your community, as an interconnected part of a bigger whole. We began this exploration but did not manage to delve deeper. Because the concept of Ubuntu was new to many in the session, certain principles of the philosophy found more resonance than others and hence the journey leads us down another path.

The session also created a space for the group to practice the philosophy and principles of Ubuntu. Loshnee had challenges with connectivity and was unable to join with a camera and sometimes sound. This presented a material complexity in the Dialogue that seemed to call on this very philosophy. When one person in a group of 20 cannot be seen it is easy to forget they are there, so within the session itself, we had to engage with the Ubuntu principles of inclusivity, empathy, respect and interdependence. The principle of community was also important where a different level of attention was needed to proactively think from the perspective of all rather than merely for self. For Loshnee, it was a challenge to co-facilitate. There was a sense of being on the outside but creating spaces to have her voice heard was symbolic of African models of Leadership – not always being seen but finding a way through.

How to Handle Conflicts as a Dialogic Leader

Timo Nevalainen, Ismo Huusko

PRE-CONFERENCE DESCRIPTION

Tensions and conflict are unavoidable elements in team dynamics, and they can even contribute to the life force of an organization. However traditional leadership styles often fall short in managing them, sometimes leading to a toxic work environment. We believe that Dialogue can be an effective approach to managing tensions and conflicts in organizations.

Dialogic Leadership provides an alternative that promotes collaboration, participation and mutual respect, crucial for both conflict management and long-term organizational health. Our dialogic inquiry session is driven by our need to develop capacity to manage conflicts within teams and we invite both beginning and seasoned dialogic leaders to share experiences and learn together with us.

CHECK-OUT

Timo Nevalainen:

I am feeling that we are only getting the dialogue rolling now, but we need to have a check-out. The check-out question is, *What do you leave this session with?*

Speaker:

I'm leaving with the aspect of vulnerability, and how people want to respond to their own vulnerability in a conflict. For example, getting pulled out into the ocean. Some people might prefer to say, *Hey, lifeguard I need help.* They ask for help. Some people might say, *No, I'm going to swim. I'm going to try.* Everybody has a different response to how they deal with their vulnerability in a situation.

Speaker:

The thing that I want to take away is looking for the questions and not the answers. Pursuing the questions and not the answers.

Speaker:

I came in thinking of conflict as opposing sides, or like resistance to change but I'm going out looking at it more like tension and awareness of that tension.

Speaker:

Well, I don't haven't a lot of nuggets to take away from this. I want to see tension as an opportunity, but it's not, for me at least. I don't always have to be in harmony about this. Tension is something good? It's good if we can feel this tension and be self-aware of that. This tension is there. The question is, how do we biologically deal with it?

Speaker:

I really like the idea of looking at conflict or tension as opportunity, a growth or evolution opportunity, something positive.

Speaker:

For me very similar. I'm mulling over this point. The tension might be needed to create awareness and new learning.

Speaker:

I'm thinking that I'm sitting with a lot more questions than answers. I'm thinking about many connected parts in this group here today and hearing the very different ways that we each individually make meaning of this. I'm attaching this to dialogue, which is about making meaning through others. I'm taking a lot away. Part of it is the experience of what it's like in this room with so many people I don't know—and sharing, being vulnerable and practicing how I make meaning, and how that meaning then contributes to the group. There you go. That's what it is. Sorry. It took me a few words to get to that.

Speaker:

That's okay, because it does, doesn't it? I'm looking at conflict as not a bad thing, but an opportunity for awareness. The word clarity kept coming to my mind, an opportunity for clarity. When conflict arises, especially as a leader, it means that maybe some clarity needs to be provided. So, instead of looking at conflict as a negative thing, strive to look at it as a positive thing and an opportunity for growth. The other thing for me is vulnerability. That's because I am one who does not show vulnerability. It is hard for me. In my position, I think that showing vulnerability makes other people concerned. I want to be sure they don't see me sweat, and that they don't sweat. If I'm going to show vulnerability, and I do see the value in it when it when it comes to dialogue and conflict . . . that is what I will take away to work on, because I do struggle with that.

Speaker:

I don't really know what I'm taking away at the moment, because my head so full of all the words that have been hovering around the room all of the time. I have a headache, and I wonder what is at the heart of all this, because so many words were spoken, and my view was kind of blinded. I don't have any words for this. I just have to process everything.

Speaker:

The thing I take away from this is that you must live with the tension.

Speaker:

I take away this statement, and I'm going to think about it, that you can use the energy of the conflict to create something positive. Thank you and do well, please.

Speaker:

I sat back and listened very intently. I didn't make a lot of comments, and I think that's because I've been kind of censoring myself during this entire conversation. I think it is part of the conflict, people come to the table and they self-sensor. For me, my biggest takeaway is to get out the entire picture and see what everyone's goal is. Even if there isn't compromise or conflict, at least you can see what everybody's goal is and what they want to get across.

Speaker:

I'm looking at my notes, and I would say there's a lot of heightened awareness and self-reflection. I think these arise when there's conflict. That is something that I, myself, will need to work on more because I think that ties in with getting somewhere once you are in there trying to have that conversation. When there is conflict, if you're not in the right spot, it's just not going to work.

Speaker:

The word vulnerability is floating around a lot in my head. And it's been there for a long time. I teach students to think about conflict as something that is constructive and important. But you know, as I'm listening to everybody talk, I am reflecting more on bringing my own vulnerability to the classroom. I think that demonstrating this can be a positive thing, but I am also keeping in mind how hard that is. Everybody who's around me is going to be in a different place and have a different capacity to be with vulnerability. That's tricky because you always want to move everybody together. It's very complex to always have to keep all of that in mind. That the person who's not speaking up can't show that vulnerability. This is where all our assumptions and stuff come in. We can play with the idea, but we just simply don't know enough. That's part of the quandary of doing this work. We're always swimming in a lot of unknowns, a lot of questions.

Speaker:

I follow many of you, what you guys have said. I was not able to talk due to my connection to this self-awareness about conflicts and the capability to deal with that, and the willingness to deal with that. I think that leaves me to practice in real life. I see this as an opportunity to put it into practice. That's the difficult part.

Speaker:

I leave with two questions. Firstly, *It isn't that we are protecting ourselves, is it?* Actually, we are harming ourselves. The other question is, *Should the dialogic leader call the elephant in the room in pursuit of helping dilute the tensions?* This has been very rich, thank you all.

Speaker:

I feel like identifying what was said. *What is your headache, or what are you afraid of?* If you could go around the room and get people to share that, then it creates vulnerability. A big part of what I take away from this is that you must be vulnerable. You must identify everybody's biases, and what's really bothering them before you can talk about group conflict.

Speaker:

I'm kind of overwhelmed. It's a lot of information, but I am thinking of what others have said about conflict being an opportunity. It's really difficult to deal with conflict. So definitely something that I need to work on as well. And becoming a leader. Definitely a lot of good takeaways.

Timo:

Everybody has checked out? Everybody has said something? Okay, what I take from this is the importance of working with tension and conflict. Observing when the tension touches my need for resolution in a way that it becomes an internal conflict.

Ismo:

Thank you everyone. I'm very interested in vulnerability and really rumble with it. Big growing comes out of all those situations, and I like how other people work as a mirror for myself. The inner work and the inner dialogue are very important, and in the dialogue system, know and learn when to react and when to hold a situational awareness of vulnerabilities.

POSTSCRIPT

We were invited by Peter Garrett and Jane Ball to host two conference dialogue sessions, and we decided to hold our session on the theme of managing conflicts dialogically. This was a very current theme for us in our work in TAMK Proakatemia. The team we work with there had just undergone and resolved a conflict situation that severely affected its work and how people felt about being members of the team. We believed that the team had worked out their conflict in the spirit of dialogue, but we also felt like we wanted to inquire further into the topic and learn together with the participants in the conference.

The theme attracted a full session, and people came to it from a variety of professional backgrounds – from corrections to consulting, management and leadership. It took a while to get the dialogue flowing but, in the end, there was quite a depth and variety in both the dialogue and reflections. Themes that became central for the participants included: one's own and others' sense of vulnerability, and how to work within tensions whilst holding open questions instead of forcibly seeking answers or resolution.

In this dialogue session, one of the biggest topics raised among the participants was how conflict is often caused by tension that could also be used in a positive way. The tension inherent in the conflicts could be made useful through self-awareness. Without self-awareness, people stay reactive and take sides in conflict situations. One question raised by a participant was, *Should the dialogic leader call the elephant in the room in pursuit of helping dilute the tensions?* This question was thought-provoking and summarized the topic of tension quite well. It is important for a dialogic leader to learn to navigate through tensions, find opportunities for growth and bring awareness to these situations.

What seemed to surprise some of the participants was that something good might arise from a conflict, and that the inherent tensions might be needed to create new kinds of awareness in the group as well as bringing about new opportunities for learning and growing together. An interesting question that remained was how to use the energy of tensions and even conflict to create something positive and new in a situation.

From Leaders to Leadership-Shifting Relationships, Power, Decision-making, and More

Leo Hylton and Tzofnat Peleg-Baker

PRE-CONFERENCE DESCRIPTION

We invite participants to explore how the leadership role may be undergoing a profound transformation in an era marked by a rapid evolution of new technologies and the emergence of complex global challenges that demand effective, collaborative efforts across diverse perspectives, experiences, and backgrounds. Leadership may replace the traditional focus on individual omnipotent top-down leaders and their aptitudes. Instead, leadership may exercise shared power to reshape social environments in collaborative and inclusive ways that harness the full potential of our diversity and ensure informed decision-making and optimal outcomes. This interactive Dialogue explores whether shifting our mindset away from the traditional emphasis on individual leaders and their personal attributes towards a more holistic conception of leadership is essential. Such a shift prompts us to reconsider who wields power, how it is distributed, the processes of decision-making and the allocation of responsibilities. Together, we will examine the profound implications of this possible shift in how we navigate an increasingly complex world.

CHECK-OUT

Leo Hylton:

It's a question, for each of us. We have the responsibility as we learn these things, to carry them with us in our lives so that regardless of what position we hold, we can walk in our leadership power. Our position is not as important as our relationship with ourselves and with others. Right. This is our official, wonderful closing round where we hear all the voices and all the wisdom in all this space! *What aspect of dialogic leadership will you explore further in your life, practice and or organization, whether or not you have the title of a leader?*

Tzofnat Peleg-Baker:

Take a minute to think about that. What specific aspect would you like to pursue or implement further, whether in your family, your workplace, your coaching or consulting—anything that has to do with systems and organizations? A family is also a system.

Speaker:

For me, it's about role modelling the practice. I'm fairly new to dialogue as a practice, although it really resonates with me from coaching work. In my system, in my organization it's very transactional, scoring points over each other, speaking just for the sake of speaking. So, I want to go forward trying to role model a more biologic style of conversation. You know, this conference has been fantastic for that. Seeing everyone try to speak in that way, and to really think about what they're saying. I must think out loud. I would love to do more of that. And I want so give examples of that to people back in my organization.

Speaker:

Your thoughts really had me thinking. My thought is that dialogic leadership is very different from any other kind of leadership—because you can lead from anywhere, like when you were saying. If you're in a dance, you can't lead from the back and dance—you have to be able to see. But in dialogue it's really listening and using your voice, and you can lead from anywhere. What can I do from my role in dialogue to empower others to help lead from where they're at? That's really what I'm thinking about right now.

Speaker:

Thank you all. I have so much to hear, about so many experiences. One aspect of good leadership is being a good listener. I think with good listening, leaders have been going further with making good decisions. I'm thinking that if I'm a good listener and making good decisions, then I can quote good thinking, too.

Speaker:

The word that I would use is inclusivity—with family, friends and work because ultimately, they all want the same. You can deal with them in almost the exact same way when using dialogue. Inclusivity must be ensured so that all people feel that they have a voice. They will give you nothing if they're just sitting there. If you have no interest, or they have nothing to say then it's like people that don't vote. They say, *My one vote? Whoever I vote for, my one vote doesn't matter in the grand scheme of things*. But it does the same thing if you have three or 300 people in an office. Everybody's voice should be heard. That's the thing for me.

Speaker:

Let me just show you all this. I wrote down an African proverb. It says, *If you think you are too small to make a difference, you haven't spent the night with the mosquito!* What that means is that what I can do is use my voice to encourage others to use their voice. I don't have to be the loudest. I don't have to be the one to have all the answers, but I can encourage other people to move forward and catch on. That basically touches everything.

Speaker:

For me, I take away the inquiry, the asking of questions to elicit more conversation, especially when it comes to family. When you think about relationships, and you think about a hierarchy, I automatically think about children and how automatically adults are seen as the leaders. This is the person that's telling the others. But try getting away from that to ask the why, the thoughts. *Do you understand why we are doing what we're doing? Tell me, what are your thoughts around this? So, what do you think?* You get more buy-in. Better to try to understand what we're saying, what I'm saying, what I'm trying to do. That's one of the aspects of dialogic leadership that I am taking from this conversation today.

Speaker:

From our dialogue today, I believe that leadership can be exhibited by anyone. It is not always someone listed or called a leader that is really the leader. It is someone who possesses the right way, the right aspects of going about it, as far as being able to communicate with others and being able to listen and not just speak. That is something that I try to implement in my daily job. I try to lead by example, even though I am not specifically a leader by any means. I do try to show others that I do this myself. I say, *It's not hard, and I'll help you through as much as I can.* I think anyone can be a leader, but not everyone is a leader. It's something that must be learned and practiced regularly.

Speaker:

Respect. I think it's more subjective than people realize, especially now in our very individualistic society. People feel disrespected for things that we didn't before. I really want to have an inquiry around respect in any function of leadership. Let's talk about that as a group. First, let's just set some definitions.

Tzofnat:

Wonderful. By the way, that's how I start processes in organizations, considering types of respect, and how we understand respect. So, thank you for that.

Speaker:

I heard a lot of things and got a lot of information apart from what I heard. What

I would pursue in the future is, not only having good listening skills as a leader but making good decisions by thinking for the future. Think of a vision for the future. That is also a good skill for the leadership. That's what I believe. I want to pursue a vision for the future. I want to practice that.

Speaker:

First, I'd like to start by thanking you. You all are a wealth of knowledge. I'm just really taking it all in and enjoying it all. Someone was talking about giving and accepting feedback. I definitely want to take heed of that outside of here, and in every aspect not just in work. When it comes down to my co-workers, sometimes I have a question about their intentions, and what their ideas may look like in the workplace. I want to get myself into a position to be able to give and accept feedback better. Yesterday in our group I learned that I potentially have rejection dysphoria, so I want to dig a little deeper into how I can reverse that and become a little more sensitive when these symptoms are exhibiting themselves.

Speaker:

I am going to continue to work on listening and listening to understand not listening to respond. But I think I've come a long way with that because I used to be in my head thinking *Oh, my God* and let them go through it. Now it is more like letting them go ahead and actually listening to understand their process, what they're thinking, and how they came to that position and appreciating why. Not what they do, or how, but why. People really have more buy-in when they understand your why, and they feel more. It's more authentic. Instead of detailing what I do and what I'm responsible for, which seems very technical, people tend to get it when I start talking about why I do it. Then it's much more emotionally driven. People tap into their emotional side. I am going to work with that in the little pocket of leadership that I have, and to influence them to understand and appreciate that it matters why.

Tzofnat:

We want to thank you for being here with us, learning with us. Remember you are not alone. I'm always open to talk with you. It was great. A lot of food for thought. Good luck with whatever you do and we'll see you in the next session!

POSTSCRIPT

In an era marked by rapid change, new technologies, and the emergence of complex global challenges demanding effective and collective solutions across diverse perspectives, we sought to explore a potential shift from the traditional conceptualization that emphasizes **Leaders** as individuals and focusing on personal attributes, toward a collaborative conception of **Leadership**. Our prompt was, *Is it essential to shift our mindset from the traditional emphasis on individual leaders to a collaborative conception of leadership?* We approached this dialogue with the understanding that collective leadership could be more valuable than a traditional singular understanding to address effectively today's complex global challenges. Held on the second day of the Conference, with the theme *What is dialogical leadership?* participants were exposed to dialogue as an organizational practice. We briefly presented the idea of **Leadership** vs **Leaders**, the concepts of **Power With** vs **Power Over,** and the idea of **Positioning** one another in the interaction.

The participants, however, seemed more inclined to continue discussing the broader concepts of dialogue and its potential within organizations rather than delving into the specific topic we initially intended to explore. Regardless of that, a more focused conversation did take place. Through the process of inviting people to share, we were able to supportively challenge participants to interrogate their own lenses, which were understandably conditioned to embrace the archetypal leader. These supportive efforts opened a conversation on **Power With** vs **Power Over**. Participants began exploring how they could help uplift the voices of those who might not feel they had a voice in decision-making spaces.

There was a shift from focusing on what leaders can do to how people can co-create a leadership culture. This change from the individual to the collective is a powerful one. Together, corrections professionals, prison abolitionists, re-entry professionals, students and dialogue practitioners spoke openly and collaboratively about how each could better incorporate dialogic practices and principles into their lives and work.

Even though the dialogue didn't focus entirely on the shift from Leaders to Leadership as we had planned, it was wonderful to feel how collective wisdom is built. With each shared story, the group grew in understanding and connection. Each voice and story were honored, accepted and affirmed with gratitude. The co-creation of this kind of connected space allowed for challenges to be welcomed and embraced. We could all leave with specific learnings that we wanted to incorporate into our dialogue practice and organization.

As co-facilitators, we complemented one another on our approaches, and we continue learning now. We believe there is room for improvement in being more focused and coherent in our prompts and questions for future sessions. Through our respective work, we are committed to utilizing dialogue more fully to support a shift in organizations from the archetypal **Leader** to a more collaborative **Leadership** model The journey is ongoing, and this interactive dialogue proved supportive to both of us as practitioners and fellow community members, who connected with each participant before, during and after this specific engagement.

How does Dialogic Leadership Build a Scaffold for Sustained Innovation?

Meg Bower & Shaketta Thomas

PRE-CONFERENCE DESCRIPTION

Organizational innovation can be hampered in many ways by instability. At one extreme, when major organizational change occurs in otherwise stable organizations, there is a heightened sense of caution and attrition occurs before the turbulence is fully resolved, resulting in a loss of organizational knowledge and contraction of innovation in those who remain.

At the other extreme, in rapidly changing industries such as Google, it is widely acknowledged that embracing "scratchy discourse" on project teams can be a vehicle to incubating cutting-edge ideas in a lightning-fast industry

How can Dialogic Leadership build a solid framework for any organization that can provide the stability needed, whether to successfully negotiate massive change or to maintain a highly honed creative edge?

CHECK-OUT

Meg Bower:

That's a perfect segue, a perfect tie-up of thoughts, and that's exactly what we want to ask all of you for. We're going to move into the check-out. The question is the one you just answered, but feel free to check-out again. The question for the check-out is based on this conversation and the panel that you heard previously, and it is about your takeaways on dialogic leadership and how it can help facilitate a healthy tension in a creative group. And also, how you will incorporate what you've learned going forward? So a two-part question, 'What are your takeaways from these last couple of sessions, and how will you apply them going forward?' Take a couple minutes and think about it. We'll use the same format where you can just put your hand up when someone's ready, and then we'll do a tag out.

Speaker:

Okay, I'm going to go ahead, and I'll start us off with one of the biggest takeaways that I have from the prior session, that dialogic leadership needs to be very porous. You need to leave a lot of spaces in everything that you do for other people, encouraging other ideas and a flow. And the thing that I would like to apply going forward is an acknowledgement of the need for tension in the room, and a little bit of discomfort, in order for creative ideas to emerge.

Speaker:

What I'm taking with me at this point is a combination of the conversation someone described that started with all looking for conflict, that was then continued so beautifully by someone else describing the dissonance that's required for harmony. They called it polyphonic dialogue. I love that phrase. I think I understand it. Maybe I don't, but that's something that I would like to explore more in future dialogues with the team that I work with.

Speaker:

I would like to get into a position to be wanted to lead a team in a dialogic way. The more I shut up, and the more I listen, eventually the team will relate to this dialogue thing, so sometimes the easiest part is also the hardest part. Just be quiet and let the team go to where they want to be.

Speaker:

I went into what was my sensation, and I found myself feeling under pressure. I wondered what I might sit with. I wondered in what ways might I start to be mindful of accidentally creating expectation or pressure in groups that I am working with when I work with dialogue. I'm just going to sit with that one for a little bit.

Speaker:

I wouldn't say I was lost through this whole portion of the dialogue, but was lost on finding the appropriate wording, as well as getting my brain to wrap around the concept, the meat of what we were trying to go for. I feel like I might have gotten it but there was a disconnect. The discord of the situation, the conflict of needing to be there. It's okay that it's there. It's needed and is what will ultimately lead to the harmony of the symphony being created, and the ideas being created.

Speaker:

What I heard here, I think, is all about harmony. It seems like that the leader must let everyone be himself. Let them go through whatever they need to, and then together they can make a beautiful sound, and an environment like this. Everyone can do, and speak, and share. That's all.

Speaker:

I see the potential in listening to all the things that were shared. I see the potential for the leader to get the greatest benefit from dialogic leadership. Certainly, the organization will benefit, and people in the organizational benefit. But the growth and all the great things that can come from trying to be a dialogic leader maybe the biggest, the best piece of it all. I'm on an 18-year journey, and I'm more motivated than ever to continue that journey and continue to figure out what this means for me, and how I live my life.

Speaker:

I wrote down something about this healthy conflict topic. What I'm grateful for is that I've realized how many of the environments that I'm in are innovative and do have this support from leadership, who try to bring out the thoughts from other people. I'm relatively new to this dialogue thing. I came into this from a different angle. The Kantor Four Player Model (the Dialogic Actions) can have a really useful role in the environments where I work to actually get that rounded. I don't know. We call them positions coming out from everyone. So thank you for that.

Speaker:

In future I like to follow the dialogic leadership approach to provide a safe container for my team, and to create, harmony, and trust, and to help them to contribute new ideas.

Speaker:

The harmony and conflict business has been sticking in my head. When we started talking about harmonies, I started to think about Berry Gordy and what made him so successful at Motown was the same element of Pixar. You had to come in and really be critical of what you were listening to, asking what was missing and what was it that was working? What was still needed? There is so much more we can do, but what is it that we're not doing? This is the opposite side of the coin. What did I not ask? What am I not doing, and Gordy was really big on that. All that is sitting with me, to go back as a leader for myself to think about these things. So thank you so much.

Speaker:

Part of what really resonated with me was when it was said that all conflict is not negative. I don't think many people realize that people express themselves differently, they understand differently, and they learn differently. I am thinking of dialogic leadership especially with the state agency. I'm new to the State. I've only been here for seven months. The whole time I'm listening and learning, I keep thinking, man, I wish some of our leadership was on this call, was taking this class—to know or to learn that one, that all conflict is not negative. Also, that dialogic leadership should have two purposes. One of the purposes is to guide and lead, but the other is also to get a good result that benefits the person as well. The reaction to your action is important, and I don't think a lot of leaders know that that your action and the reaction that you get is important to your growth. Move, follow, oppose, and bystand ties it all together.

Speaker:

It's been a lot to digest, but I what resonated with me most was what was said about the leader learning to be quiet, to observe, to listen, and to let others share. I think that is super important to create psychological safety. That's something I try to promote on a daily basis. With my staff, and I work in community supervision, I work in the highest risk area in Washington, DC. It is essential to make my staff feel that they have a voice and use that voice, because truly, it's life or death. It's important to provide them with the ability to do so. I do my best to continue to show up in that way with them and to create in that space. And I'm a huge believer that conflict is necessary. There's no change without challenge. I think that's an important space to operate from. It allows for everybody to put their perspective out there, because you don't know what you need sometimes until you hear it from someone else.

Speaker:

I think we could have a kind of an idea that innovation involves some big production, some important, gigantic, significant breakthrough that no one ever saw before. But I suggest something else, which is that I think we can all get hypnotized, easily, by doing the same stuff over and over and thinking we're doing something useful. Maybe within the limited band we are. But I think of the clue you gave at the beginning. Move, follow, oppose and bystand. If you have all four of those happening in a conversation you're probably not going to be able to just do the same old thing. It could be as simple as that. To be innovative is to make sure you're not doing too many of any of the actions, move, follow, oppose or bystand. Or overdoing any sequence to the exclusion of any others. Do we have the balance? Thank you, guys, I think that was terrific.

Shaketta Thomas:

Thank you so much. You hit it right on. That is the way to create functionality within a team where you allow people to explore and go different places. Be mindful of your dialogic actions. Thank you so much.

Speaker:

It's hard to follow that, but my check-out as a leader is to ask myself how I can create a space for my team for authentic exploration of ideas. That's where the tension is not shied away from, but it's put in the center of the conversation. That's my check-out. Thank you.

Shaketta:

For those of you who are new to dialogue, I welcome you to keep participating in learning more, and you can always reach out to any of us. To become more equipped with all the skills, and to be functional in your spaces. Thank you so much for joining us. We'll reconvene on the hour.

Meg:

Thanks for joining us.

POSTSCRIPT

The session aimed to explore the role of Dialogue in maintaining stability during periods of change. Recognizing that change is inevitable and chaotic, and that organizations must accept change but also preserve brand integrity and productivity, this session explored how dialogic leadership can establish a stable structure, while embracing (rather than resisting), innovation.

The Dialogic model assumes that opposition (one of the Dialogic Actions) is essential for generating the best creative ideas, because innovation happens when you step outside how things have always been done to generate new ideas. The group also recognized that, while conflict is essential, it is often seen as negative and creates a feeling of tension in the workplace that is uncomfortable for most. The group acknowledged that conflict can be healthy or unhealthy, and that one role of the dialogic leader is to ensure that discussions a) include opposition and b) are conducted in a healthy manner.

The group identified that the dialogic leader must hold two roles—creating a safe container within which the team can work and guiding the discussion so that the outcome is useful to the organization. Creating a safe container requires the leader to relinquish the role of holding the answers. The leader must, instead, encourage team members to contribute authentically and listen to the input, and be open (our group used the word "porous") to new ideas. This stance allows the leader to benefit from the knowledge and input of the whole team, which perhaps makes the dialogic leader the greatest beneficiary of dialogic meetings. A safe container also means transforming potentially unhealthy conflict into a healthy harmony. Accomplishing this requires the dialogic leader to listen well and to provide any missing dialogic elements in discussions. The group named this healthy, dissonance-embracing dialogue "Polyphonic Dialogue"—giving voice to all.

The non-linear nature of most dialogic sessions runs counter to a typical business meeting's pressure to go somewhere deliberate in a certain amount of time. The lack of overt "outcomes" made the participants of our Dialogue uncomfortable—a situation that occurs frequently when incorporating dialogue into business meetings. The dialogic leader must manage external expectations of results with the internal productivity of the team, guiding the discussion in a way that allows new ideas to surface while resisting the pressure of time. Trusting in the dialogic process can help the dialogic leader balance the need for results with the non-linear nature of generative dialogic discussions.

The greatest takeaway is that in today's business environment, it is the dialogic leader's role to bring opposition into the room. The leader must model healthy dissonance, demonstrating the value of disagreement and opposition for optimal idea generation. By championing constructive conflict and embracing differing viewpoints, the leader plays a pivotal role in steering the team toward innovative outcomes and fostering a culture where change is seen as an opportunity, rather than a threat. If opposition is not welcomed, most so-called "creative" groups will simply yield to the strongest voice(s) in the room, discarding possibly very good ideas for the prevailing ones.

A related takeaway is the lack of skills in most groups for disagreeing. The dialogic leader will likely need to teach team members how to engage in healthy contradiction prior to engaging in creative sessions. A mock debate or silly argument using the Dialogic Actions can provide a framework for the group to use later, which will facilitate incubation of all ideas, instead of those that are presented by the "loudest" voices in the room.

Opportunities and Challenges of Dialogic Leadership

Joseph Walters and Laura Little

PRE-CONFERENCE DESCRIPTION

Leading a diverse team of individuals in a collaborative work environment creates both challenges and opportunities. Organizational and personal success is dependent on the ability of the leader to effectively share necessary information and expectations while also having the opportunity to benefit from the experience and perspectives of all team members. This requires the skilful use of effective communication strategies to engage best with the full team. Dialogue provides a structured process that facilitates communication by creating an environment where all team members are encouraged to actively contribute toward a shared goal or mission. This session will explore the challenges of team leadership and how to utilize dialogic skills effectively to create opportunities for shared success.

CHECK-OUT

Laura Little:

The check-out question is, *What is one thing that you take away from this session?* Anybody can start when they ready, and then you can invite the next person to speak.

Joe Walters:

Laura, can I lead us off? Is that okay? Alright, I'd love to do that. I want to say that I truly appreciate the sincere way that everyone approached this Participatory Dialogue. The topic that we talked about, how we engaged together and the thoughts that were brought into the room. I think every single person contributed their ideas, which is exactly what you would want. And I've appreciated the opportunity to spend some time with you today to learn a little bit more about you. I really think that your approach, your ideas, your thoughts about this topic are exciting. I'm glad that you have brought them to this group today. So, thank you for that.

Speaker:

I follow all of that. I did like this idea of psychological safety that was bought out, and I really have to keep that in mind. I did enjoy everything that everybody said, and I learned a lot today.

Speaker:

One thing that Mr. Walters said is that leadership is a behavior, and I never looked at it that way, but that really is sticking with me. It also makes me want to analyse myself when I am interacting with others, especially with my staff and other individuals within the district who look up to me as a leader. Now I realise that it is a behavior, and they're feeding off that. Especially because, like I said, our staff is getting younger, so they're looking at us older ones as more as a leader, and someone that they would like to emulate. I have to remember that.

Speaker:

Where do you start? To put this in a nutshell, as far as I know, I'm the only person in Australia who's into this dialogue stuff. So, being able to learn more from those who are further along in their expertise in this particular skill is what I will take away from this today. Also, a lot of what I heard about creating that trusty environment, psychological safety, and using different strategies. All of these, and behaving as a leader. I think I would group all those ideas collectively into being deliberate in using dialogue in your leadership, and in your behavior as a leader. I think I walk away challenging myself to be a lot more deliberate about it.

Speaker:

I follow. I have learned a lot, and a lot of things were new to me, and some of the things were reminders from previous sessions.

Speaker:

The talk about psychological is very important. Psychological space, intentional space. A leader providing intentional space is very important. That was a good reminder for me. Although we practice it, respect is very, very important. Giving respect to each other and providing people with opportunities to grow naturally or vertically, is equally important.

Laura:

For me, communication is the key for building a good team. Communication is the key, and the most valuable component for any leader in any team.

Speaker:

What I take from today, like Joe said earlier, is basically that a good leader creates the environment of feeling safe from the top. Between you, Mr Walters, and you, Laura, you did that right off the jump. I felt like everybody was authentic in here, and they felt comfortable expressing things about the organization they are from. I feel like you did that from the top. So that's what I took away from this.

Speaker:

I am thinking about examples of exemplary leadership. What was said about leadership being behavior-based made me think about some other things as well. Also, people talked about performance energy and citizen energy. We do have to be consciously aware of what we bring to positions of leadership. One of the things that has helped me tremendously is to be aware of social awareness. Self-awareness and relationship management are important in that you have to be aware not only of what you bring forward, but how you are perceived by those people you are leading. Self-awareness only comes when you can really look at yourself. You look at the way that you are performing in front of people, and you look at the way that people receive your message. Through dialogue your tonality is very important as well when you're speaking because you could have something really important to tell someone. However, if you convey it improperly, or in a way that they are not ready to receive, they don't hear you. Conveying our message through dialogue is very important. And we definitely need to stay aware of the performance energy as well as the citizen in energy that we bring. They are synergistic. So those are the things that I take away from this discussion.

Laura:

I thank everyone for participating, and if anyone would like to leave any comments, we have a comment section in the conference centre, and you can leave a comment if you like. If you want to leave a comment, please do so.

Joe:

I wish everyone all the best. It was a pleasure to get to know each of you a little better over the past hour or so, so wish you all the best, and enjoy the rest of the conference. Thank you very much.

POSTSCRIPT

This dialogue session provided an opportunity for all participants to consider the opportunities and challenges of dialogic leadership. The participants in our group were able to share their personal experiences and opinions while learning from others. This included examples from past leadership encounters, serving in a leadership role or hearing about how critical effective communication is to the effectiveness of any organization.

The participants pondered on the concept of Leadership versus Dialogic Leadership. All the participants agreed that effective communication is necessary. A Leader's behavior can either positively or negatively impact the culture of any organization. Leaders can make people feel safe, worthy and heard, or belittled. However, a Dialogic Leader will create a space where folks can voice their concerns and value others' perspectives. A Dialogic Leader understands that diversity is a key component, and we can all learn from each other's experiences, regardless of our age, race, gender, and values. A Dialogic Leader will incorporate the teams' ideas to achieve the agency's goals.

In achieving goals, Leaders must be proactive when dealing with challenges and opportunities. A Dialogic Leader understands that crucial conversation is necessary to overcome issues as well as being able to embrace changes. A Dialogic Leader should be able to utilize their leading energies—wisdom, visionary, citizen, and performance. In addition to being aware of their leading energies, a Dialogic Leader should be able to recognize the strengths of the team, and delegate assignments accordingly.

Overall, this participatory dialogue session made each participant feel that we are all connected in some way. The foundation of any successful organization is grounded in how we interact with others, and we must be willing to listen and respect each other's views. These strategies will help achieve shared success which ultimately is more lasting and important than the individual success of any member of an organization.

How Can Your Leadership Impact the Quality of Dialogue?

PJ Manning

PRE-CONFERENCE DESCRIPTION

A leader has the vision and sets the pace and the tone for others to follow. A leader creates the environment that is needed for growth and provides the avenue for subordinates to feel confident enough to trust their voice, and to feel that what they contribute matters and is respected.

How can a leader make change if people are unable to express what they see as the *missing link* to move the organization forward? As a leader, are you aware of the effect you have on the quality of Dialogue within your organization? The quality and content of a dialogue will be more fruitful if the subordinates are able to provide genuine thought and not a generic response.

How can you make the necessary adjustments as a leader to allow your subordinates to help you thrive? When we discover the benefits of dialogue in our organization, it becomes a representation of the way we lead.

CHECK-OUT

PJ Manning:
We're going to check out, and we're going to reflect on some things that we can take with us from this session. We will conduct a „tag" check-out, and then once you have checked out you can raise your (Zoom) hand, so we'll know everyone has checked out. That's our little accountability piece.

Speaker:
Can you repeat the check-out?

PJ:
We're reflecting on things that we plan to take away from this session. Anything that stood out to us during this session that we can build. What

we're going to do is use the reaction to raise our hand once we have checked out.

Speaker:

What is very important for me is to be aware of the effect. It's important because I know that whenever I am communicating with my team, or any individual person, my voice carries because I get so passionate and excited about what I'm communicating. I must continue to check myself and be self-aware of my voice tone. A lot of people are not used to an excitable personality, and that is what I would call myself. I can raise my voice because I'm used to talking loudly, coming from the Big City. I'm very vocal and I must be mindful of my voice tone, and my levels of volume, whether I am communicating with a group or an individual, so that my communication won't get lost in that and make me ineffective. That's one of the most important things that I'm going to take away. Like Director Clarke said yesterday, your voice can either drive or hurt. My voice levels may hurt someone. Hearing that tone and delivery all day may lead people to miss the pieces, the ingredients of what it is that I'm saying. That's what I'm going to do. I am going to be self-aware of what I have to offer in my safe container.

Speaker:

I think the value that people bring to the table needs to be taken into consideration. Everybody's voice, or their input, is very important. And again, the title does not guarantee leadership. We must empower people to lead.

Speaker:

I take away growth, expansion and change. Change is inevitable. For some change is scary, but change can be a good thing. Growth, because dialogue is always going to grow. You don't ever want to stay stagnant or complacent. You want to advance, and you want to expand because the relevance is worldwide. It's not just in one department, it goes from your personal life to your work life, to every aspect of your life. So, growth, expansion, and change.

Speaker:

I think this gave us some insights into where we've been. I know one organization that's going through the storming phase of dialogue. We've all been there. This is not an easy undertaking. I remember it being described as turning a large cruise ship around. You can't do it by just whipping the wheel, because it's too large to change the direction suddenly. It's a journey, not a day trip. It's a whole journey, and it begins with each individual. I always tell people, *If you think you're a leader, look behind you. If there's nobody there, you're not a leader, you're a pusher. Everybody's in front of you!* We must make sure whether we are enhancing the dialogue, or whether we're hurting the dialogue. I think it's important for us to be focused.

Speaker:

I guess the biggest takeaway for me today is that we're all leaders when it comes to dialogue. But I do feel that we need one to lead one. I think that's one of the biggest takeaways that I see, because we do have supervisors in our dialogues. But are we leaders? Are we leaders? Because a leader can be anybody if they put their mind to it.

Speaker:

PJ, you said something earlier along the lines that our topic is that dialogic leaders should be able to lead and not be misled. Otherwise, their supervisor will overpower their dialogic practice or their use of the dialogic skills. I feel that's something that needs to be reiterated. A lot of our workplaces could have a smoother running operation, and some of these institutions are a home for people. There are issues with communication. People need to get back to dialogue and talking to people like they are humans, and not like we should just post the work for them and expect them to do as they're told. At the end of the day, we're all adults. You have to talk *with* people. You can't just talk *to* people and think that they are supposed to listen to you just because you have a supervisory role. Supervisors have a voice, and so does everybody else. That's something that I took away from today. Leaders being able to lead, and not losing sight of the dialogue that we need to be practicing in the Virginia Department of Corrections.

Speaker:

So many takeaways. But the most important for me from today is how we're still learning and growing. No matter where you think you are in that spectrum, you are both a teacher and a learner. You're both a student and a teacher. So even when you think, *Hey, I'm not the expert in the room*, you're still teaching. You're teaching, and you're learning.

Speaker:

The one thing I'm going to take away is what was said about bringing someone along to help further the goals and to try to change the culture of our agency to make it more dialogic. That's my new marching order. At least bring someone along. And I do appreciate the samples of the learning team plan. I really do appreciate that. So don't be surprised if I reach out and you get an email asking you to provide me with those samples.

PJ Manning:

I have a lot of things to take away, too. We talked about how to deal with resistance. We talked about how to build rapport and relationships with staff so that we can provide a certain comfort level when we are in the midst of dialogue with people. We want to be able to sit in a circle and dialogue with people and have them know that they're still in a safe environment, even though we as leaders are present, right? So that was great. And then, turning the large cruise ship around. It gave me an image to picture what it really means to change a culture, what it really means to dialogue with people. It is not a process that is going to happen overnight. We will have to continue to model and demonstrate this. Then growth, expansion, and change. How do we do that? We get the voices in the room, and we see what issues need to be addressed. How can we address them? We all work together. This was a good session. I am so happy you were able to join me today!

POSTSCRIPT

As I worked to generate a title for this session, I reflected on how important leadership is in an organization. Trailblazers, enforcers, delegators and influencers are some of the characteristics I associate with leadership. They have the responsibility of guiding a group of people to success or failure. We have dialogue as a tool to extract great ideas, insight, and conclusions. Yet, there is still a chance for someone to misuse this gift. I posed a question, *How can your leadership impact the quality of Dialogue?*

As the participants pondered on the question, we eventually produced quality content. We discovered that sometimes we can abuse our power. It is possible that our first and only language can be one of power. We have to understand that as we all work together to achieve a common goal, we each have an ingredient to add. We also realized that the quality of Dialogue depends on how we present ourselves. Our tone, facial expressions, and gestures make a difference in the delivery of any communication. As leaders, we show more *consideration* when we consider how people on the receiving end would feel about our delivery. People also appreciate knowing why an idea was turned down, thus producing the „why", which adds value.

We explored inclusion and how we choose to invite individuals into communication, and what that looks like for a leader and a subordinate. One of the participants reflected on change and how it is inevitable. The participant went on to explain that it is not good for an organization to stay complacent, and that change is necessary if you want to evolve/advance. This reflection was a result of examining the paradigms, and how people are most likely to invite those they know would most likely prefer their own way of working. Opposition is not always welcomed. This realization was consistently brought up throughout the week. As subordinates, however, people feel valued when their opinions are heard, and acknowledged by leadership.

One of the participants quoted our former Director Clarke, *Your voice can either drive or hurt.* This is a reminder of the accountability that comes with being dialogic. It also expresses an expectation to hold ourselves accountable as leaders to produce a quality representation of the use of Dialogue as we maintain the fidelity of the skills. We hold an organization back from prospering if we misuse Dialogue to comfort our egos.

This session did not have many participants, but the content was rich. We were challenged to evaluate ourselves and how we show up dialogically. When we hold a mirror to ourselves, we can see what we are assembling before us. Our goal in the Virginia Department of Corrections is to change the culture to be more dialogic, and one participant used an analogy of a ship in comparison to the culture. *You can't do it by whipping the wheel because it's too large to change direction suddenly, it's a journey and not a day trip!*

Could Anyone Provide Dialogic Leadership? If So, How?

Peter Garrett, Jennie Amison

PRE-CONFERENCE DESCRIPTION

This inquiry is about formal and informal leadership roles in an organization. In any situation, the formally named leader is expected to determine what needs to be done, to make the necessary decisions to deliver specific outcomes and to ensure everyone understands and plays their part. That is effective leadership. But what is Dialogic Leadership? Clearly, with one leader and a lot of followers, everything depends on the skills of a single person, the leader. Perhaps Dialogic Leadership creates the space to include the contribution of others. Drawing on the collective experience, ideas and intelligence of the team, or everyone involved, may be far more effective. The leader may still have to make or confirm any decisions, but others could play a more active part. What would that look like? How would it work? What experience do you have of Dialogic Leadership?

CHECK-OUT

Peter Garrett:

Last conference we recorded the check-outs from each of the Participatory Dialogues, and later invited the co-facilitators to reflect on the Dialogue they co-facilitated. Both were included in the book Dialogue as Story. We'd like to have a check-out now, to hear everyone's thoughts about the conversation we've been having and to put them, potentially, into the next book. So, I'm inviting you to become an author at this point. We've had a good conversation, and we've been asking, *Can anyone provide Dialogue Leadership? And if so, how?* Perhaps you could reflect for a minute about what you've drawn out of this conversation. Not so much a summary as what you and I have found of value in the thinking. Each check-out will be recorded automatically. What is one thing you can do to get to dialogic leadership in your organization? Hopefully, we'll have time to hear from everybody. We've got about a minute each.

Speaker:

What I'm trying to do right now in my organization is to bring the stakeholders in early to support the work. It's going to take a long time. I want to get them engaged. The panel earlier today helped—intentions matter!

Speaker:

You have to teach people the skill to make a move.

Speaker:

I'm trying to think through in my mind how I'm going to present this. I am working on a way to introduce the concept of inclusive dialogue at the Department of Corrections, to employees and leaders all. We're all leaders. I want to convey an understanding of how everyone can take leadership in the dialogue practice with the purpose of creating a more and more inclusive culture in this organization.

Speaker:

Be the example myself. I'm totally going to steal that one. But also, I'd like to build on it and say embrace what to use when and raise awareness of what it is that I am using—if it's conversation, debate or dialogue—so that the learning filters through to others.

Speaker:

I'm thinking that if I work in an organization where the leader wants to be a dictator, I try to bring him or her into the container and into being a part of a team. But if the leader is not a dialogic leader and the team is not in a dialogic position, then I try to choose an action, like 'move or 'follow. It all depends on the container. Be dialogue! And I try to be the container, to be safe and be dialogic anyway if I can't do anything else. Sometimes the situation is so bad!

Speaker:

As was said, you should lead by example. I agree with that. And you should know your audience and also promote cooperation. That is a huge thing as well.

Speaker:

The bit that I'm struck by in the context right now in Scotland is that there are about 10 or 12 new policies that have been created around how to shift the whole of the education sector. It affects me because I'm a chair of one of those universities. But there are 18 others in offices in other universities, and I think, even as chairs, how can we see the whole? This notion of fragmentation is an issue. All these policies have been looked at individually, and they're going to descend on the whole sector and affect everything we do in Scottish University and Tertiary education. What I'm taking away is this whole piece about fragmentation. But is there a way to create an architecture where we could have dialogue around the implications of what these policies mean? Because everyone's anticipating all the individual pieces. Seeing the whole picture, even starting with us as chairs of the universities together, might be an intervention, a good step to take.

Speaker:

I am thinking about the definition of *leader*. Who's the leader? The guy who speaks the loudest, or who controls the topics? Who can be trusted in the conversation to always lead the way? So, what is a leader? It all goes back to a conversation about the smartest people you know. Sometimes the really smart people are the ones that make the other people think they are the smartest. They may make other people think they are leading the change, but maybe the very quiet people could be leading. I'm thinking we need some clear definition of a leader and of dialogic leaders.

Peter:

I think it's down to you and me, Jennie. I'll come next if you're happy with that? I really like what you just said. Although a leader might have followers, I am not convinced that a dialogic leader creates followers. If they do, I think they haven't understood dialogic leadership. I think a dialogic leader creates other leaders. If you're a great dialogue leader, you create other great leaders. It's not just communication—I think you help to create an architecture. One thing I can do is help people realize that an architecture is needed. By that I mean there need to be forums and places where you meet and talk. However well you communicate, if you were in the Virginia Department of corrections with low retention, and something like 7% of people coming in every year from a completely different culture, and then 14% after 2 years and 21% after 3 years . . . You can't hold a dialogic culture on that basis unless you have places where people talk and think about how they contribute and why they should behave in a particular way. Places and times are needed to bring people together to think about what we're all trying to do, and to commit to it. It's not that somebody doesn't need to lead us. We need to think about how leadership is shared.

We come to Jenny's closing comment. Just before we do, I want to say Jenny is a most unusual lady. If you don't know her, you should take the time to get to know her. She has a wonderful history, which she uses to great advantage. But also, she is unique in another way. She is the first employee from the Virginia Department of Corrections who joined the Academy independently of the agency. In her own right she said, *I want to be a member*, and she paid up to be a member. Almost all the other members are through the Department's corporate sponsorship. She's not usual!

Jennie:

I just want to continue to model the way and to use the practices to take care of things. And my closing comment: I want to be the work instead of doing the work. Thank you!

POSTSCRIPT

As Co-facilitators we prepared well beforehand, we had a sense of each other's strengths, and we felt confident going into our session. Working together has given us confirmation that we can easily work well together in the future. We had a smaller group of about a dozen people, which was conducive to engaging in an online dialogue. Larger groups can sometimes require more attention to ensure that everyone has the chance to express themselves, whereas in the smaller group people are often more sensitive in making space for each other.

A general concept that leadership is provided by people appointed to leadership roles was initially present, but that transitioned to a notion that through dialogue anyone could shift or deepen the consideration in a significant way—by asking a good question, by-standing the situation, contrasting what we say with what we do, skilfully opposing, proposing a different approach or picking up on something that was said but habitually overlooked. This notion, in turn, seeded the general view that anyone could provide leadership in this way, and that this is what we meant by Dialogic Leadership.

As facilitators, we also asked about situations that are not handled dialogically. When pressed for clarification, we asked participants for examples of situations where they experienced leadership as dictatorial, and dialogue seemed impossible. Eventually, Jennie provided a first-hand experience that people clearly understood. It was an early example of leadership where she herself was dictatorial in style and unwilling to listen to others' ideas.

We pressed on with the question, *How do you provide leadership in such circumstances?* This inquiry elicited few responses. People were uncertain about what could be done and were still openly considering this question as we approached our check-out. (After the dialogue, our reflection as co-facilitators was that one obvious approach would be to provide offline coaching to the leader involved). A notably different approach, which appeared in the check-out, was about providing leadership through ensuring an overview perspective of the whole situation. The participant involved described a series of pending changes to an educational policy at national level, and the lack of a whole perspective during this process. She then explored how she and others might provide such an approach through assuming a dialogic leadership stance.

This dialogue felt like a good contribution towards understanding the whole idea of dialogic leadership. It distinguished between good leadership provided by good leaders, and dialogic leadership provided by any participant. Understanding dialogic leadership this way does require both formally appointed leaders and other participants to see and play their roles differently, to everyone's advantage. There are distinct roles for formally appointed leaders to confirm decisions (and their authority and accountability are not affected by dialogic leadership), and to make sure there are suitable times and places for people to think together in dialogue about issues that matter to them.

This is a large step beyond the currently dominant idea of *ensuring that everyone has a voice* (that is about the individual), to *anyone being able to make a contribution to understanding the situation and finding the best way forward* (that is about the whole). This content felt innovative.

DAY TWO

What is Dialogic Leadership?

Why Does Your Organization Need Dialogic Leadership?

PART THREE

Co-hosted plenary session

CO-HOSTS

Harold Clarke (USA), Academy of Professional Dialogue

William Isaacs APDP, APDPA (USA), Dialogos

Harold Clarke:

Welcome back to all of you. As you may have heard me comment a second ago, my breakout group was very, very dynamic. I really enjoyed it. It was quite fruitful. I hope yours was as well. Bill and I talked about how we are going to proceed. Please take two minutes to think by yourself. Write down what you have taken away so far, especially from your last breakout session in the Participatory Dialogues. Just take two minutes to write that down.

The room was quiet for two minutes as people wrote.

Harold:

Now, I'd like to ask Bobby to put you in break-out groups of three people, and what we'd like you to do is to take the next nine minutes with the three of you in conversation, sharing the information that you just wrote down.

Participants went into break-out rooms for 9 minutes.

Bill Isaacs:

Welcome back. We want to have a conversation together, which implies two or three things. One is that we're not going to call on you. That's not a conversation, that's a classroom. This, however, implies doing something challenging, which is listening for when it's your turn. It's always an interesting question. How do you know if it's your turn? You get this feeling. There's a little tap on your shoulder and you kind of go. There are two versions of that; it's your turn and you feel a little reluctant, and there's another one where you can't wait, which might well mean it isn't your turn yet. You might want to relax that impulse for a minute and see if it comes back.

We want to encourage all of us to have an inquiry together, and to remind ourselves that there's a difference between inquiry, which is asking a question to which you do not actually know the answer, and advocacy which is putting out your point of view. Sometimes there is advocacy disguised as inquiry, like *Do you really think that's the right thing to do?* That's not really a question, right? There are always parts of us that want to show up well and be smart, or be provocative, or be interesting or whatever. It's perfectly normal that such things would be there. You might want to notice the degree to which there are those 'protective instincts' in you. They're in everybody and in a context like this, which is both oddly intimate and completely artificial, it requires a little skill. So, managing those protective factors in ourselves, or those performance-oriented ones, is about noticing that they are going on and acknowledging them. We don't have to do anything about it. Just chill and open it up so that we can hear what you were thinking and what occurred to you in your conversations. Let's see if we can do that all together. So go for it. We can use the chat also, so if you have comments you want to add, that's fine. We're going to stay concentrated on being together, but if comments come up in the chat, that's fine, too. The floor, or the zoom space, or whatever the metaphor is, is open! *What was striking to you about the idea of dialogic leadership that you heard from the panelists? And that you heard from your colleagues in the last few minutes? What's occurring to you? What's coming clear to you?*

Speaker:

Yeah. It's about what was talked about at the beginning of the panel. The panelists tried to come up with leadership and with dialogic leadership, and their experiences of dialogic leadership. All the examples they brought were about a person or a team or a leader who came to this wisdom. So, I should go to dialogue like in BP? They were worried about their position and their future. Another leader was losing something, so he tried to protect the damage, and that was dialogic leadership? I'm from the Middle East, and I think there is another concept of leadership here that worships the damage. Sometimes they wish to have the damage. Sometimes they are sensitive to damage, but sometimes they don't even sense the damage. For them damage is okay. They want to get money, and they are not worried about changing the environment, they are not trying to do something better. Do you know what I'm saying? There's no doubt about the wisdom that we should change and that we should achieve something better but the achievement they are trying to reach is not something that speaks to the decent. They want it to be profitable. I wanted to achieve something, but some managers and some leaders here in the Middle East don't want it. They even like the damage, you know. You tell them, *Okay, you are leading an organization but you're going to lose something, you're going to lose the profits.* But they say, *Okay, it's our ideology. We'll pay for that. It's okay if we lose the profits, but we get something sacred. Our belief is valid.* I live in Dubai, and it happens here.

Bill:

Well, I think it's certainly not just in the Middle East that people are invested in their beliefs, sometimes to the detriment of themselves, their families and the people around them. It's not limited to the Middle East.

Speaker:

Perhaps the conflict is good news for us. The wisdom was top-down when the leadership sensed that they should change and that they should bring dialogue. Perhaps we can call it a conflict, or perhaps the challenge of making leadership dialogic.

Bill:

I think that's a great start for this conversation. Often the words are, *Let's be inclusive, and let's hear what everybody has to say*, but the behavior isn't that, right? You know, sometimes the words aren't that either, so what a good inquiry to pursue! What do you do about that? Others? What's occurring to you as you hear this?

Speaker:

What I'm hearing goes back to the question I had posed yesterday, which Director Clarke brought out, *Why are there pros and cons to dialogic leadership?* Because you have leaders that will use it in a malicious way. It'll seem like they want to do the right thing, but that isn't their intention. What's inside them isn't really aligned with what dialogue is supposed to be. And so that's kind of answering that question. It's about the person who's introducing it. That's going to determine the success of dialogue being introduced in any entity, what's in the heart of the person as they are doing it.

Bill:

Another great question, divisiveness or something that's somehow not in line, for whatever reason, shows up. What's the stance of leadership you need to take, relative to that situation? What do you do about it? A really good question to sit with. A few others. Let's keep it going.

Speaker:

I happened to be together with a Canadian in the Participatory Dialogue and in the trio, and the two of us were joined by someone from Mexico. I started telling him about the conversation we had about how to deal with tricky questions. I asked him what it is like in the Mexican culture raising tricky questions. We had found that our Canadian and Swedish cultures are quite collaborative but very afraid of conflicts, and we were wondering what we could learn from that. As he perceived it, there is a totally different culture in Mexico where they are not afraid of conflicts or raising difficult questions, but they have some problems collaborating.

Bill:

Right background matters. A deep cultural background definitely influences things.

Speaker:

There was a big conflict between Sweden and Canada, but we didn't deal with that. The ice hockey, I mean!

Harold:

If I may, I would like to go back to the issue of the leader using dialogue for his or her own motives, their own interests. The question that needs to be asked is, *Who is responsible for the dialogue? Is it the leader, or is it all the participants?* If the response is the second, all of the participants, then the question needs to be asked, *Are you inquiring? Are you following up? Are you by-standing?* Because if you're doing those things then you can check that leader and that leader's motives and intentions. My answer to who's responsible for the dialogue is everyone, not just the leader.

Speaker:

That brings into question, Harold, the preparation and the capability of those who are asked to dialogue, to build and hold a container and to have the trust needed to allow the dialogue to ensue.

Harold:

Exactly. You're correct.

Speaker:

Harold. If you go from the lens of everyone is responsible, then everyone is a leader. Then everyone is responsible.

Harold:

So, we prepare ourselves for that conversation, and for those moments when we must inquire of that leader, and when we have to by-stand as well.

Bill:

Indeed, I think it shifts the meaning of the word leader. We have this sort of lone hero on the hill picture with leadership, you know. Or a mama duck and the baby ducks following.

Speaker:

I also think that by and large most of us are looking for strong leadership in our communities or our organizations. Those of us who want to be heard, those of us who are lower on the ground, more inexperienced or have less tenure, or whatever. I think that it's also important to realize that in our organization we do need strong leadership to set the tone and set expectations.

Speaker:

But I thought that one of the fundamental attributes of dialogue is that we all come to the table on the same playing field. Even though I might be sitting next to a director or next to someone on the executive staff, I should be able to communicate authentically, right? That is why I follow Director Clarke's premise that everyone is responsible for the dialogue. It is a conversation and it's fluid, and it's supposed to allow for ideas that are free-forming.

Bill:

This does appear to be a bit of a contradiction, right? Are we responsible, all of us together, or do we need strong leadership to tell us what to do? Or is it more complicated than that?

Speaker:

I wasn't necessarily saying we need a leader to tell us what to do, I was thinking along the lines of coalescing our goal or our mission within a framework that allows for dialogue, equal dialogue.

Speaker:

The role of leadership in a dialogue changes from that of directing to one that is facilitating. That is getting people together at the table and inviting individual leadership, not controlling the outcome.

Speaker:

I'd rather use 'decisive' leadership, not strong leadership. Decisive because the strong leader dictates something to the team, but the decisive person has an awareness of what the team is going to do. Sometimes good leadership with a dialogic mindset can have control without pushing people, without pushing their ideas to something. I don't use strong, but I use decisive. People with decisive leadership and a dialogic mindset can lead the team to a due destination.

Bernhard:

Could you say that a strong leader tries to speak first, and a decisive leader dares to speak last?

Speaker:

It can be. Yeah. It can be just that the dialogic leaders should try to be aware of the atmosphere, like a controlling influence. Controlling means knowing where the team is going. Sometimes he will start at the beginning, and sometimes he will speak last, but there's no interference between being decisive and being dialogic, I believe.

Speaker:

I'm sitting with something that was said a couple of minutes ago about the container. I'm wondering when we say a strong leader, if what we mean is a strong container.

Speaker:

Yeah, because I think that dialogic leadership for me is allowing it, not from a place of control, but a place of letting go of control. Being able to sit comfortably with that and allow space in the container. It plays to a different kind of leadership for me.

Speaker:

Dare I say, the way most systems and organizations are designed, when you come in it is clear who the leaders are. You know their pictures are everywhere and when they come around, we have to clean up, clean up every time one of the leaders is coming. But I feel like, if we really want to push that everyone is a leader, then that same energy should be given to the person that just got hired or the line staff. They should be as empowered as leaders as the people at the top are. But you really don't get that same energy given to the line staff.

Speaker:

I've got a by-stand to offer, and I guess it has some move in it. It has some of my agency, I am aware of it, but we're doing a lot of externalizing about 'he' the leader, or 'she' the leader, or 'they' the leaders. What about when we think about ourselves and our agency?

Bill:

What do you think about yours?

Speaker:

Well, I'm using it now, and I'm aware of my underlying interest, and what I want to tell. I'm aware that there's a lot of telling here in me but, also, I want to offer it as a dynamic that is here in the group. I see that. In fact, I said it in our smaller group I was feeling a sense of frustration that we were not getting into 'we and I' together, but rather spending lots of time in 'they' and 'it'. So, what do I think about my own leadership? I sit bang in the middle of a large hierarchical organization—I have very little formal power, no budget and no direct reports. I'm creating a program with a group of very senior leaders, and I can do that because I have a leader who offers me a safe container, who trusts me and my skills. But you know it wasn't enough for her to take up my own agency in the system. I had to let go of the part of me that was fearful of the system, the part that said I can't step out of line here because they would sack me. In government you basically have to break the law to get sacked, I know, but they could minimize me and they could sideline me. So, I did the work on myself and said, *Well, you know, am I going to stop? Am I going to stop moaning about all the people who aren't doing this thing or the other? Am I going to stop othering everyone else? And am I going to step in and take up my own agency?* That was a big thing, and it still is. Some days I just want to hide under my duvet. Anyway, I've got really loud. I didn't mean to get loud, but this is bubbling in me. How long are we going to sit and pontificate about *they* and *them* and *those*? Let's get real about us. We're all here. We're all here!

Harold:

I really appreciate your comments, because, in essence, that's what it comes down to. We are leaders. What responsibility are we actually going to take for dialogue? Are we always going to point the finger up the chain and up the ladder? Because often when you're pointing the finger up the ladder, those people may not even realize all the struggles you are going through. What are you doing to bring those things alive and to work to take action to resolve them?

Speaker:

Is shared meaning what we are really looking for in dialogue? If we're unconditionally inviting people, then everybody has a voice and we're looking for shared meaning. That's where – get the richness in this – it is evolutionary-thinking together. Yet what is the leader doing in that? The challenge of either general facilitation or purposeful hosting. It's not just, *I'm looking for and meeting my agenda.* But in the final analysis, Harold, the leader still needs to be able to summarise what that shared meaning is and to say this is where we need to go. By saying I've heard everybody, and this is where we go, the leader shows up. But in the midst of a dialogue, it's much more subtle. Yes?

Harold:

Very well said.

Speaker:

I was in the session with a deputy director from the Department of Corrections and he brought to the forefront that leaders in dialogic leadership are behavior-based. That was something that we all discussed because we probably had never thought about behavior. Then he went further to talk about the performance energy within the citizen energy and I thought that was a very profound statement as well as a very enlightening and eye-opening statement—because sometimes as leaders, we don't look at our role in leadership from a self-aware perspective. One of the things that I brought forward was that sometimes you have to use your voice, and this goes back to the practice of voicing. You have to use your voice, even if you're not invited to the table or if you're not looked at as a leader. You use your voice because you do have the agency, as an innate leader, to say what you have to say and to advocate for those people that you need to advocate for. Sometimes in leadership, we sit back and just listen without doing anything actionable to move the needle forward. And sometimes you have to take that initiative as a leader in order to do that for the people that are in your group, your organization or even just some employees that don't have the confidence to speak for themselves. I think that a lot of times we look at leaders as authorities and dictators and things of that nature, forgetting the humanity of them. They are people, too, and sometimes they just need to be reminded of that when you find them not to be approachable. Particularly, I guess, when they are not seemingly working with the people, but just rattling off orders. We've all had that type of leader. But when we look at ourselves, and we look at the behaviors that we contribute to whatever the situation is, I think that's important not to forget about leadership as well.

Peter:

I'd like to bring in a slightly different element around leadership, if I may? I'm looking at you, Harold. I can see you on the screen here. There's a consideration about Harold bringing a new idea into Virginia, how he behaved, how he engaged people and encouraged people to talk and think together. But another aspect of leadership is what I call the infrastructure. Somebody has to create the forums where people meet. Someone has to create the sequences of engagement. If Virginia is successful, it is not just because Harold is good in a room with dialogue. There is more than that. People who come into the department go through an induction. There are forums where people can talk. There is that expectation in the whole organization. If you only have the room, then you deal with the architecture within the room, the container, the check-in, and so on. If you have a bigger sphere of activity, like a whole organization, how do you manage the architecture of developing the dialogue? That's not only skills like move and follow, vision and performance. It is answering the question, *How do you create the settings for people to come together?* If we hadn't created this conference, we couldn't have this conversation within it. I like the idea that we don't choose who speaks. Instead, we just speak to encourage the developing process. And we need infrastructure for it to work. That's my big acknowledgment to Harold Clarke and also to Dave Robinson and their colleagues, who really have enabled this to happen.

Thomas:

For me, this all is going very fast. I saw a question in the chat, which I think is relevant, *Who determines the leader?* From what I'm hearing, I'm getting a little bit confused with what we are meaning by leader as well. I hear that the leader, my leader, is only my leader if I choose to follow him. If not, he's my boss or maybe he is my manager. I often hear people in human resources talking about human capital and immediately afterward talking about the headcount. So, I realize that human capital is just a new fancy name for an old meaning of people just being resources. Something very similar can happen with leadership. Who determines the leader? There's no leader without people who follow, who choose to follow. So, I determine the leader. With that realization, leadership stops being a noun and becomes a dynamic verb because we will have leaders in different situations. We will choose leaders in different situations. We will be leaders in different situations if people choose to follow us. We will observe that in a dialogue as well. Everybody who is bringing up something that nurtures the general system will in some way be acting as a leader in the dance in the dialogue.

Speaker:

I want to just mention something related to what you said about the dance in the dialogue. I feel like diversity and inclusion, which is something that is at the forefront, is being explored heavily in management. We know that transformational leadership is key to a very inclusive organization. But diversity can also look like you're just checking the box because you have a cross-section of the population in your organization. But are you asking them? If you think of it as a dance—now you've got your dance list. You've invited people. You've got your diversity, but are you asking them to dance? That's the verb where you're not sitting back pontificating but you're actually going to do something about it. You're going to dance. You're not going to just invite them to the dance and say, *Wow, look! I've got diversity.* You're going to engage and ask them to dance.

Speaker:

I want to respond to that because I'm the chairperson for our Diversity Council, and you're right. Diversity is inviting them to the party. Inclusion is asking them to dance, but all of that is for naught if they don't feel comfortable and welcomed in the environment. A lot of times people are invited, and they are included. Think about all the policies and the processes. But if people don't feel like they belong, you've already missed the trust factor that enables people to buy in. You can't have one without the other. You must have all of the tenets covered in order to be effective and for real action and change to take place.

Speaker:

I agree. I've been thinking recently about who says we have to dance and who owns the dance hall. We talk from such a white perspective, like inclusion in what? Who says that I should own the thing that people who are not like me think I should own, and thereby be included? That in itself is a construct, that we need to unpack. If we still keep talking about inclusion, as if the majority power base owned the thing for everyone else to be wonderfully included in then nothing's really changing there, right? I'd far rather come to your dance, or whatever it is like at your party, than invite you to mine, because mine's pretty stale and boring.

Speaker:

Can I pick up on that? We talked a lot in our groups about role models. And how when you model a behavior you actually create a space for others to follow suit to be those dialogic leaders. My question is, *What happens when we put policies and processes in place and we talk the talk around diversity and inclusion, or whatever it is, but we don't model it as leaders?* What is the impact of that? My sense is that the impact is even worse than if you don't talk about it at all. What's the negative impact of saying something, but not following through on it?

Speaker:

I work with diversity and inclusion at the Department of Corrections, and I embrace the model of using dialogue as a tool, especially in the workspace as a tool to bring about inclusion. And to take it further, I'm contemplating the concept of inclusive dialogue, which is really tying it all together. That allows for the safe container, allows for all the authentic voices and participation from all of the stakeholders. Also, I'd like to talk about dialogic leadership. You can look at it as a leader who is dialogic, or you can look at it as someone who is leading in dialogic practice. That's when you change, when you are leading in your actions and your behavior. You are leading the way by modeling the behavior that creates that safe container and creates that dialogic environment where everyone can feel safe to speak up.

Bill:

We're heading towards the end of the time. A couple of people have noticed that conversations have been moving fast or moving around. I think it'd be worthwhile noticing for yourself—what you're noticing and what you're feeling in yourself, in the first person. Where are you? I mean, there are all kinds of conversations and concepts like diversity versus inclusion. All that stuff. But, *How are you feeling, now in this moment? What are you feeling?* I think we're being very earnest in endeavoring to find definitions and so on. I think it's useful to pause and notice that there might be quite a swirl of different ideas, from attitudes to infrastructure to who's going to create the conditions in which whatever's supposed to happen is going to happen. And then what if people don't want to play or have a different point of view? There are all these challenges. I think what's interesting is that this sort of intensification going on here. It feels to me not so much a resolution, but more of a building up of stuff without necessarily a focusing. That raises for me that dialogic leadership, in my view, is riding the wave that's running all the time, running in and through us. We talk about something moving through us. Well, there is something moving through us now, and it's really interesting to think, *Well, how aware are we about it? And what even is it? How do you articulate it?* I appreciate the intensification and the desire to master it, whatever the 'it' is. Anyway, that's what I'm noticing. Harold, do you want to add something? We have a couple of minutes,

Harold:

Bill, in addition to the comments that you made about, *Where you are at right now and how you are feeling with all of this*, I'd like to also pose a question, Where am I in terms of being able to influence what's happening around me? And if you don't think you can. you should ask yourself a further question, *Why not? What are the real barriers that are preventing you from influencing things?*

Bill:

I think it's worth pointing out that Harold uses the phrase *healing environment* as a theme that covers a lot of the infrastructure, practices, training, and so on. And I think you hear him, even in this minute, including the energy of challenge. Where are you? Are you taking responsibility for yourself? Now, this is really interesting. Do you have a healing environment, comply, sit back and have everybody look after you? No, it's actually quite the opposite. Take responsibility for yourself. There's a bit of calling you up in yourself to another place.

Harold:

I just want to say, that this conversation, as you all know, could go on for a long time. There are so many parts to it that we could touch on. But I want to go back to something that Peter talked about earlier. And it's about structures. You know, we must create structures. effective structures to be successful. If you say you're going to support re-entry or you're going to support dialogue, what structures are in place to support dialogue and to support re-entry? That is something that leaders do deliberately—working with others to put these things in place. If we had more time, we could talk with you about the structures we've put in place to support dialogue. We did a lot of creating, and they're still there to support those things into perpetuity. For example, the meetings, the structure of the meetings, the type of meetings, and so forth, and who is invited to these meetings—who is invited to the dance? All those things were put in place, things that were not there before in order to support the development of dialogue. Keep it in mind as you think and plan. You need to have structures in place to support what you're trying to achieve. And those structures, hopefully, most likely will outlive you. So that's something we need to keep in mind. And I go back to what Bill was saying about challenges. We always tend to look outside the window as opposed to looking in at ourselves. When it comes to healing, we have a responsibility and a duty to heal others as much as we seek our own healing as well. I just want to leave that with you.

Before we stop, I want to share some information with you about the Academy. It won't take long.

The Academy is an educational nonprofit organization. We have a range of educational offerings that Jane will tell you more about tomorrow. The conference theme this year is, *Your Organization Needs Dialogue*. If you believe your organization indeed does need dialogue. you can do a couple of things. One is to register people from your organization onto a public course or program—or inquire about an in-house course or program for your organization. If you want to enhance your dialogue skills, you can register for one of the short courses and become eligible to become a member of the Academy and continue your educational journey. Additionally, should you want to become an Accredited Professional Dialogue Practitioner, register for the six-month program, *A Different Way of Working* to become an accredited dialogue practitioner.

Bill:

I appreciate that Harold, and I appreciate everybody's contribution to our conversation today. We're in the midst of a process here. We started yesterday exploring, *What is dialogue?* We've moved into, *What does it mean to lead dialogically?* Leading dialogically might involve handling greater intensity and thinking about it. Tomorrow we will talk about dialogic decision-making with my co-host, the one and only Peter Garrett. We'll take a further step in thinking about how to take conversations, which explore possibilities or create space, and turn them into action, turn them into results, turn them into something different from what might otherwise occur. How does that translation occur? Well, I think we've taken a step today to make the space for that. Thank you all very much. Thank you, Harold. Thank you all for your attention and participation. Much appreciated.

TWND! 6: Your Organization Needs Dialogue!

DAY THREE

What is Dialogic Decision-making?
Why Does Your Organization Need Dialogic Decision-Making?

The third and middle day of the conference tackled the key issue of dialogic decision-making and was co-hosted by Bill Isaacs and Peter Garrett. People are employed by organizations to make decisions, so to take dialogue into an organization, which was the interest for most participants, it is necessary to understand the relationship between dialogue and decision-making. Without that clarity, the dialogue tends to become a talking shop, whilst the decisions are made independently by others, independently of the dialogue. Used well, dialogue can lead to better informed, more sustainable and generative decisions. Somehow the dialogue must be central to the decision-making process without eroding the organizational delegation of authority and accountabilities to specific individuals – since these are made in all organizations for good reason. Given that, a consensus approach is rarely applicable. So, what is dialogic decision-making, how does it work and why is it needed?

DAY THREE

What is Dialogic Decision-Making?
Why Does Your Organization Need Dialogic Decision-Making?

PART ONE

Plenary session with a panel of four practitioners

HOSTS

Peter Garrett APDP, APDPA (UK) – Dialogue Associates and Academy of Professional Dialogue

William Isaacs APDP, APDPA (USA) – Dialogos

PANEL

Mine Bolgil (UK) – Air bp

Laura May Brown (USA) – Virginia Department of Corrections

Marcus Reisle (Switzerland) – Swiss Agency for Development Cooperation

Efrain Jimenez (USA and Mexico) – National Network of Mexican Migrant Federations and Organizations in the United States.

Peter Garrett:

Good morning, Bill. Good morning, afternoon or evening to everyone, wherever you may be. If you weren't here right at the beginning, you might not have realised that the beautiful piece of music and singing is a tribute to the hundreds and thousands of people who go missing every year through political action, kidnapping, war, migration, and so on. It feels good to bring something more serious into our conference at this stage, as we come to the middle day. It is not always fun and games, is it? Scott Frakes was one of the panellists yesterday. I remember a little while back when there was an incident, and the death of one of his staff members happened in an unfortunate way. He held some dialogues for his people to reconcile their experiences. It can enable a profoundly cathartic difference to do something like that.

The big thing today is dialogue and decision-making. Would you like to pick up after this, Bill? First, I'm suggesting that we go into break-out rooms quite promptly to get everyone warmed up on the subject of dialogic decision-making. I suggest we each have a think about our own experience in our own organization. We'll put you into trios or pairs, depending on how it works out. The questions are, *How do you help decision-making?* and, *How do you hinder decision-making in your own organization? How do you improve it? And how do you trip up decision-making yourself in your organization?* Okay. I think you will have about 7 minutes.

Participants went into break-out rooms for 7 minutes.

Bill Isaacs:

Alright. Welcome back. Could you get more direct today? I think the word we heard yesterday was 'crunchy'. As you guys were in the break-out groupings, we were just speaking together here about almost four decades of exploration into dialogue. Put into a single sentence, dialogue is a means of letting awareness change. A way of recognizing that there was a way in which awareness could be shifted if human beings listened for the obstacles between them, and began to suspend those obstacles, began to listen for something underneath or behind that. We had some experiences of it, and we experimented in various contexts over quite a few years. It turns out that things can be profoundly transformed if you figure out how to let that happen in a group of people. Something happens that no one would have ever predicted. You have breakthroughs you wouldn't have expected, whatever the situation. However. while that's developmentally helpful and enlightening, it doesn't actually change things. Individuals come from different starting points, with a different sense of what's possible, and in organizational contexts where there's direct conflict you have to do more than that. You have to translate what you're hearing into a kind of creative space and into action. The question is, *How to do that?* How do you not just go back into the normal modes of decision-making that are either light on data or use feelings to bash one another with? Anybody can have bad discussions, but how do you have good ones? How do you have enlightening ones? How do you make decisions, in other words, that come out of a different experience altogether? How do you cross that divide? That's kind of the territory we're going to explore today.

Peter:

On Monday we considered the questions, *What is dialogue? Why do we need it?* On Tuesday we started to look into dialogic leadership. Today the theme is dialogic decision-making. One big question is, *What's the relationship between dialogue and decision-making?* Do you have dialogues on one side, and then decision-making somewhere else? If you do, dialogue will never be more than a talking shop or a place to feel good. This is the rub. How does dialogue relate to decision-making? That's the inquiry through the day today. We need to crack that one so that we can start to do something useful.

You may have heard the term 'fragmentation'. Maybe you're very familiar with it, or perhaps not. It is a term that came from an insight of David Bohm's. What he realised was that there is widespread fragmentation in human consciousness. We're exploring fragmentation in human beings working in organizations, but what does fragmentation mean? What he meant was that something has gone wrong with our thinking. We think we're independent and can get on and make our own decisions for our own benefit but actually, we're interdependent. We think we can just get on and do the best we can with what we've got, but we're interdependent with everyone else. If our decision-making is based on the assumption that we are quite independent, then we're going to have very different results from decision-making that takes into account our interdependencies. So, this gives you a clue about where we're going.

We've invited a panel of four very different people with interesting and varied backgrounds, to hear a bit about how they've been using dialogue within their decision-making processes. If you are ready, Bill, I will ask Bobby to pull up our panellists by spotlighting them. First Laura May Brown, who I'm told is not really in her garden, despite her background. Efrain, you're from California and Mexico.

Efrain Jimenez:

Yes. Right now, I am in Salvador, but I'm mostly based in Cancun, Mexico and in Los Angeles.

Peter:

Okay. And Marcus, welcome, Marcus Reisle. You're in Switzerland.

Marcus Reisle:

Yes, I'm in Switzerland.

Peter:

And Mine Bolgil is in the UK. Good. I know you all, and I know why we've invited you all, but maybe a quick introduction would be helpful to everyone. Your organization, your role and where you are, as a quick round, please, and then we'll come back and ask you to give us a little more insight into how you work. Are you happy to start, Marcus?

Markus:

Yes. I live in Bern. I'm an anthropologist by profession, and I have worked my whole life with persons on the move, so to speak, with migrants and displaced refugees, all within international organizations and in multilateral global contexts. I work with the Red Cross on refugees and asylum seekers in Switzerland and in West Africa. I worked for the Swiss Agency for Development in Rwanda, in Switzerland and in New York, mainly on migration issues but also on international negotiations. Decision-making is always a challenge, and it is even greater when cultural values and contexts are not the same for the actors involved. If you come from different angles, you tend to be more aware that processes take time, and explanations must be shared.

Peter:

I see Marcus as a senior diplomat based in Switzerland and a world expert in migration. He's just come back from the United Nations in New York where he led the negotiation with most countries in the world about how they allocate their grants of money for development, and so on. He's a very interesting guy! Who wants to come next?

Mine Bolgil:

I can go next. I'm based in the UK. I work for BP, a very different massive organization and I am the Vice President of Commercial, which means I have a global team looking after the fuel supply and the pricing to our customers.

I have been working in BP for 25 years in different parts. It is very, very different from Marcus's work but I still have different cultural elements because we are a global organization. The decision-making that we talk about is much more on the commercial side, about what we buy, what we sell and what we make as a company. I'm in London today, actually nearby in Sunbury. Is that enough for now, Peter?

Peter:

Yes. I can give you my story of Mine as well if you like. She is a bright, sensitive and ethical person in BP. This is an organization Bill and I both know well, and one that gets a lot of criticism, and she is managing a high-powered job in a key commercial field and doing it extremely well, I believe. Okay. Efrain or Laura, who would like to go next?

Efrain:

Yes, thank you, Peter. First, thank you for inviting me to be here. I am the Coordinator of the National Network of Federations and Organizations of Migrant Descent in the United States. The members are mostly umbrella organizations that represent thousands of Mexican migrants in the United States and are working to improve the well-being of our communities in the US and Mexico. We are working with governments on both sides of the border, and we treat everyone in those organizations at the same level. I call it that way because they always have something to say about any issue and the challenge is to align our efforts. I'm the facilitator of all this network effort.

Peter:

Okay, thanks. Perhaps you would like to hear my story of Efrain as well. Efrain is a great character. If you want a great night out, if you want to get something done, he's got courage, he's got conviction, he is ethically sound. If I had an army of 1,000 cavalry on horseback, I would put Efrain in front. He can really move things. He's a remarkable man. Jane and I were with him in Ecuador, in a remote part of the country talking with people to understand their experiences of migration. We had Spanish-speaking people there and he translated into English for us live while they were speaking, and our words into Spanish live whilst we were speaking. I didn't speak and then stop for him to translate. He could just carry on talking at the same speed as I'm talking now, except I was talking in English, and he was saying the same thing in Spanish while I just kept on talking. I don't know what goes on in your head when you do that Efrain, but you are brilliant! Immediate translation for half an hour or more. Now, Laura, we are over to you.

Laura May Brown:

> Good morning, everybody, if it's morning, wherever you are. I work for the Virginia Department of Corrections, and I'm located in Henrico County, Virginia, a little south of Washington, DC, the capital of the United States. I have worked with the Department for going on 40 years and my commitment, purpose and passion have been to work with the re-entry of released prisoners back into the community and working with families of people who are incarcerated or on probation and in the community. Also, I work with a whole range of associated community partners.

Peter:

> Thank you, Laura. A quick story on Laura. If Laura's been in the department for 40 years, why wouldn't she be the director by now? Partly because she is very modest, and partly because she can see where the real action is, which I believe, is working directly with offenders and the offenders' families – not supervising people or making up policy, but direct hands-on work. You may not know this, but when you go into prison it's a crisis, what Jane and I call the 'crisis of entry'. That is when going into prison. People don't realize that it is a crisis coming out too. It's a crisis coming out, re-establishing yourself and then having to reconnect with your family or community, who have views about you. Laura is also working with families who have the crisis of re-engaging with their family member coming out of prison, maybe after a long time. How do we reshape things to receive this person back into our daily lives? How do we manage this? A real crunch situation, close up, with live women, men, children, and so on.

> Okay. We have our panel, and I hope you're interested in what they have in common about their decision-making processes. Bill, why don't I hand over to you to orchestrate how we hear these stories?

Bill:

> Very good. I think the question we have for you is to hear what really stands out for you in this matter of turning dialogue into decisions. You each have strong experience in engaging people in unusual, non-standard contexts. You know something about that and you also know that you must turn that non-standard way of engaging people into something that produces a result. In fact, it may well be that the way you engage people has that intention in mind. I would be willing to bet that's the case. So, it's not like there's dialogue over here, and decision-making over there. I suspect in your minds they are one thing. I am very keen to hear how you think about it. How do you put

that together? How do we produce results that otherwise would normally not occur? Maybe we can hear from each of you on that front, starting with Markus?

Markus:

Okay, thanks. My story deals with a process within the United Nations in New York in late 2020 and I need to make a couple of introductory remarks to give you the context. The most important job of the United Nations is to assist governments and countries to face and overcome their developmental challenges of poverty, poor health systems, poor administration, public services or whatever, and the UN development system includes over 30 different UN agencies. You may know the World Food Program, UNICEF, UN Women or others. This system, as a whole, is guided by instructions from the Member States every fourth year, in the form of what is called a resolution and this resolution covers a wide range of organizational and normative frameworks, setups and guidelines, operational requirements, thematic priorities and reporting and monitoring issues.

My task in New York was to facilitate that resolution, based on a proposed text, which has more than twenty pages and 100 paragraphs covering all these issues that I just mentioned. The drafting of the text was the task of the countries of the South, the so-called G-77 and China, who basically benefited from that resolution through the support of the countries of the North. The negotiations involve all the important groups or Member States of the UN. I've already mentioned the G-77 and China. Then there is the US, and of course, the Russian Federation, the EU and, as an entity, Canada, Australia and New Zealand form one group. Then Norway, Mexico, the UK, Korea, Japan and Turkey, are amongst the other important countries. They often hold different and conflicting views and positions, and they have to be managed somehow.

I had less than a month to lead the negotiations to a successful end. I succeeded. And how? That is where professional dialogue comes in because the process did not start when the first text was sent off and the negotiation began. It started months earlier before I was even appointed as the facilitator of that resolution. I used all the instruments of professional dialogue to involve the relevant actors; to create opportunities to exchange views to deepen a mutual understanding of different positions; to create a trusted network beyond ideological borders and to develop a broader understanding of issues and positions and a sense of common purpose. That took place in smaller groups, informally at the Swiss Mission over lunch with people. My main task, I often say, was listening. Not deciding right away but listening. The negotiation itself allowed me, as the facilitator, to use different roles and I followed the model of professional dialogue. I opposed destructive trends, I by-stood promising trends, I followed constructive proposals and I moved towards consensus and a decision on a certain paragraph on a certain topic. The more the exchange between the representatives of the different countries turned into a skilful conversation, and also a Generative Dialogue, the bigger the chance was of finding a compromise. Some had to reduce their ambitions so that others could gain from the collective situation. There was an overall balance throughout the resolution. Some had to say, *Okay, on these issues, like human rights, we have heard enough. We cannot have more than three or four paragraphs on this issue. We must also take into account other things, and not end up with a resolution of 200 pages. We must stay focused and balanced.* So, I succeeded, as I said, and the resolution was finally adopted at the General Assembly in December 2021. Of the 168 countries present, 167 countries were in favour. One country abstained from its position, and that was the Russian Federation.

Peter:

Wow! But that is an impressive story! I should point out that Markus is not an accredited professional dialogue practitioner. We met up in a migration lab over only a few days, but he recently showed me copies of the models we shared with him and others, and he told us he was using them directly in the work he was doing.

Bill:

An incredible result. Remarkable, thanks, Markus. There are lots of important themes in what you're saying which we will bring out in a few minutes. Mine, let's hear from you. Tell us your story.

Mine:

Thanks, Bill. In contrast to Markus, my story is very different. I am VP of a global organization where I manage the aviation fuel marketing side of things. As context, in 2020 we had the biggest organizational change in our hundred-year-plus history when we aimed to flatten the organization. This is all very good, except for the substantial challenge of moving away from what previously was probably more of a command-and-control type of decision-making to a much flatter organization with dispersed decision-making, thereby making dialogue so much more important. I thought, my time has come! There is a great need to bring people together.

My story today is related to the sustainable aviation field. As we all know, we have a climate crisis on our hands, and aviation remains one of the most difficult areas to decarbonize. To make aviation fuel produced from renewable feedstocks is thought to be the main way. We can therefore understand why the decarbonization effort is so very important for the world, and why it is very important for BP's commitments to getting to a net zero for the energy transition. The problem statement, then, first of all, involved the fact this relates to developing markets and there are lots of uncertainties that we haven't dealt with before. Nobody really knows how it is going to function. So still, to this day, we are in the middle of making that market happen. There is a little increase in production. Within the company, we had to decide how to participate. Whether we should try to run some renewable feedstocks through our own refineries or whether we go to try to buy from others, and that's not so straightforward. And who do we try to sell to? What's the story or proposal that we use? And how do we use it to build partnerships with our customers, who could be commercial airlines or general aviation customers such as people with private planes or business aviation, or even firefighting departments with their helicopters, etc.?

I didn't get back to a specific model. What was coming naturally to me, from what I've learned over the years, is that it is very important to have representation from each of the groups involved to have a sound decision-making process. I deliberately said, *I'll take the lead*, and I set up a staff task force for the short in sustainable aviation fuel. It was a tight-knit group to start with, and we discussed everything with a small number of people who were experts who should bring their knowledge into the room. Everybody was tasked with the same thing, which is that you bring information into the room, you learn in the room and you take that information back out to the group that you're representing. We have a large organization, so this is a massive exercise to do, to learn and to do. The one thing that I dedicated myself to is to ensure that there was consistency. People knew where to come for that hour each week, that we would always hold this session and that we would bring in information and make decisions on what to do. From that tight group, the word started to get out over time. It's been brilliant to see!

The group has grown, although it was kept deliberately tight knit to start with to be effective in decision-making. What's enabled us to do well is that those who arrived more recently understood that there was something that was already working. They came to observe to start with, and then they knew how to participate in the consideration. It has been unlike pretty much anything else that we do. We have been religious about keeping brief notes, which are circulated to everybody in the wider group. Not everyone can make it every week, so we make sure they can keep up with the storyline. They get to follow what's happened and how decisions are reached. Not everything's perfect. One thing we did was to develop a framework about what inputs we needed to make sure we were clear. We have a limited supply of sustainable aviation fuel, we have many potential customers and there's more demand from them than we can supply to them. How would we make the right decisions about which customers we should agree to partner with strategically? That was a matter of consideration. Then we developed data around the value represented by the short-term and the longer-term relationships. This is an ongoing effort. We have been going for three years. We're now selling something like 45 times more sustainable aviation fuel than we did three years ago. It's an exponential growth, and hopefully we're doing it well.

The learning I have is that it takes real consistency of approach so that the group recognizes this also. Do, learn, do. We consistently applied the same framework. At times, I think I did not push enough, and the group or others have not called out enough. Some factions feel a bit excluded, and so of course they complain and say, *Well, hold on! How come they get the fuel, and I don't?* We continue to work through this today.

Bill:

Thank you. Excellent. Just to be clear, does the word "factions" mean different customers or other stakeholders and account managers within the organization that are the voices of the customer? Ultimately, anyway, it would be a customer conversation somewhere that is coming into the room. Excellent. Again, many really rich themes to bring out and look into. Efrain let's hear from you as well.

Efrain:

Yes, thank you. We are a national network of federations and organizations based in the United States, and we were able to create a three-page set of nine-point proposals for the Mexican Presidential candidates. As some of you might know, in 2024 we will have elections for our Presidential candidates, and for the first time ever in Mexican history, we will have a woman as President, because all our coalitions or political parties have women representing them. Creating this nine-point set of specific proposals took us probably two months. The national network involves more than 90 organizations with different backgrounds and with different political views. So, it was quite a challenge to produce this document. It is important to say that we brought it to the attention of the political candidates just 10 days ago. I was seated next to one official, a woman who would be one of the candidates for President, and I presented to her in the name of all my colleagues. Just a month ago, I presented the same nine-point proposals in front of another of the candidates. Two other women travelled to Los Angeles to meet another candidate. We are 12 million Mexicans living abroad, and we do influence elections in Mexico.

You may ask, how are we able to do that, being all over the United States and still to come out with a three-page nine-point set of proposals? That's quite challenging. Especially when people ask, *Why this word? Why the other word? Why these proposals, when the Mexican agenda is a big one?* First, we decided to bring the leaders into a new model of governance that encouraged collaboration, and the active involvement of leaders' opinions in the decision-making process. As you know, this is an original and strong contrast with most traditional top-down decision-making from a few leaders. We invited the leaders from these organizations and other leaders of opinion, like radio hosts and TV anchors, and some small business owners into the dialogue.

We created this equal platform through a WhatsApp group, because it's a national network, and with this national WhatsApp group, we began to listen to each other and to promote dialogue. Then we said, *We need to avoid debate at all costs because the truth is not in one single person.* So, there is dialogue and no debate. Constructive dialogue. And there is also collaboration, not competition. We started discussing the issues and then came the challenge. There were so many things that everyone wanted to prioritize. So, we created another seven different and separate groups, with seven different commissions. We put a facilitator in each commissioned group, who was the coordinator, but like I mentioned, on the same horizontal level. What we tried to promote was the need to have this document, and for that, we needed to promote this equality platform and we needed also to promote a deliberation that was done in a constructive way. We needed to have a more informed dialogue with all the facts that would lead us to a more comprehensive decision. That's why we were able to say that equal rights for Mexicans living abroad need to be there. We need to have the right to vote. We want health benefits was another of the nine points.

Once we began to dialogue, there came common ground. We were able to identify what was agreeable for everyone, even though we came from different political parties. It is also important to say that in order for us to be able to do that, the ones who facilitate or coordinate these groups need to be accountable because once there is a decision to be made, it needs to include the collective will of that commission – specifically so. That is possible because we listen to everyone. Everyone has something to say. We are very flexible, to the point that sometimes when something is already agreed upon, even the next day, somebody can come out with something and, if everyone wants to, we can agree to a different version. We are able to do that. To do that, it is important that we are very transparent in the decision-making.

All the people are in the plenary. The plenary is the big group. The other seven are the commissions. When there is something new about any of the issues that we are working on, people would go straight to this group to share whatever they have. They don't have to go through the leader to put in the information. Everyone there is a leader. We have been able to really bring all the voices in to add to the effort. For everyone and to focus on specific proposals, we were able within the four years that we've been organized in the United States, to become a political push factor – to the point that now we have 11 Congressman at the Federal level in Mexico representing the Mexican migrant population living abroad. We never had that before.

Bill:

I think this is a great first summary. It gives us the spirit of, *Why to be transparent and inclusive*. It is compelling. There's a tidal wave of inclusion here, and a very useful one. Now let's give Laura a chance to speak, and then we'll come back to everybody. Laura, please. What's your story on this topic? It should be fairly brief, please.

Laura:

In 2012, as part of my duties, I began facilitating community family reunification events. I quickly determined in my work with family members, that family members of those who are incarcerated and are releasing into the community receive little support and education from our organization or from the community at large. I made a commitment to address this gap, and I have honoured that commitment since dialogue was given to me as a tool to help family members address their thoughts and feelings and make decisions about their loved ones coming home. This past June, for example, our 28th family event was facilitated at a conference room in a rural Hanover County public library, and we had about 80 guests invited. Nine family members attended, which is a good turnout for these events, as well as an assortment of professional guests, several probationers recently released from jail and staff members from both the Hanover and Henrico probation offices. After reviewing basic dialogic concepts, actions and practices, family members were arranged in a circle and given a handout listing questions to assist in the consideration of their concerns.

Then we just went around the room. We've done this dialogically since around 2014 when we first started using dialogic tools in these events. An example? Questions might be, *What will be different in my household when my loved one comes home?* Another one would be, *How can trust, be rebuilt?* At this event 'trust' quickly became a topic of intense concern for a mother of two sons, one of which would be coming home soon whilst the other would remain incarcerated for a while longer. She felt ill-equipped to make decisions for herself or her family. She expressed fear and frustration at their inability to make positive change, stating, *I'm through with them!* and *This time, one step out of line and he's on his own. I'm tired of this. It's been going on too long*". A recently released probationer responded. Drawn to the mother's concerns, he replied. *I can relate to that. I gave my family trouble for years in and out of prison and jail. This time, before I was released, I decided to do something completely different — to strike out on my own. I chose to release into a long-term sober-living situation. I'm here today with my house manager and sponsor. I guess what I'm saying is, that your sons have choices they need to make. They may need some help from others that have been there and done that, to make those choices.* The mother listened. and the other persons in the circle as well. We continued around the room.

Bill:

Excellent! This is quite a wide range here in all your stories. I have to say that a theme occurs to me as I listen to you. In each case, you're doing some preparing of the ground. You're doing something that cultivates a possibility in people's minds before they engage with each other. Typically, you show up for a challenging exchange but you're doing the work before that pivotal moment arises, and you are creating potential that might not have otherwise been there. In some cases, there are also capability gaps. People don't know, or they don't know what to do. In other cases, it's cultural or subcultural differences and divides. People are all over the place and don't recognize the degree to which they're in different places. So, you're creating a context in which those differences can start to be noticed. Not changed but noticed. I heard that in each of your stories. I think there are a couple of really interesting themes here, with the quality of the decision being a function of what happened leading up to it. You're doing some work upstream of the action so that the action can occur in a way that it would not otherwise. Peter, what's your take as you listen?

Peter:

Well, I was thinking earlier that there are somewhat different speeds of decision-making going on. Marcus worked for an extended period to reach one agreement with many stakeholders, as did Efrain. Mine is working with a whole sequence of decisions, as may be Laura. Then I am thinking about Mine's comment that it works if you get all the different parts of the system represented in the process. That was pre-defined for Marcus. It was every nation that belongs to the United Nations and impressively of those involved all but one agreed. I believe this is a good model for dialogic decision-making. If the whole system isn't there, you're not going to get the full answer. I heard Efrain doing that as he got his groups together. All the different political groups, social groupings, and so on. And if they're not there, bring them in. As a result, you can tackle high-level political figures and say, *This is what we need,* or, *This is how we think we should do it.* It's not partisan advocacy, it's a full representation. It sounds to me like Laura is definitely in the preparation phase you mentioned Bill, getting it together before the difficult meetings occur. The family is not yet with the returning man or woman who's coming out of prison or jail. They are still preparing. When they do come together the crunch will be there, I guess. But how interesting and how different each person's story is. 900 organizations and where's your website? Efrain told me, *We don't have a website. We simply communicate with each other.* If I want to find out what Markus came up with, I look on the United Nations website. There is a huge variety here, and the right question is the one I think you're asking, *What is in common here?* People are using dialogue in their decision-making in quite different yet similar ways, in very different yet essentially similar situations.

Bill:

Perfect. Let's open the chat. Please feel free to put comments in the chat at this point. Do raise your observations, not just your questions again. There are no promises that we will address every question. In the spirit of what's been said, let's include everybody and hear what everybody has to say. Whatever it is you have to say, let's hear it and see what emerges. I'd also be interested in the panellists thinking. You have been listening to each other. While people are writing, what do you hear that's in common, or perhaps that's different?

Markus:

To start the conversation, I think what is in common, and I maybe didn't say a lot about it, is that I did not do my work alone. I had people who supported me. You need a surrounding that enables you to run through the process and the decisions. It's equally important if you have to make decisions, to make sure you have the necessary support so that you're not alone somewhere. You are part of a system, and you are challenged but also supported and encouraged. That is a very important element of a successful process or dialogue.

Bill:

I think that's right. Also, I sometimes hear people making policy decisions in a business context and they say they have consulted with everyone. What they mean is, that they wouldn't talk to everyone, but rather they more or less heard what they were hoping to hear, which everybody kind of knows is the case, and the consultation isn't very real, right? It's a performance. Here we have a more genuine quality of inclusion.

Peter:

There's something about being transparent as you say, Marcus, so that everybody can see what's happening, just as Mine was making sure that new people can see what's happening to get a feel for the kind of process involved or someone who misses a meeting can track the new information and the learning it stimulates. Being open and inclusive with participation is quite a big part of it. I think.

Bill:

I thought, Mine, that what you were saying was interesting. The idea is that you created a group that has the dual responsibility of contributing and learning. I think that's a very useful paradox to offer to people because people often want to bring only their expertise and their point of view. But then you give them the challenge to, *Bring your expertise, by all means, but also bring your questions and what you don't yet know. Bring that, too.* That is a qualifier for the initial core group. I thought your service structure was really good and also the point about consistency. These processes are emotionally very taxing. If there's something stable that people can rely on, then they don't have to reinvent it every time, and that takes away some of the pressure. It's like wearing the same colour socks every day. You don't have to think about it. You minimize the amount of energy needed by focusing the energy on the bigger stuff. That's the premise, the economy of energy.

Mine:

Apart from the economy, there was the consistency of always having a group to provide clarity to an organization that didn't know how decisions were going to be made now that command-and-control was no longer present. Because there was now a bit of a question for people like, *Well how do we get decisions made?*

Bill:

That's a really important point. If you take away the scaffolding supplied by one person, the highest-paid person in the room, who decides everything, then you better put something else in place that's trustworthy.

Peter:

It is an important question, *How do decisions get made in any organization?* I think, Markus, you found it takes people quite a while to work out how the United Nations works and to understand how a decision gets made there. It is also true locally in a team. How does this team make decisions? If we don't know how we make decisions that is a problem. And in a family where it's even more complex, how are decisions made? Laura's right in the thick of that question, when there are experts in drug-related issues, the care of children, and so on. So, what is the relationship between dialogue and decision-making? How does it work?

Bill:

Maybe for just a few minutes, Peter, let's make some space for comments from people in the wider circle here, based on things they're reading in the chat or what they've heard from us. I think that would be good. Let's hear from some of you. And the same rule as yesterday, which is to just speak up when you are ready.

Speaker:

What I experience in a dialogue is that you come into a space while sitting in a circle and bringing in a point that transcends perspective. It is a beautiful place and a beautiful way of letting go of the ego and preoccupations. For me, dialogue doesn't lead to compromises, or it seldom leads to compromise, instead, it leads to consent. It can be that a compromise is this and consent is that, but you come to a higher perspective. And so, it's more than just engaging with each other.

Bill:

Exactly. What struck you as you were listening, what touched you? What rose to the surface? Gave you a bit of an Aha!

Speaker:

I heard a common theme between all four panellists and that was the collaboration between the stakeholders. Everyone is a leader, and there is a consistent process. Also, for each one of them, the practices and the actions were being used and that's how they got to a common ground in their decision-making. It really struck me and impressed me, especially with Markus, the multitude of work that he's doing with so many people. And Mine, the work that she's doing, and all of you really, each one of you was doing basically the same thing.

Markus:

What I forgot to mention in my presentation, but I see it now as I listen, is to get the data right. Get the information right because any compromise is not just about what the group of people are thinking at a given time and in a given framework. There are also overarching values and we have borders or limits of what is possible and what is not possible that decisions need to respect. The wisdom is how to differentiate between the limits that need to be broken and the limits that need to be respected.

Bill:

Hmm. That is a hard question and an excellent one. A decision or a choice implies cutting off the other choices. So, I agree with a lot of the comments. I would just like to distinguish what Laura's story is showing because I think there is one way in which dialogue leads to collective decision-making.

Speaker:

Markus, you had to take the time, and everybody apart from Russia agreed and signed up to this resolution. But Laura's talking about a dialogic process that leaves every individual family member better informed so that they make better individual decisions out of a collective process. Sometimes the collective process leads us to come up with a decision on nine points in three pages that goes to the Presidential candidates. And sometimes I leave with what I'm going to do, and it is clearly my decision that I take away from the dialogue. I think Laura is quite different in that regard.

Bill:

It's as much about making the decision as building the confidence that one can make it. Often what happens is things wander around in the process and stay vague forever. All these cases built collective confidence either to move to a singular focus or, as you point out, a separate focus. To me, it's all about building confidence to move forward as opposed to, *Well someone will be unhappy therefore we can't*, or, *Someone will be excluded, therefore we can't.*

We are now at the time where we should stop.

Peter:

If this panel has worked well, you probably have more things you want to say and want to think about. Fortunately, next, we have the Participatory Dialogues where you can do just that. Then when we all come back together, we'll pull the panel members up again so we can all see them and remember what they were talking about. And we'll keep going with these questions, *What is the relationship between dialogue and decision-making? What makes it easy, and what makes it hard to do? What makes it doable and what gets in the way? What are the obstacles?*

DAY THREE

What is Dialogic Decision-Making?

Why Does Your Organization Need Dialogic Decision-Making?

PART TWO

Seven concurrent participatory dialogues

Thumbnail sketches

Thumbnail sketches to introduce the seven Participatory Dialogues that follow:

PJ Manning APDP (USA) and Jane Ball APDP, APDPA (UK) drew on their very different experiences of role, nationality, age and race to engage all in their room in a stimulating consideration of dialogic decision-making. At the heart of the enquiry was a desire to understand dissent and opposition in the process. Rather than ignoring what was happening or becoming defensive, people recognised they could give the time, effort and courage to listen, and hence to learn why people were opposing. Discovering that would help include them and improve the quality of decisions.

Susan Dandridge APDP (USA) and Tom O'Connor APDP (USA) explored the challenges of getting all the relevant voices into the dialogic decision-making process. People realised this does not necessarily mean everyone speaking, but that your thinking is included, even if it is presented by someone else. The practical keys are the intention, whom to include, how to organise the process and what to do before and after making a decision. Some responses may only appear after the decision has been made, so reviews or a survey about the sense of inclusion can be helpful.

Laura Little APDP (USA) and Wendy Hendrickse (South Africa) proposed that acknowledging and receiving the many voices present in the room is the first step to reaching a meaningful decision. People agreed. They appreciated the energy, respect, transparency and vulnerability they experienced in this session. They saw the value of the outsider's voice, and of celebrating difference, not trying to sound the same. Differences can enhance, not feel like 'a thorn', and easy words, like saying an exchange was 'crunchy', are more accessible than academic terms.

Tecora Davis APDP (USA) and Troy Adams APDP (USA) considered the Working Dialogue in depth. This is a structured process where everyone seeks a mutually beneficial solution to a named challenge. Some present used Working Dialogues regularly to great benefit, whilst others heard about them for the first time. One lamented the need for judges and probation staff to be in the same purposeful dialogue, whilst another advocated including their city's media, judges and law enforcement in a Working Dialogue. In essence, whomever is affected needs to be included.

Ali English APDP (UK) and Carroll Macey APDP (UK) led a sensitive enquiry into the challenges of organizational decision-making. Leaders can help by creating the framework and forums, being vulnerable and authentic, not always seeming to have the answer, and not accepting silence to be consent. All could aim for a level of authenticity where what they say is the same inside or outside the room. A little harder, as people follow the implications of any decision, is naming and suspending cultural assumptions that people did not realise they had, but that affect the decision made.

Timo Nevalainen and Ismo Huusko (Finland) wanted to explore the use of dialogue in making tough decisions, based on experiences at their TAMK Proakatemia workplace. Participants were encouraged to know there is a dialogic decision-making process where courage is needed in the face of uncertainty. They thought that not all fires should be put out quickly since discovering the self-evident can take time and often provides important learning. In contrast, someone from the UK described the experience of asylum-seekers in an opaque decision-making process.

Shakita Bland APDP (USA) and Helena Wagener APDP (South Africa) successfully introduced an experiential session about the value of being distracted, and participants clearly enjoyed the freedom of relaxing, laughing and learning together in this way. Some committed to reducing the impact of their distractions on others, some felt more tolerant of different ways of attending and yet others saw creative possibilities in distraction. A further line of enquiry may be about the key role of boredom in distracting one from the current activity to allow new forms of creativity.

How Do we Truly Include Other Perspectives in Our Decision-making?

Jane Ball and PJ Manning

PRE-CONFERENCE DESCRIPTION

Decision-making can be a difficult task. We may find it most difficult when we have to make decisions that affect an organization, where there are many hierarchical levels and departments to consider. It is important that we are inclusive in our decision-making. We should welcome the voices of those who do the work and can provide insight to inform decisions. Even knowing this, it can be challenging for leaders and managers to relinquish control and welcome the perspectives of others. Why? What would be required of you to welcome other perspectives?

We will be considering this question to raise our awareness and think about the new habits that would improve the way in which we make decisions with others, how we talk with them and what we are willing to talk about.

CHECK-OUT

PJ Manning:

> We're going to check out now. We want to reflect and we're going to use the same reaction process that we did earlier. When you have checked out, could you please raise your Zoom hand, and then that gives us that measure of accountability, and it helps us with time as well, so we won't have to search and find someone who has not checked out. Would someone like to start us off?

Jane Ball:

> We want to hear any reflections, takeaways or learnings.

Speaker:

> I can start my reflection on this dialogue. We may need to relax a little bit on the decision-making process. I think some people feel the urgency to make a

decision and to make people more inclusive. To do so requires us to have more inquiry into why others may oppose, and maybe what they're feeling. What I took from that is a need to also to engage ourselves and see where we are as well. There were a lot of good meaty things considered, a lot of the other things said that I could elaborate on, but for time's sake I won't.

Speaker:

I'm going to challenge myself to invite the disruptors into the room.

Jane:

Nice.

Speaker:

Oh, I'm sorry. I didn't even give you a chance to choose.

Jane:

That's alright. You were being disruptive, which I thought was in the style of your commitment to modelling.

Speaker:

Yeah, I was just thinking about how inclusion takes time, effort and a lot of listening.

Speaker:

I really appreciate everyone's perspectives that they brought today. I think that allowing disruptors into the room is a good move because it ultimately helps to gain further consensus and makes sure everyone's voices are heard. But, as I mentioned at the start, sometimes people are just going to be negative, or they are just not going to understand the process. Taylor Swift, recently re-released 1989 and one of her famous lyrics in there is, *You know, the haters are going to hate sometimes, so you just had to deal with it.*

Speaker:

Oh, I'm so excited for the Taylor Swift shout-out. I've got a teen at home and that's been a big thing in our household over the last couple of weeks. So, I think that one of the things I'm going to take away came from the panel, but also from this conversation, that it's so important to keep a learner's mind. Keep that idea in my mind, but also be sure to cultivate it in the mind of everyone who's in the room. They are learning while they're in the room and they should stay open to new ideas and other things that come in. I think that will underpin the ability of people to have a voice who might otherwise be excluded. So that's my takeaway.

Speaker:

So many takeaways from this discussion! We talked a lot about getting to the whys. That takes skill and it takes courage to face that during a meeting, during a dialogue. That's a big takeaway for me.

Speaker:

My takeaway has been to allow time for the actual process, and not just focusing on the finished product.

Speaker:

I like the idea of trying to get the people who it seems want to oppose and trying to really talk to them and figure out why. Find out exactly what's driving that, really.

Speaker:

For me I think it is threefold. One is identifying the intention of the participants at the start of the dialogue. Then setting the expectation. I call it expectation management, but making sure that everybody has an understanding of what kind of decision is going to be made. Is it a vote? Is it me hearing everybody's considerations or everybody's voice, and then considering them but I'll be making the decision, or whatever? However, that decision must be made, so making sure that the room understands that. I wonder sometimes if it doesn't turn out their way, then people automatically think they haven't been heard. And then lastly, revisiting the decision. Relaxing the time frame and making sure that everyone knows that we can come back to it.

Speaker:

Thank you. I've learned so many things. First, I'II reconsider decisions if we all conclude that we need to reconsider. That is what I learned.

Speaker:

One is inquiry, really inquiring about why – especially for the ones that are wanting to oppose, or that are constantly opposing.

Speaker:

I love this round-up. I really love that I've been writing while you've been talking. I appreciate it so much, so many takeaways for me. A big takeaway is realising again, and imprinting it in me again, how important the preparation is. To set everything in line, to coach the responsible person, to have the right tone of voice, in the invitation to set the tone at the beginning. All these things make it make it easier for that flow to be there. Then you can let go. and the dialogue will take care of itself. So, this preparation is really at the front of my mind now.

Speaker:

My takeaway is the more you reflect the more complicated things are. Let's stop. Being authentic is not a bad idea, and then let's combine that with a good design, including preparation.

Speaker:

Just embrace that challenge as the dialogue practitioner when you have a person that's just going to be a serial opposer. It will help make you into a better practitioner. Also, you may be able to find something very valuable from that person if you can help them onto the right path.

Speaker:

I agree with everybody. I think the biggest takeaway is following up and focussing on the ones that are the opposers. I do believe that will help. We all know that the opposers are the negative ones that are kind of like the cancer in the facilities. They always have something negative to say. Naysayers. I think if you could focus on them and get to the core of why, I think that would really help the dialogue.

Jane:

As a consultant and practitioner, I'm very used to dealing with the opposition in the room on behalf of other people. But I do know it's more difficult when it's my own leadership and decisions I'm making in some roles that I have. So, I'll keep working with that. I do think this idea of transparency helps. If I have done okay, but I know I was a bit grumpy, then let's come back to it in the next meeting, take a bit longer and make sure we get it right. Being willing to do that, and to have the intention to come back to it and get all the people who are affected included. If that means you must go back on a decision because we forgot to include somebody, then apologize. That should be the most important thing, not worrying about losing face in some way because we didn't get it perfectly right the first time. Then an early comment about who decides who is relevant. Because in some of the groups I work with, there are people who feel like and believe they are excluded. I believe they are, too, for whatever reason. I am using the position I have, whilst I have it, to ensure that all those different perspectives are included. We map stakeholders but I think there are sometimes groupings that we miss. So, I'm going to be more thoughtful about that. They're like your blind spots – I think I'm doing all this so well – but I missed this thing . . .

PJ:

I agree that it is important for us to understand the why. I think it is important for us to take ourselves out of the equation just a little bit and understand that people may be opposing the process and not us. If we can come in with that frame of mind periodically it helps, and then during the dialogue to do a self-evaluation to keep ourselves in check and bring awareness to the inquiring a little bit more. Okay, what's happening here? Sometimes we need to take a pause. And that's something that I learned in the first session today. Pause for a little while.

So, we enjoyed you all, and we appreciate you all for joining our session. I think we had some great takeaways from it.

POSTSCRIPT

We came to the theme of Dialogic Decision-making with different experiences and perspectives. Primarily, Jane is an external consultant and PJ is an internal practitioner. We are of different ages, race and nationalities. Jane is one of the authors of a process for dialogic decision-making called the Working Dialogue and PJ is employed in the Virginia Department of Corrections, where this Working Dialogue process is followed as a regular business practice. Including our different perspectives to find a relevant question and co-facilitate a diverse group of participants, was a rich and enjoyable experience.

PJ raised the theme based on the reality she saw at work. In the Working Dialogue process, people who are impacted by an issue should be invited to participate in finding solutions. Staff need to break with the compliance culture of a hierarchical organization, and leaders need to listen and include other perspectives in their decision-making. These are great principles, but we were interested in what really happens, and why it happens that way. The word _truly_ in our question was significant. This also meant we sought a practical consideration based on first-hand experience, rather than theory.

In the session there were common patterns of people not being truly included in decision-making – for example, they had been invited to talk about an issue and the decision had already been made, or they found they and everyone in the meeting agreed with the view of the leader, yet they knew there was dissent in the organization. Interestingly, when asked, everyone in the session said they were good at including people, but they knew people who were not. The risk was to end up talking about 'them' rather than 'we' – our assumptions about why other people don't truly include others in their decision-making. Jane brought in personal experience of being in a leadership position, how that was different to being a consultant, and times when she had been less inclusive than she would like to admit, and this encouraged others to consider themselves.

We noticed the common view was that not including people was a way to avoid disagreement. This may be because different views are not given any value and are dismissed out of hand. Others said it is hard to hear opposing opinions, so you don't invite them in. Or people who disagree may be seen as troublemakers with a personal agenda rather than having a legitimate view. It seems that truly including others who disagree therefore requires thinking differently about the situation – recognising that better sight of the big picture is achieved when we have different angles. It requires curiosity about the perspective of others and careful consideration of each one to understand their understanding. It may also require acknowledgement that I don't have all the answers on my own, the self-awareness to notice when I am becoming defensive and a willingness to work on being open to others.

The final area of learning for us was about the time and timing of decision-making. Including others takes more time, and this requires more planning and less last-minute, reactive decisions. Also, the way we make decisions is habitual, and changing these habits takes work.

Dialogic Decision-Making: The Challenge of Including All Relevant Voices

Tom O'Connor and Susan Williams

PRE-CONFERENCE DESCRIPTION

Ethical decisions are the endpoint in a complex set of operations that includes, paying attention to what is happening in our situation, understanding our situation correctly, having insights into the range of actions we could take to advance more goodness in our situation, feeling our way into the values that each of these actions would realize, discerning which of the possible actions we should take, deciding to choose that action and finally carrying out the action. Some decisions are best left to an expert, but most require a collective approach. They also need the active input of everyone directly affected by them. Dialogic Decision-Making is the process that people with the power to make decisions use to engage everyone affected and reach a collective decision. Too often this process fails and decisions are compromised. Come and explore the challenge of including all relevant voices in collective decision-making.

CHECK-OUT

Tom O'Connor:

> We're just about 20 minutes out and it's probably a good time to start moving into the check-out. I wonder if we could include something in the check-out about the challenge for each of us including all the voices. There's something there that is really interesting.

Susan Williams:

> You may have heard in the previous days, but today might be your first day so I'll repeat that we are going to be making a book that will include many of the check-outs from the sessions. We'll be writing postscripts that go into the 'Your Organization Needs Dialogue' book. So, part of the check-out is gleaning the information that people took from the session. It's not going to identify people by name. You'll just be identified as a speaker. So don't worry about that. Just

think about what all we discussed today in terms of dialogic decision-making, the difficulties with dialogic decision-making, the importance and the principles of dialogic decision-making. And what do you think? What has it made you think about in terms of including the relevant voices and getting people together to make that sort of dialogic decision-making? What do you want to share of your reflections? And we have 20 minutes so you don't have to hurry, but let's make sure that we get everyone in.

Speaker:

What I think what I'm getting from this discussion is that when different people are involved, I should make sure that every sound is heard whether they are in their room themselves, or maybe they have some representatives there, or at least make sure before the meeting the sounds from the people who are involved are heard. This is the thing that I get, and it is very interesting for me. Thank you.

Speaker:

One new idea that I picked up is that not necessarily everyone has to speak. Do speak up, but to make sure that your idea is presented. Make sure your voice is heard, even if it's not you speaking but it can be coming from somebody else. Also, I liked the idea of conducting a survey afterward. It is such a simple thing, yet you can get so much information from it.

Speaker:

What I gathered from this session is not to be afraid of the follow-up when a decision has been made. There may be other things, but this is where my mind went to first. When we make decisions as a department, as a unit, we do include those that are stakeholders. But also, let's understand that we won't see some things until the decision has been implemented. From that, stakeholders may have even more to say. Don't be afraid of it. We can revisit it. You all have probably dealt with that sometimes. People don't like going back over their previous decisions. They want to stay staunchly with it. Let's not be afraid of revisiting it. That's a takeaway for me personally, and just being willing to help guide others through that so that they do not take it personally.

Speaker:

For me decision-making is like activism, asking more questions and welcoming new ideas. Respect each other, and each other's ideas. But usually, the decisions are coming from top to bottom. We need a process where people have the courage to raise their voice or get into the dialogues. That's what I feel. Thank you.

Speaker:

This dialogue has really helped to remind me and to reinforce just how valuable a dialogic culture is to support dialogic decision-making. It seems like it is almost a requirement. In order to have true dialogue-decision-making through an organization, the culture must be there to support it. That's my big takeaway, and I'll keep working with that one.

Speaker:

Thank you. It's been a great conversation today, and I think that the dialogical decision-making process is an awesome tool that includes and values staff. It affects them. It's a slow process, but when used correctly, I think it's a very valuable beneficial tool.

Speaker:

There is a decision that needs to be made, but it's not a final decision. There are different things that can help change it. A decision is there, but it's also up for being changed, or fixed, to make something other than just that one decision. So having a voice helps that. That's what I take away.

Speaker:

Even if decisions aren't made in a dialogic format, we need to understand. Being able to have those conversations with whomever is affecting your team, to be able to listen to what it is, to listen to their voice, right? Perhaps your voice wasn't heard in the room when the decision was made, but your voice is being heard now. Even if it is reactive what is said, how do we move forward with this decision that we're having to implement, or with this change that we're having to implement? How do we listen? How do you get your voice into the solution, if that makes sense?

Speaker:

Definitely. We need to promote a more democratic participation and to ensure that we have decisions that reflect the collective will of the group. We really need to listen to everyone and of course we need to be flexible. Be flexible and apply the thinking, if there is political will, there is a practical way. We need always to be aware of the meaning behind the words, the true meaning behind the words, because sometimes we are very sensible and that's why we begin to debate. So democratic participation is definitely something that I will focus on.

Speaker:

I really like the takeaway of having a survey afterward. That was how you gauged if you're really being effective, right? Because you're thinking that you are coming up with these great concepts for the team, but they might be sitting there thinking I'm not getting anything out of it. That's a great way to see if you are effective or not.

Speaker:

If an organization or a team wants to include all the relevant voices, I think a dialogic culture is very important. Without a dialogue culture, we can't have dialogic decision-making. I've learned a lot from this conversation. It was very interesting for me when it was mentioned that the decision doesn't stop just there, and we should follow up with what goes on after that. I'm sure there are other types of decision-making that suit some situations. We don't have to use the dialogic-decision-making all the time. And the last thing that I realized is this is not a simple process.

Speaker:

What I'll take away from this session, and it was fantastic, was that it's not the end of the story if it's an ongoing process where you can implement changes and have input. And the other thing is what was said about making sure that you talk to people that you represent and bring their voices into the room. I thought that was an excellent session.

Speaker:

I took notes. I like the idea of speaking for the individuals that aren't in the room. I hadn't thought about that in the dialogic practice. If a decision is made, don't be afraid of the follow up. Be inclusive, and I like the survey. You can think you're doing this grand job, and then you get feedback. Perhaps I wasn't receptive, or people didn't feel like their voice was in the room.

Speaker:

What sticks with me was that although we create the space to have everyone included, we also respect those that may need some time. Let them take a pause and not feel pressure to put their voice in immediately.

Speaker:

What I take with me, apart from many things that have been said already, is that you have to be clear on what the decision is all about. What the intention behind it is. The goal and everything else follows from my point of view, including who to include, how to organize the process and what to do before and after the decision-making. I think this is the primary thing to consider.

Speaker:

Well, I take away the wish to keep momentum and the faith. When not all parties are yet ready to engage in dialogue, to keep on going.

Speaker:

To save time, you need to invest time. That's a bit like investing in anything. If you want something to develop and improve, it needs investment. Whether it's relationships with people or a bank account, you've got to put something in it to get something back, right? If you don't put anything in, you get nothing back. So, in this case, by investing some time into something in the long run, you save time. I think about being deliberate. How do I, how do we, do this? And I think it's about being deliberate in fostering that culture of dialogic engagement and giving it the time that it deserves. And giving people the time that they deserve within that dialogue engagement within that culture that you're trying to foster. So that is my takeaway, summed up.

Tom:

I like the dynamism with which it was put on the table, that the decision is a decision, but there are more decisions. It doesn't stop. This is a process. The other thing is about feeling that you are being heard and being taken seriously. It's not about debating every point or telling people they are right or wrong. There's something different about being taken seriously and being heard, rather than debating. I think the personal challenge for me is time. I really do like that meditation at the start, it just settles me, but time is the challenge for me when we're all moving so fast. Either I am in myself, or I am out of myself. If I'm out of myself, I get frustrated in the conversations. So how do I stay centered? That's my challenge.

Speaker:

These are all great points, and I've made notes as you guys have spoken because it informs my own thinking. I'm sitting with the idea of many cultures. I work with teams and organizations, and there's a lot that can be done at a team level within an organization without support from outside the team. So, starting small, starting where we are, and then thinking of it as an experiment. It's one experiment after another, like it's one decision after another. And how can we create some experiments around dialogue that inform our next steps?

Susan:

> I want to thank you all for joining us today. I want to thank my co-facilitator, Tom, who reached out to me to do this today. I really appreciated your opening breath, and I will be using that breath exercise. I really enjoyed that. I agree with those who have talked about taking the time to make the dialogic decisions or take the time to make the corrections. But I also want to say something that hasn't been said that dialogic decision-making is having the information in the room and sharing that information. For example, I wanted to share with you all about what is going to happen with the check-out, with the check-out information. By sharing that information, you could make your decision about what you wanted to share. I hadn't thought about it before, in terms of dialogic decision-making and getting your voice in the room. How can you have an authentic voice and contribute well if you don't have all the information that you need?

POSTSCRIPT

Some decisions are best left to an expert, but most require a collective approach. They need the active input of everyone affected by them. Dialogic Decision-Making is the process that leaders use to make decisions that impact more people than just those with the power to make the decisions. The process engages everyone who is impacted, to reach a mutual, synergistic decision. When leaders and organizations do not take a dialogical approach (a common occurrence) they reach compromised decisions.

There are several challenges to including all the relevant voices in a collective decision. There are also ways to meet these challenges. One of the initial challenges in a dialogue is making sure it is inclusive; everyone impacted by the decision needs to be part of the dialogue. This does not mean every individual needs to be present, it does mean that every perspective needs to be represented. For example, the Parent-Teacher Association became stronger, and more attentive to school needs when it became the Parent-Teacher-Student Association. Including the voice of the students, gave the association a much better understanding of how to improve the school.

People must feel comfortable expressing themselves while others need to focus on listening. Some may feel uncomfortable voicing and feel fine if others have represented their views. Ideally, however, there should be enough space and time for people to pause, reflect and speak their voices into the room. When people do voice in a respectful manner, others should listen with an open mind and try not to take things personally. To be truly dialogic in the decision-making, people must be willing to share and not hoard their information and knowledge. Sharing with an open mind, also known as suspension, allows everyone in the room to know what you're thinking and arrive at a shared understanding. Others can then use their authentic voice to add and build on that understanding.

Another challenge is to properly prepare the soil or the ground for the dialogue beforehand. This includes the following: a) being clear on the goals or intention for the dialogue, b) scheduling an appropriate time that will not leave people feeling rushed, c) being deliberate in creating and fostering a culture of dialogic engagement that focuses on the practices of voicing, listening, respecting, and suspending, and d) gathering the people who can represent those who will be affected by the decision. Each individual has the responsibility to listen not only to the words being spoken but also the meaning behind the words. Respecting people and feeling respected are important. There is something special about being taken seriously and being heard rather than debating with someone.

Lastly, there is the challenge of following up on the dialogic decision-making. Sometimes when people make decisions, they do not follow through with the actions required for those decisions. For example, every new year, there are people who say, *I have decided to lose weight and get in shape*. As we know, that certainly doesn't mean that they will lose weight or get in shape. Active follow-up is necessary to support the decisions made in a dialogue and to make sure the changes are implemented as decided. If these changes do not turn out as planned it is time to revisit the dialogue, if the changes work it is time to amplify them.

The Value of the Voices in the Room

Laura Little, Wendy Hendrickse

PRE-CONFERENCE DESCRIPTION

The collective knowledge pool and the diverse thinking achieved when the broader collective in a company is acknowledged, could add to a deeper and clearer understanding of the challenge being faced, and consequently to reaching a more meaningful decision. This session will explore various parts of the collective decision-making process and allow others to express their thoughts, so everyone can be heard, seen, and valued for their input.

CHECK-OUT

Laura Little:

We have ten minutes left, so I want to proceed with the check-out. We are going to check out like we checked in – using the tag method. I'll start the check-out with a question, and when you have spoken, tag the next person to speak. The check-out question is, *What's one thing that you take away from this from this session that we had today?* One thing that has really stuck with you, that you will really use. Anybody can speak first, and then you invite the next person to speak.

Speaker:

I'll go first. The one thing that I learned is that being an 'outsider' in a group can be a positive. You can bring a different or unique perspective to a group that has already formed. It's okay to be the other person stepping into the room. I'm taking that from here and being willing and always trying to come as my authentic self, even if I'm new to the group – versus just always sitting back and listening.

Speaker:

I'm doing just that. I'm looking at the question. I'm ready. I'm ready to listen. You know for me there's so much that I'm taking that I can't just choose one thing. I like the energy. The bagels are like mine with extra cream cheese. I like the respect that has been given to Leo as an incarcerated person. The fact that he continues to earn that respect, that people continue to afford him that opportunity and he takes the opportunity. I think the realisation that I am introverted came to me in this session. I don't know how. I don't know why. It was just a realization. So, I accept it, and I move forward with it.

Speaker:

I guess that most of the time I don't really notice that there area lot of people here from my organization. It's just kind of always been that way, and I've been coming enough times to know that. But what I noticed today is that when I get into a little break-out room, if it's all people from VADOC, something in my brain says, *I want to meet other people!* I love all of you VADOC people, but I want to meet other people and hear other people's voices. I can imagine that may sound obnoxious, and I hope you don't hear it that way. That was the most on my mind.

Speaker:

One thing I'm taking away from the session is more accessible language. Someone used the word *crunchy*. She explained it and I found it very relatable. Every time she spoke, we could all pull this image in our heads and it was almost comforting. I know I'm a person who's very academic, and I love my big words. I love science – all types – and the words I use sometimes reflect all of that, but it's not so accessible. Now I can see how more accessible language is really encouraging to others. I'm taking the use of accessible language away with me when it comes to dialogic decision-making.

Speaker:

This feels good, that there is something that I'm really taking away. As I leave this session, I'm carrying with me a deeper appreciation for the power of meaningful inclusion of difference. Because that, for me, is what this is right here. There is real power in the meaningful inclusion of difference. We do ourselves a disservice by trying to sound the same rather than being intentional about honouring the difference that people bring into the room. The breakthrough in this session was that moment of realising we're different, and that's not a bad thing. It's a beautiful thing. So, this experience, the connection and the sharing are fantastic, and the key to so much. I'm bringing all that with me as I leave, and dialogue is what made it possible.

Laura:

Yes, that's awesome.

Speaker:

Well, I am sitting here, and I am full. I am. I think this is probably the best session that I've had in these past three days. I appreciate the transparency of the group. I appreciate the vulnerability in the group. I take away the fact that I will not shun my voice to fit other people's ideas. I will not. I am very thankful to everyone who was a part of this session right here. Leo, I appreciate your advice, your sharing. I appreciate it because you've been here longer than I have, doing dialogic stuff. You're probably like one of the captains, with the hat on and stuff.

Wendy Hendrickse:

My daughter was the one that really taught me to stop and listen. She said, *Mom stop and listen.* I can be quite a strong personality, so she told me to stop and actually listen. As someone else said, maybe somebody's got something to say that I can learn from. Maybe I don't need to have all the answers! That for me was very scary and liberating at the same time. Not needing to have all the answers and just hearing another perspective and another point of view. That led to me having the boldness to approach governments. As I said earlier, I'm an advocate and an activist. I was going into a place of strict law, where people don't listen. And I was saying, *No, you need to listen.* But as somebody mentioned earlier you must have respect to connect. I went respectfully into that environment and achieved things that others had not been able to achieve because they had been going in antagonistically. And I've kept on saying, *You must hear me!*

I really think that this was really an amazing conversation, an amazing dialogue, and I feel very close to all of you.

Laura:

I guess I'm the last one. Last night I was worried about this session. Even though I've been a dialogue practitioner for a while, I get nervous every time I get ready to do a session. But all of you made me feel so comfortable. All of you just made me feel at ease in my mind a little bit, and I enjoyed speaking and listening to what all of you had to say today. I really appreciate all of you. This was a great participatory session. The takeaway for me is that we must take the time to listen to other people. Other people have different perspectives, and they have different ideas. They have different ways of doing things, a different background and different values. So, we need to take the time to listen. And that's what I've done today, and I did learn something from each and all of you.

POSTSCRIPT

Laura's positive energy, with which she started the session, had an incredible effect on people. People sensed her eagerness to hear them and responded. It was truly a reflection of a *collective knowledge pool and diverse thinking* coming into play. From that perspective alone, much was "achieved".

The experience was a beautiful example of what is possible when people feel that others want to hear them, and that they have something to contribute even when they originally felt they didn't. The effect of the idea, *We want to hear you not because you agree with us but because you have a voice to be heard*, was powerful. One could see that people did not feel they had to make a "wow" statement to have a voice. Others hear their "wow" even when they did not themselves.

The uniqueness of the group was enjoyed as well as a shared understanding – which we all agreed on – that it is important for all of our voices to be heard. The youngest in the room (a 20-year-old) made some powerful remarks towards the end, which was a further indication of the value of hearing all the voices in the room. Value of voices is no respecter of age.

The session made us realise that we all must take the time to listen and respect each other because we all have something to share.

The month following the conference was a near-daily confirmation that we can engage with others who think very differently to us and grow with this, without it "threatening" our core beliefs. Difference does not have to be a threat. Different can merely be different without changing anything. Differences can enhance life and do not always need to be perceived as the "thorn".

Engaging with diversity and diverse thinking in a positive manner can be "merely" a fun, exciting and engaging experience without fundamentally changing us or it can cause us to grow or pivot. Going in positively without any expectations leaves one more open to hearing diversity rather than being clouded by our bias.

Diverse voices are important even if just to remind us that there are more than "three" ways of thinking about something. We don›t need to listen to agree or disagree. We merely need to hear the other and value their voice. When we hear alternate views and don't change ours, it can be a beautiful reminder that we can be different and still comfortably share spaces. A reminder that blue is not better than red but that each contributes to the beauty of life.

If we are not hearing the voices in the room, the diversity that is life, can we honestly say, *I have considered and decided . . .?* How limited and biased are our opinions, thoughts, decisions and more? In an organization, group, etc, who are we then making decisions for if we are not hearing diverse voices?

Interestingly for me, Wendy, the first part of everyday at the conference was often frustrating as I was hearing people speak but I could not engage effectively to explore what I thought I heard. The size of the room, format and time, did not allow for those meaningful engagements. It made me question the value of what I was hearing as I could not clarify my perceptions of what I was hearing. It was my interpretation, biased. And as a result, I questioned its value to my thinking. Where is the value in only acquiring data which we self-sort with no "testing board"? It seems like it could merely fortify existing biases.

Would merely hearing diversity without exploring its diverse thinking be empty?

Organizations need Working Dialogues

Tecora Davis, Troy Adams

PRE-CONFERENCE DESCRIPTION

Organizations are by nature fragmented, which can hinder effective decision-making. Poor decisions lead to more problems and less profit. Therefore, good decision-making skills are paramount to the success and achievement of organizational and community goals. It is important to have tools and resources that address the challenges faced when it comes to problem-solving and making tough decisions. Through Working Dialogues organizations can empower their leaders to make quality decisions which increases effectiveness and improves overall outcomes.

CHECK-OUT

Eddie (Troy) Adams:

We want to hear all your voices following our consideration today. What are your thoughts now about Working Dialogues? And how might you use them in the future in your area of work or expertise? We have a small group. So, whoever wants to go can start.

Speaker:

I can start by saying, thank you very much. I really liked the way you presented things, and I think I will have a big use of it when I work with the teams in in the future.

Speaker:

We use them regularly, and I'm going to continue to do what we've been doing. Like he said, it is democratic and gives everybody a chance to be heard.

Speaker:

Considering that I'm on the road to becoming a Dialogue Practitioner, this is one of the first ones I want to try to orchestrate or facilitate, or whatever.

I want to put it to our judges and the probation staff. I don't know whose approval I need to do that but I'm going to get there. There are certain things that the judge is ordering when instead he could be trusting that the probation officer will see to this person's needs more effectively, so that doesn't make any sense. I'd like for them both to get into a room, and let's talk about this.

Speaker:

You know, I believe you will get there. I think whoever is the employer is probably pretty lucky to have you! As for me, this level of structure and control in the Working Dialogue is really different from what we typically work with. I'm really grateful to you for explaining it right through. There is an element in our organization where perhaps we are not giving quite as much structure as this. For some of our leaders, this might be the way in. I think, Eddie, you were trying to find the right words for old people, and I don't have them either. But we have similar characters in government in the UK, as you described. And so, it's definitely useful for me to sit and think if maybe there is a middle ground between that old culture, command and control, and dialogue. Somewhere in between for them to meet up, which you guys are explaining.

Speaker:

I find it very interesting too, as well as eye-opening, to have dialogue guide the way to a resolution. I've been taking my notes and listening very carefully. It's my earnest desire to be able to facilitate dialogue at our plant to make some much--needed changes, and I'll say it again, *I wish some of those people were here in this conference.* It has been very helpful.

Speaker:

I will speak on three levels. One, with basic branch and team case assignments, that's the most granular level. Then I would like to see this also in our agency. It seems that even if we're cohesive as a community supervision branch, we're dragging it along to make sure things are working properly. We're sort of banging our heads up against the wall when it comes to HR, finance or the training department. It's almost like, *Are we working toward the same common goal?* So, gaining some common ground there, and a dialogue about us being part of the same mission. I don't think that I'm ready to facilitate it yet, but I am very passionate about it. Then I would love to see all the stakeholders in a dialogue where it concerns criminal justice. I don't know if anybody listens to the news, but the criminal justice has received such a beating down in the last few years! There's something going on. I would love to have the media and judges and citizens, and all the people who feel like they know how to run criminal justice agencies there. Let's have a dialogue about what's going on with the crime problem here.

Speaker:

Amen to that. I hope that for you, for all of you. I hope for that so deeply, and not just about criminal justice. We could take this all the way to the Middle East, right? But maybe we don't have time.

Speaker:

Yes, I definitely agree. For me this whole process has been enlightening. I feel like a lot of people who make decisions. have never really walked in the shoes of those who do it, and I mean no offense to anyone. It's just my personal opinion. I feel you should not be a warden if you've never been an officer, because you don't know what we do. You don't really know what we experience, what we go through, the stress, the everyday life of an officer having to really make decisions on how to run things or how we should be —as officers, or sergeants, lieutenants, captains, majors, whatever. Personally, I want to continue learning and giving my opinion, because I think it's needed for the lower levels to speak out and voice their opinions. It's very helpful to hear other people's perspectives, other people's point of view, and their opinions, when it comes to certain situations. For me, personally, I'm going to continue to dive into the whole dialogue community.

Speaker:

I just wanted to add that in Paris, if you want to become a warden, you must work as a prison officer for one month.

Speaker:

How often, I wonder. Like just one month ever in your whole career, or one month every five years, or I don't know. At least it's a question of saying that a warden must actually understand the way it is for staff.

Eddie:

Well, thank you guys. I find myself learning from everybody else all the time, even when I'm leading dialogues. When you're on the dialogue journey, the learning goes on and on. What I've learned from you guys is a different perspective of how this can work in other situations besides just the Virginia Department of Corrections. I had never really thought about that. Somebody mentioned two things where the world right now could use a Working

Dialogue, and I had never really thought about that. If we could get there, if we could get countries to sit down and participate in something of this structure as somebody mentioned... I never thought about getting the media, the judges and law enforcement, maybe even in just one city, to get down and do a Working Dialogue. What we could accomplish! I'm not sure it's going to solve all the world's problems, but like I said, *I've never participated in a Working Dialogue where we didn't have some good ideas and make some things happen.* So, these are some things I've never even really thought about. I've always just thought about how to use Working Dialogue in my workplace and my job. But you have all helped me to have a better understanding of how it can be used outside my agency, out in other parts of the world and in other parts of the work environment. Thank you for that. I appreciate all the input today.

Tecora:

I echo some of the same things that Eddie did. I have not really thought about the global. I have thought about children, about introducing dialogue to children, because I think that it would just be amazing to enlighten them or to help to train them in a different communication perspective. That may create some movement for future generations. What I have gathered between this session and some of the other sessions in the previous days is the importance of experience and perspective. Someone said it is so important for those in upper administration to have some people from the field come up. Everybody can't just be coming in without knowledge of what we do and how important it is. You can't replace experience. That's been an ongoing theme. It reminds me of how important it is no matter where you stand. I look forward to some of you becoming a warden. I may not be around at that time, but you make sure you send me a shout.

Speaker:

I'm going up there and I'm going to make sure that everybody who has helped me along the way is recognized because we need to recognize those who help us. I give accolades all the time to all my supervisors who have truly impacted me as the officer that I am today. So absolutely, I'm getting there. I'm getting it.

POSTSCRIPT

Being a part of the whole impacts both individuals and organizations. Just as fragmentation impacts organizations, individuals can also experience fragmentation. Increasing awareness of the whole at a conscious level, by bringing individuals together to experience the whole, creates growth and generates more effective decision making. Dialogue provides the platform and creates an environment where a more in-sync or harmonious process can evolve in both the individual and the organization.

It is important to identify who the individuals are that need to be included in a Working Dialogue environment. The title of an individual may require them to be there, and the duties of a position may mean that someone needs to be involved. Whomever is affected by the decision needs to be directly involved or to be represented. Given the diversity that may be involved, the role of the facilitator is to create the right environment for everyone to participate effectively, to help them to find their voices and to contribute to the outcomes determined.

As co-facilitators we have been pondering on the check-out. One speaker stated, *It's definitely useful for me to sit and think if maybe there is a middle ground between that old culture, command and control, and dialogue. Somewhere in between for them to meet up.* That, of course, is what a Working Dialogue provides. Another stated, *I feel like a lot of people who make decisions have never really walked in the shoes of those who do it.* Both statements resonated strongly with the need for an environment, a common place, a platform where all voices are equally heard, valued and acknowledged as such and where everyone seeks a mutually beneficial solution. That is what is provided through the structured process of the Working Dialogue. This further solidified the notion that organizations need Working Dialogues.

What makes Decision-making One of the Top Challenges for Teams?

Ali English, Carroll Macey

PRE-CONFERENCE DESCRIPTION

Margaret Wheatley's work in *Leadership and the New Science* identifies that in today's business environment the world is getting ever more complex and global, and that change is the norm. Where once it was assumed that decisions were linear and ordered, we now understand more about the nature and impact of networks and systems. People's conscious awareness is limited by how much of the whole they can see. We each only see some of the data points that are salient to any decision. Dialogue helps to broaden the collective span of salience and reduce fragmentation for better decisions to be identified and taken. Dialogic decision-making brings greater clarity, direction, and rigor for teams and organizations.

CHECK-OUT

Carroll Macey:

> Just take a moment to think about what we have talked about today. As we check out, we'd like to hear no more than two sentences so that we can hear everybody's voice.

Speaker:

> I think everyone has a ladder, a ladder of vulnerability, that is unique to them. Once you learn what your ladder is, you know the difference between asking someone for help and just raising a concern. They are two different things. I said on day one that suspension is really important in dialogue and in communication. I think that we don't give it as much energy and attention as we should. It is critical in leadership roles. Once you learn what your ladder of vulnerability is, then in the later stages you can say, *I've been being truly transparent in conversation*. My biggest takeaway today is how my decisions impact others. Being consciously aware of that. I think all leaders need to consider that when they make decisions.

Ali English:

So that we can hear all voices, let's 'sentence' rather than 'paragraph', if we can, please.

Speaker:

Okay, sentence one: I promise leadership is responsible for creating the framework. Sentence number two: Dialogic decision-making reduces fragmentation.

Speaker:

My takeaway from this is that leaders must have the courage to be vulnerable, and teams must come to a common understanding with their managers on how to make decisions.

Speaker:

I have a great question that I'm thinking about. The question is about culture at large. I imagine an organization that is safe enough, has a safe enough container, has a dialogic leadership. But my question is: does this mean that we can make a direct decision?

Speaker:

So, it starts with the leader, and it starts with them showing their vulnerability and showing their authenticity as well. And this is dependent on the relationships between everyone in the room.

Speaker:

For leaders, it is important to be authentic, to show vulnerability, and not to always have the answer. The other most important thing is the preparation on the ground. I think these will help a lot with the decision-making.

Speaker:

On my road to self-discovery, I realise that I'm not doing well. I'm trying not to talk so much in meaning, and it's not working. As far as this is question is concerned, I'm really taking away as a leader not just being vulnerable, but when decisions come, using dialogue to move and inspire the team to go forward, even when those decisions are not wanted or desired.

Speaker:

What I heard is that we probably need to take several steps back from the decision and start with building a container so that voices can be heard and considered with humanity and safety. I'll leave it there.

Speaker:

I am thinking around how the organizational and systemic culture impacts the way decisions are made in a team.

Speaker:

The one that comes up for me is really understanding the potential barriers to decision-making. When you're creating that safe container, you try to create it from your perspective, but that's not the only perspective. You must be aware of cultural barriers. It sounds like an easy concept, but often it takes a lot of work to do it well.

Speaker:

For me it is also the building of a safe container. I think that's the foundation. And I really loved what was said about silence not being taken as consent. I normally do not think of it as that way. Thank you for that.

Speaker:

I guess deciding if you have enough of a container depends on whether you're together for an hour, or together for a day, or a year. Do you have enough of a container for your taxi ride? If you have, you'll be fine. Do you have enough of a container for a two-day project or not? I think we only really need to know each other well enough to function well within what we are trying to do. In terms of being authentic or genuine, I would like people to say in the room what they say outside the room. Then I think we've got a sufficiently genuine voice. The key thing when making a decision is to try to see the whole picture as well as our own. We need other people to represent parts of the picture. *Do they represent enough of the picture for the decision?* If not, how do we get the rest of the picture in here so that we don't have to deal with it afterward, which takes more time and energy than doing it now? I think that's so. I'm thinking of the right level for what we're trying to do. I feel we know each other well enough in this Participatory Dialogue, led by Ali and Carol. I think we did fine in that regard.

Speaker:

Our leaders have to set things up in a way that it makes it possible for us, under their leadership, to get into the whole process.

Speaker:

How they set the tone, I guess, would be my thing. You know, it depends on who you work with. Here in our district, our chief is very hands on. She makes it very comfortable for people to participate and get into the process. So that's a good thing.

Speaker:

I'm sitting with culture, systems, hearing about leaders creating containers – and all of that is true. But culture will trump anything that's new to an organization unless people allow all voices to be heard. For me, dialogue will be successful if leaders say less and encourage people to say more.

Ali:

I'm sitting with a couple of things. That piece that was said about the importance of the use of conscious, or subconscious power, and how it affects decision-making. I'm also thinking about the system and how to encourage voices. Encouraging people to speak their truth. One little extra one, I can't get away from my curiosity about who that baby was that we saw briefly on the screen. I may have to message afterwards to find out.

Carroll:

Well, better education for the next generation as well! My last thoughts cross over quite a few things. The word assumption comes into my mind. That is the gift of suspension. Quite often in a system, there are lots of assumptions that are unspoken. If we're able to suspend those assumptions and voice them, that helps. The leader needs to be able to encourage people to voice those assumptions. That comes back to the dynamic of the container and of transparency. Quite a big cake of different things is how I would wrap that up and summarise decision-making. I've learned so much from today, listening to all your different perspectives on that. Thank you, for a rich dialogue. I'm sure things are going to bubble away more as we go through the conference.

Speaker:

Could I ask one question, Carol, just before we break? I don't know if other people agree, but I thought this session worked well. The two of you led it in a way that people said what they wanted to say easily. What do people think that Ali and Carol did that made our 80 minutes-long 'team' work? They were like the leaders of the team. Why did it work?

Speaker:

Well, I'm going jump straight in at that invitation to say I think they created a container that allowed us to dialogue.

Speaker:

I think the intro was great. Ali came in with the check-in in a very bubbly way. Carol, your story was very relevant and relatable to, with so many affected by the pandemic and the shutdown, and about going back to work. I think that provided a lot of thought and allowed people to open up about their own experiences and share.

Speaker:

There was a connection. When folks came into the room late, we took a pause and welcomed them, got them up to speed, brought them in, and heard their voices. I thought that there was some really nice by-standing. A few moves and lots of observation from the two facilitators helped us understand what was going on.

Speaker:

They just made us feel comfortable enough to be open and to have true dialogue. It was a smooth balance. I think I can speak on behalf of everyone by saying we felt engaged. We felt that you were listening to us as we shared our ideas, our thoughts and opinions, and you also talked less and allowed others to talk more. I thought that was great.

Ali:

Thank you for your comments!

POSTSCRIPT

In our dialogue we wanted to explore the group's experience of dialogic decision-making in today's business environment, along with the questions raised in our pre-conference description. Several useful points emerged.

Leadership vulnerability is important in decision-making. Acknowledging the need to ask for help and support, using suspension in communication, and knowing where on the ladder of vulnerability a leader is sitting, all enable a transparent conversation. Decisions impact others on multiple levels and through dialogue, having this awareness can transform the effectiveness of decision-making.

We need to start with building a safe container. and being aware of cultural barriers, through the use of the dialogic practices of authentic voice, respect, listening and suspension. This will help to encourage all voices to be heard with humanity, and the different perspectives to be shared, thereby reducing the fragmentation within the decision-making process. Recognition that silence does not equal consent. People need to be able to say in the room what they would say outside of the room. In that way, dialogue provides the space for the bigger picture to emerge to enable a more effective decision.

In our approach of working with teams to enable effective decision-making, we now have a greater understanding of the importance of creating a container and taking the time to establish this as a foundation for dialogue. Frequently leaders are put into a position where they feel they need to hold accountability for a decision. Ultimately perhaps they do, yet there is another choice. They can share the perspectives, vulnerabilities and impacts of the ripple effect of a decision if it is done well and if it is done poorly. Exploring all these aspects of a decision through dialogue will engage support and ultimately enable the decision to be made with greater integrity.

How Can Dialogue Help in Making Tough Decisions?

Timo Nevalainen and Ismo Huusko

PRE-CONFERENCE DESCRIPTION

Tough decisions often have far-reaching consequences for teams and organizations. Traditional decision-making processes may not suffice to address the complexity or diversity of perspectives involved. Dialogue can lead to more well-rounded decisions that are also accepted more readily by those whose lives the decisions impact. This can contribute not only to better immediate outcomes but also to fostering a culture of participation and responsibility. Our dialogic inquiry session focuses on the role Dialogue can have in the decision-making process, especially in complex or high-stakes situations and we invite both beginning and seasoned dialogic leaders to share experiences and learn together with us.

CHECK-OUT

Timo Nevalainen:

A question for our check-out is, *What are you leaving this session with? What are your takeaways from this?* I can begin this round with my own so far, which is that I'm leaving this with a question of how I can bring more of the whole into decision-making. Even weekly, when it's needed, even in situations when it's not conducive to bringing in that whole. How can I bring a little bit more of it to the decision-making? That's what I take away with me.

Speaker:

Like I said in my check-in, I'm in a privileged position of not having very difficult situations for decision-making. But I think this has been quite a helpful overview of the challenges and opportunities of dialogic decision-making. It seems that your situation in the organization is that making a decision makes a big difference to the kind of framework and principles that that can be used. There is a lot to learn from experiences of different types of situations, and what kind of principles to use. So, I think this has been very helpful to gain a better appreciation of that.

Speaker:

What I take from this conversation is that dialogue might uncover the decision that you already know that you have to take, right? Which means that you can reduce risk. Still, you need the courage to take the decision in the face of uncertainty. So, I leave with a question, *What does it take to have the courage to take a decision where you're alone?* I think dialogue helps me with this uncertainty.

Speaker:

I'm leaving with a lot of food for reflection and more questions than answers, which is a very nice place to be for me, and with excellent answers to the questions I came in with. Also, this has been a very nice pace for me too. Thank you all for having created this space.

Speaker:

I'm delighted to be in the session, particularly with all the experience that's present in the room today. I'm continually encouraged that there is a dialogic decision-making process to use when making decisions, the toughest decisions. The reality is that the dialogue can both help the decision and benefit the collection of decision makers included. What Harold said about inclusion kind of blows the mind a little bit, about including people in your executive meetings. And the impact for the people who are involved is as important as the quality of the decisions themselves. So anyway, I'm empowered by this time together. Thank you so much.

Speaker:

What I'm taking from this is that within the context of dialogue, dialogic decision-making is new to me. I am thinking about when to allow dialogue and how it empowers those involved to take ownership of whatever entity they are a part of. I'm trying to do that with my guys, because there is a situation for me and them. I'm trying to create a feeling of ownership throughout the staff and inmates, and I know that will lead to greater productivity. They are from different cultures, so we will create something new.

Speaker:

It has been really helpful to reflect and break it all down to understand it. I'm very conscious of the two areas where I volunteer at the moment. In the world of families seeking asylum and in the National Health Service. Every single word you guys have said today has expressed how frustrating and sad and difficult it is for people in that situation. They have absolutely nothing of what you've mentioned about knowing how their cases are being dealt with, and whether they'll ever find out. How sad it is to be so lost in a decision-making process that is holding your life at risk. I'm just really noticing that. With the National Health Service, which is our UK healthcare system, so many doctors run the risk of being sued. Most General Practitioners have a lawyer for when someone thinks they don't get it right. I'm just fascinated by how we can get some of the most fundamental things right in our lives. How could they be changed to make some more transparency and openness? Harold, I loved your ideas of inviting the observers to a meeting, just observing so that they recognise it as fair. Lots to think about. Thank you.

Speaker:

Some of the things I'm taking away are about the difficult decisions. Ones that lend themselves to dialogue, and that's not always the case. When it is, you must ensure that you have not only all the voices, but the correct voices in the room, the ones that can impact the change. I feel that you have to allow the process to create the outcome, not have the outcome drive the dialogue. The other thing that comes to my mind is that once that outcome is discovered, you have to be committed to making that change and be committed to following through. I was reminded of a situation that I was in several years ago, where a small-town private school was on the brink of closing for financial reasons. We came together and saved that school. A lot of those dialogic practices were in place then, although I didn't realize it at the time. It was a success. So that's what I've taken away from this.

Speaker:

Listening to you all, I had two reflections that I'm leaving with. They are questions, I suppose. The most difficult decisions, and what I mean by that are the ones that have possibly the biggest consequences as a result of taking them, benefit from the use of multiple perspectives and require dialogue to draw them out. The next thought in my head was about inclusion. How do we draw out those multiple perspectives? Because not everybody feels safe voicing what they're thinking in a group. So that's the reflection or question I leave with. How can we use dialogue to make it safe for everybody to contribute?

Ismo Huusko:

First of all, thank you everyone. It has been amazing to be part of this conversation and also to partner with Timo. Very amazing and, to be honest, I'm just happy to be here listening to you guys who have so much experience.

I want to keep it short. I'm going out with this. All the fires should be put out, and the ones that cost us the most need learning about more. And as a quite young person, two years into dialogue, I want to bring new ideas into organizations and to challenge those older beliefs. So, finding a balance on that is my interest too. Thank you.

Speaker:

A couple of things. One, a reminder that it's important that we be true to the needs of our internal dialogue. I think often we can forget that, and perhaps not be as true as we need to be to nurture that internal dialogue, and to take all aspects of it into consideration. Secondly, I was reflecting that all organizations are different. They're structured differently, and although a logic process can work in all of them, there will have to be some differences as well when decisions are being made. There's a lot that can be said about that, but it's too long for a check-out.

Speaker:

Thank you for holding this lovely little moment that we have had together here. What I'm really struck by, honestly, is the thought that this can be scaled. I believe that 20 years ago this was countercultural. But now it's doable. There are all sorts of variations in it as you get more precise about the form and circumstance, the situation requires a choice of timing, and so on. Then there is the scope of the problem, but the basic spirit of it is gettable. I think that's what is evident to me. It takes experience and capability. Capability and confidence go together. If people have more experience of it, they think, *Well, I can do that.* I think we are wired to do it, but we must be introduced to it. It's really lovely to see the fruit of that showing up. That's what I'm mostly struck by. Also, this idea of vertical and horizontal inclusion hit me as the way to broaden the space to make it easier. There's a lot more I'd like to unpack. Thank you again.

Timo:

Thank you everyone for taking part in this. Alright. See you, thank you, and bye-bye.

POSTSCRIPT

We selected the theme of this session – tough decisions and how to make them dialogically – because of the challenges we had previously faced with the team we were working with in TAMK Proakatemia. It seemed that it was relatively easy to work through dialogue with issues where there was plenty of time and that did not involve strong emotions, but when those decisions involved money and needed to be decided on quickly they were more difficult to handle dialogically. We had learned previously about dialogic leadership in VADOC. In VADOC dialogue was encouraged by the management, especially in tough management situations, and that made us interested in engaging in dialogue about this with the participants at the conference. Below, we try to distill some of the core learnings from the dialogue.

One crucial question raised in the check-out was, *How can we use dialogue to make it safe for everyone to contribute?* When we are making difficult decisions, it is very important for people to feel safe when bringing in their ideas and perspectives. Safety and active contribution in a dialogue can bring a heightened level of awareness among the people. With this improved level of awareness, it is easier to make tough decisions together, minimize conflicts between participants and create a common understanding of the situation.

This shared awareness is especially important in situations where the stakes are high and that involve a high level of uncertainty. While the usual reaction to these situations is that the leaders must carry the burden of uncertainty and quickly make the right decisions in all situations, being able to engage in effective dialogue would often bring about better results – especially in the long-term. Bringing in multiple perspectives on a tough issue might even make the required decision self-evident.

When we are making decisions through dialogue, it is equally important when hearing everyone to have the right voices in the session, those who are impacted by the change and those who can make change. Changes are more difficult to make without these people and it then demotivates people to take part in the dialogue. Dialogue sessions should not be driven by the outcome but by the process. When you go through the process of dialogic decision-making and you get to the decision together, following through becomes a necessary next step for all involved.

In the end, dialogue enables teams, organizations and communities to transcend the fragmentation that is often caused by hierarchy and include diverse stakeholders and their voices in high-stakes decisions.

Distractions as an Aid to Dialogic Decision-Making

Helena Wagener, Shakita Bland

PRE-CONFERENCE DESCRIPTION

Let's discover together if being distracted and chasing rabbits means we are not totally invested in the Dialogue process. Rather than get into medical terms or diagnosis about the distracted mind we will delve into the art of distraction and the ideas that resonate from distracted Dialogues. This enquiry is about people and the millions of things we all have going through our heads every second of every day. What impact do these distractions have on our ability to have productive Dialogues and to make decisions? Do distractions take away from any aspect of professionalism or a person? Or could they settle us and bring fresh insights? This enquiry matters as we often find ourselves being categorized, either by others, who seek to understand distractions, or by ourselves, as we try to navigate our own distractions to fit into what we are told is the norm.

Wonderful Dialogue Distractions
by Shakita Bland

Some think eye contact is necessary in a conversation,
*   but fail to realize the chaos going on behind the eyeball station.*
Some people find it hard to maintain that type of focus . . .
*   doesn't make them bad, just a product of the "sometimes we just don't notice".*

Well, Helena and I are glad you decided to join us on this journey,
*   of what we are unsure, but hope you have fun as we unravel this story.*
On how to become wonderfully distracted and remain attached to the fact as if in a daydream,
*   and all that appears may not be what it seems.*

Is this dialogue? Well, it very well could be . . .
*   don't we make the rules within the scope of order?*
We shall see and may we all become new explorers,
*   seeking adventures even within our minds.*

As we take steps to break all binds,
   escaping into this unknown world we call dialogue distractions,
   becoming wonderfully taken away for only half the fraction,
   just remember it's all about learning, having fun, and oh yeah, the dialogue practices.

Thank you for your time and interest . . .
   so, without further ado here's the first of the wonderful dialogue distractions!

CHECK-OUT

Shakita Bland:

As we check-out, please give one example of how you will practice being wonderfully distracted in the future. It's totally up to you if you want to use it in a personal context, or you want to use it in a professional context. We're not making that decision for you. So, please give us any one example of how you will practice being wonderfully distracted in the future. Anyone can start and we would like to have everybody participate.

Speaker:

As soon as my budget is lifted (because I put myself on a budget), I'm going to order myself a ventriloquist's doll. I'm so serious. She's going to have braids, and I want to make sure she has a yellow shirt just like mine. I'm going to take this thing around everywhere. I'm not kidding, mark my words! Next year I'm going to have a ventriloquist's doll. Okay, watch for it.

Speaker:

Picturetopuppet.co.uk is the UK site. They may be able to tell you about someone in America. They make it to look like you, and they are amazing.

Speaker:

I feel I'm distracted too much. The question is, should I be less wonderfully distracted? The question has made me think. This has been the best session so far for me, thank you so much.

Speaker:

Well, distraction is certainly a very interesting topic, and I felt sometimes more or less distracted. I learned some things about distraction. It's an interesting topic to follow and in parts I think it was quite fun talking together.

Speaker:

I'll follow and say that this has definitely been one of my favourite breakout sessions so far. I will try to be more mindful, maybe observing what other people's distraction triggers are – because everyone's just different.

Speaker:

I think I will focus more on trying not to be a distraction, and to pay more attention. I have all types of stuff all around me, right now. I have candy, popcorn, my iPad, my work cell phone, my personal cell phone, a notebook. I think I'm going to try to slim down some of the stuff around me so that people won't think I'm not interested.

Speaker:

I've observed a few times when I had big projects, I was so totally into working on those projects that I completely forgot my daughter. She only has me, and she is now big enough to tell me to put my phone away because she wants my attention. There are times when I am working a straight 30 or 40 hours, and I just drop her at school and pick her up. But really paying attention to her is something that I have not done during these times. I have just come to the realisation that I have to put a stop to it. When I am doing so much and I'm stressed out, my daughter is a very pleasant distraction for me. She has to do everything with me. So, I'm thinking that I need to sort things out properly so that work is work, and personal is personal. I must differentiate between the two and give equal and deserving time to both sides of my life.

Speaker:

Listening to everyone, I never thought about distractions being negative or positive. I guess it just depends on the situation. I would need to understand the difference between what can cause a negative distraction versus what can cause a positive distraction. For example, what can cause a distraction, which can give you a new idea, versus something that would take away from an idea? So just having the self-control and the balance of knowing the difference between them.

Speaker:

As we're sitting here talking, I'm fidgeting with a pen. Instead of being a distraction for everybody, I focus on doing something different and in this way keep myself focused. But I'm also clicking the pen and I now know that can be a distraction to other people. I'd like to work on that. When my husband and I first got together he had the leg kicks. And ten years later I've got over that. I realize that he's going to do it whether I try to control it or not. That's just his distraction kick. That's what he does. So, I want to focus more on that.

Speaker:

I'm not sure what to say about being wonderfully distracted, but I can say that I'm going to be more mindful and tolerant when things are distracting to me and recognize that is maybe how the other person is coping – how they distract themselves rather them not paying attention. I'm going to stop judging those things. You all can't see me because you can only see the top half of me, but I've been bouncing and swirling in my chair this whole time. Some people wouldn't be able to work with me because I bounce constantly!

Helena Wagener:

There's so much going through my head right now. There's something around how distracted I get when I'm not sure why people are doing the things they're doing and how important it is to them. There's something around checking in if that pen is really driving me nuts and if it's only a small irritation then to let them get on with it, or at least have a conversation, so that both people know what's happening for the other person, and then you can go somewhere with it. I'm going to sneak an extra comment in because I was really touched by what someone said about her daughter. I have to constantly remind myself of my daughter as well. She wants to show me things when I'm stressing about work. She wants to show me that little video on TikTok or whatever. I want to start making the time to just watch it with her.

Shakita:

As I go about my day, I will use my humour to help someone to be wonderfully distracted along with me, like Helena. So go play with your toys and have a break until the hour when we meet back in the main session. That was so good, seeing you all.

POSTSCRIPT

One of the main questions asked during the session was how do distractions add to your professionalism? This was an important question because it opened the dialogue by presenting opportunities for participants to think about distractions. What do distractions mean to them? How can distractions sometimes lead to various ideas outside of a more normative thought process? We discussed the importance of recognizing that distractions are not bad, only stepping stones to something potentially greater. During the session, we encouraged participants to allow themselves to become distracted, to talk about what that feeling or thought meant to them.

Distractions are an important part of helping individuals focus their attention on numerous ideas at once, and to many, this doesn't seem to take away from their professionalism. Sometimes shame may overtake an individual during the procession of becoming distracted. In today's world, we therefore call certain distractions multi-tasking as this may sound a bit more acceptable than being distracted. It is also important to note that in a capitalist society, we are encouraged to 'productively' multi-task rather than distractedly multi-task. In other words, a professional should be able to split their attention to do two billable tasks together but should not split their attention between a billable task and fiddling. Unbillable distractions, however, are a necessity when it comes to professionalism as they ensure that participants are able to remain open and aware of what is going on around them, and can therefore help others access alternative levels of activity during a process of engagement.

True frustration comes when we try to limit our ability to regulate through distractions and this can lead to good ideas not being acted upon. For example, as facilitators not having to keep everyone, including ourselves, focused on particular aspects of meaning, not having to try to closely track people's experiences or contributions, or not feeling impelled to take control of the process and how it unfolded was relaxing and rewarding. Participants also commented on the sense of freedom and ease that arose from having no particular agenda or need to produce meaning. Someone mentioned that never before has she laughed so much in a dialogue, and that she left feeling accepted, while also learning a lot about how important it is for us to accommodate and accept each other's forms of expression.

DAY THREE

What is Dialogic Decision-Making?

Why Does Your Organization Need Dialogic Decision-Making?

PART THREE

Co-hosted plenary session

HOSTS

Peter Garrett APDP APDPA (UK) – Dialogue Associates and Academy of Professional Dialogue

William Isaacs APDP APDPA (USA) – Dialogos

Bill:

We'd like to hear from you about what was stirring and expanded during the Participatory Dialogues, and thereby to continue them. There's a tendency to report on what you talked about. You could take a report mode, or better still you could just continue from the conversation you were in. Speak from where you are and what you are thinking about. It's subtle, but it changes the nature of the conversation. It's about continuing the conversation, except it happens to have more people in it now. The fact that people don't necessarily all have the same context is fine, they'll get it. We'd love to hear from you. What stimulated your thinking about this subject? You don't have to raise your hand or anything, and panellists please feel free to make contributions if you hear something that you think we want to follow up on.

Markus:

Maybe I will start. Looking at the world, we are confronted with so many, let us say bad decisions. And what can we do about it? We came to the conclusion that on the one hand, you have a responsibility if you are in a position to make a decision. On the other hand, it is important to prepare things and maybe to review your decision once you see that it is not going in the right direction. This ability to review things is what we need in many places. For example, the bad decisions made that started a war, or whatever it may be. As people on this planet, we must start making good decisions and reviewing bad ones.

Bill:

That opens up a gigantic topic, and a very rich one. Let's hear, *What struck you?*

Laura:

Our group was about the value of the voices in the room. As individuals, we know what our style is. As we go into a dialogue, which may have very simple decisions to be made or giant decisions to be made, or it may be a Generative Dialogue, we need to take our authentic voice to the room and be respectful of other people's voices. If we let certain people like Laura, meaning Laura me, speak too much, we miss out on the other voices and run out of time to hear everyone. It's so important to hear everybody's voice, whether it's a dialogue in a giant corporation or a small one to do with a localized issue. We agreed that we need to self-check. Whoever's facilitating a dialogue also needs to find the balance and make sure that all the voices are heard. That's my two cents' worth.

Efrain:

I would also like to share my thinking. What I have taken out of this is also about including all the relevant voices. Every single voice in the room is important and we should never, ever underestimate either the person who is washing the dishes or the boss who is the executive officer in the organization. What I have seen is that for us to do that, we have to ask every participant to leave their credentials outside the door when they enter the room – even if they have a master's degree or a Doctorate, or even if they have a basic education like myself, even if they are the President of Mexico, or they are in Congress. We have to set a level of being equal when it comes to us as humans to find the decisions that can work for all of us. So definitely, this democratic participation is something that we need to have in order to have better decision-making.

Bill:

Excellent, excellent. Let's hear from a few others, including people who haven't yet spoken or who are still trying to figure out how to bring their voices into this conversation. I invite those of you who are fairly quick to speak, not to speak, and to take some responsibility for broadening the inclusion here in the room and inside yourself. That equally applies to the people who are reluctant or worried. Maybe English isn't your first language, or you don't have a completely brilliant thing to say. Let's all of us make room for that.

Speaker:

I met somebody from Belgium, and she brought a very different perspective. In the room I went into, we talked about what makes decision-making one of the top challenges for teams. Just listening to her perspective on her organization was very interesting and eye-opening, about all the challenges not only that she has but that she deals with in her organization.

Peter:

Let's hear from more like that. There are some who are following the closed caption text at the moment, so they're hearing the words, and then reading them to understand the meaning. That takes time to come through, so it might be 10 or 20 seconds later that they know what has been said. If you're in that category, you're welcome to raise your hand so that people can see you want to speak.

Speaker:

In the Participatory Dialogue, one thing that stuck out to me was how important it is to hear every voice and also to recognize that in certain situations some people have far more experience. I'm at VADOC (Virginia Department of Corrections), and I shared that I think it is important for higher-ups to go through the process of being a correctional officer, to understand the daily struggles and issues that we face, the daily tasks that we have to accomplish and what it takes to deal with the inmates. It is on a different level than being in headquarters or Human Resources.

Speaker:

I'll share something. I have a little coffee time courage, so I don't mind sharing today in the big group. I was in a group where we spoke about, *Whose decision is it?* The description of this group really resonated with me. I don't work directly with VADOC, but I'm contracted through a health system to work there, so some things are just a little different in the hierarchical way that everything falls down to us. A huge, huge takeaway for me was a question someone asked. When we go into meetings, a lot of the time it is a monologue. A lot of voices don't get heard. The really good question was, *Are there clear expectations to make a decision, or is it just a conversation to bounce ideas off one another?* I want to ask that question at the start of every meeting so that there is more transparency about expectations. Otherwise, we are just sitting there, getting nothing accomplished, never feeling like we can speak, or as if we may get reprimanded if we say something. I definitely want to move to a place where we truly create a safe container. We say that a lot of the time, but is it really safe? If we're too scared to even open our mouths or if you have to have someone who is your accountability partner to tap your leg in every meeting, not to speak, is it really safe? I want to operate in a space where I can utilize courage to continue to show up with my authentic voice, in my authentic self, and not be so concerned about everyone's rank or title. Thank you for letting me share!

Peter:

Thank you.

Speaker:

Can I share a wish here? I wish I could see you panellists come up with a true scenario, or even a false scenario, and go through this decision-making and dialogue – so that I could observe how the panel tries to discuss issues, and how they try to make a decision practically.

Peter:

Good. Umm.

Speaker:

I need to hop off in a couple of minutes, so if I can shake things up a little bit on my way out the door, I am happy to do it. In our dialogue around the value of voice, we had a participant who felt very overwhelmed by the presence of people from the VADOC. It was fun to be able to engage with the idea of how important it is to honour the difference, the beauty and the difference, and to value having an outside voice who doesn't speak the same language as everyone else in the room. And there is a particular joy to have a prison abolitionist hanging out with a whole bunch of VADOC folks – and really not letting that be a disconnector, but rather leading with love and community to intentionally engage and learn together with everyone there. I really appreciate the variety of voices and the honouring of voice that is made possible through dialogue.

Bill:

Thank you.

Peter:

I was just wondering . . . Some people might not know your organization and your situation. I don't know if you feel comfortable bringing that out, or not.

Speaker:

Sure, why not? I'll throw it out there and be very open about it. I am currently incarcerated and 15 years into a 50-year sentence for a crime that I committed five weeks after my eighteenth birthday. I've been in for 15 years. Now I am a restorative justice scholar and practitioner, which is deeply dialogic. And yes, I come to this from the standpoint of wanting something better and envisioning a future that does not have prisons. Understanding that there needs to be intentional growth, we need community capacity to hold people accountable meaningfully for repair and healing outside the criminal legal system. In the meantime, it takes all of us to make that possible. Working on the inside from this perspective, with people who run and work within the system, is fun and takes some navigating. And I appreciate your question. It is something that means a whole lot.

Peter:

Thank you for contributing and participating as you are. No doubt there were some decisions in the past that are irreversible, and still, you are managing your current situation well. We'll all hear more from Leo tomorrow because he's on our panel about dialogic culture.

Leo:

Yes. You'll see my pretty face again tomorrow!

Bill:

How about others? What occurred to you as you we were talking about this dialogic decision-making continuum, that may be a way to talk about it?

Speaker:

In our session, we talked about the challenge of including all relevant voices. Listening to what other people said here and in the breakout group, there are some common themes to make sure that the relevant voices are included. But thinking even broader than that, do we care to hear those voices? Are we motivated to actually listen to those voices and make sure that those voices are heard? Not just mine, but other people's voices. Are we going through the dialogic engagement process as a tick box exercise, to say, *Yes we heard all the voices,* or do we actually care what those voices saying? Isn't that the ultimate outcome of dialogic engagement? The culture that we're trying to foster is to encourage people to share their voices with each other, and that can be really hard when there is a hierarchy and a very definite power imbalance. Do we care about the decisions that we make that impact people who are incarcerated or that impact people who are more junior than us in our workplaces, or whatever the case might be? I think that if the underlying motivation carries through to there, then it accentuates the authenticity of the dialogue process.

Bill:

Good point. What others?

Speaker:

Well, I was hoping that someone from our group would speak, but I feel compelled to, so I guess it's going to be me. In our group, the topic was about distractions within dialogue, and what purpose they serve. I had a preconceived notion in my head of what we would be talking about, but the way the conversation moved was amazing. It bought in the idea of comedy or comic relief in these spaces. We were talking about how the conversations have had a serious tone for the last couple of days but in this room, I'm telling you, you would have thought it was a bunch of kids in there playing around. We had little toys squeaking, and we had a puppet show. It was amazing. We were in there laughing, and we were able to conclude that distractions in the midst of dialogue are sometimes important. For a lot of reasons, we just need them to shift our mind away from so much about focus, focus, focus.

Sometimes we need to laugh a little, or, you know, smile a little. So, I really liked the concept of distractions and looking at them in a positive way when it comes to dialogue. I truly enjoyed that session!

Bill:

I think what hit me as I was listening in my group was that we are faced with decisions of all kinds all the time. Some of them we don't want to make. Some are really tough or difficult ones. Sometimes we have to figure out how we get a lot of other people to play with us. That may be what we're faced with. And we're looking at the question, *What would it take to change the quality of those decisions, and the impact of them?* We're talking about dialogue as a kind of context-generating change system, a way to shift that. So, one thing that occurred to me, and I don't know if it's occurring to you, is that if you focus too narrowly, you can't see the potential. I think we can get narrow because different parts of us get fearful or reactive and feel under pressure to make a move right now. So somehow that pressured reality makes the decision and prevents you from figuring out what to do in a way that might be a better way to go. It's about how to generate a different kind of space, partly by including people, partly by calming yourself and everybody else down. I think this is the interface between dialogue and action. Most people don't have access to any alternative to the way they have made decisions every day. We're talking about broadening it out.

Jane:

I think this is what Markus was talking about in the session where we were together. We were talking about the process of being willing. Markus, you described how to take ground in your case study about the United Nations. We've made this part of a decision, but we haven't made these other decisions yet. At that stage we need to let go so people are willing to do more and be fluid with the process. As you said, Bill, it's about a kind of courage not to be rushed. Taking the time to include people. Being transparent and willing to say, *Oh, I think I messed that up.* Maybe that wasn't the right decision. Can we go back? Can we do it again? There are all sorts of ways, but they should always come from the intention that the decision should be a good decision, whatever that means – sustainable, including people, thoughtful, timely. I think that the intention is really key.

Peter:

I like the idea of small victories. Take the small victory, take stock and make progress – as opposed to thinking it's all based on one comment. I was describing earlier, David Bohm's realization that something had gone wrong with our thinking. We think as if we were independent, on our own, doing our own thing. Yet we are actually interdependent. Markus, in the United Nations, how many countries did you have in your ongoing negotiation for your resolution?

Markus:

About 15 to 20 countries were in the negotiations.

Peter:

Now, every country in the United Nations believes it has the sovereign right to make its own decision and that's the problem. Clearly, countries are interdependent in terms of the economy, in terms of climate, in terms of migration, in all sorts of areas. But each one acts as if I'm independent. I've got the right to decide what I want. I'm pleased we have the United Nations, but it's faulty thinking that we come first. We have an obligation to support the collective reality, that is the fact. We are not separate. Now, if you take that down to the local level, isn't that what's happening? Me in my situation and in my job? My main point here is that we should also think about others and change our thinking about where we sit in the larger mix.

Thomas:

Now, that can be taken also more into the micro. I was in the same group with Bill, and this point about inclusiveness and including people came up. There is the point about intentionality as well, which I really think is important because one of the main complaints today from executives and people all around in organizations is the number of meetings they have daily. They say, *I don't even know why I am being called into a meeting. What do I have to do with this meeting?* Nevertheless, they are called and spend their days in meetings. Those who call the meetings also say, *No, no, we must make this decision together.* But the intention there is diluting responsibility. That has grown enormously with uncertainty. Those who couldn't make decisions on their own want to make them in a group – not because they really invite involvement in the decision, but because they just want to say, *We took the decision together.* Yeah. So, there is a very fine line here to pay attention to. Why are we calling the meeting? In the spirit of dialogue, or for some other reason?

Peter:

I think this is a really important point.

Bill:

I remember times in my own organization when I would say, we're just doing this, and people would respond with, *Well, this is an organization about dialogue.* I said, *Yeah, but we don't need to talk about this, we just need to do it.* This generated a big surprise on people's faces like, *Oh, all right.* I think it's quite an interesting notion that inclusiveness can dilute responsibility. I see this in international development organizations where the inclusion 'consensus virus' is so complete that you have 25 people show up for pretty much everything and you can't get anything done.

Speaker:

I don't have a skilled way to say this, so I'm going to put an apology first, but regarding the last few contributions from you, Peter and Bill, I question how much we are prepared to check our privilege here. It took my mind to the situation in the Middle East right now. It's all well and good to talk about safety and the responsibility to contribute and not to be individualistic, but if you're someone in a war zone right now, can we really expect that we don't operate in the space of looking after our individual safety and the safety of our families? I have to hold the awareness of my own privilege in this. Nobody is dropping a bomb on my house right now, and I can walk out in the street, and no one's going to chase me or hunt me down just because of the way I look. But that's not everybody's reality.

Bill:

True.

Speaker:

I greatly I agree that organizations need dialogue, and you're supposed to plan for it when you're having these meetings. Afterwards, you go and do it, and then you study what was done and you come back and act upon what you find. So, when you say, Is it getting diluted? It will get diluted if you don't make a plan for the outcome.

Jane:

Maybe I have caught the inclusion virus, but I can see someone who has had their hand up for quite a while, and there hasn't been space for them to bring their voice in. I want to use my privilege to help you to do that, if I may.

Peter:

Thank you, Jane.

Speaker:

I agree with the gentleman earlier who talked about voices in the room. In dialogic decision-making I feel that voices in the room are necessary, not only to say that the decision was made democratically, but because everybody can put their two cents' worth in as well as leadership – just as we can now in the meeting and have our voices heard – but ultimately the leader is making the decision. Having a personal voice in the room guides me towards buying into the situation. We call it the buy-in. Not just talking based on what we feel, but what we've come to understand. So, I think voices in the room are important in a decision-making situation.

Peter:

Good point.

Speaker:

I'll go back to Bill's comment about inclusiveness, and I agree that including everyone can be counterproductive. I live by Jeff Bezos' two pizzas rule, that you should never have more people in a meeting than two pizzas can feed, because it's not effective. However, I also do believe that you have got to have the right voices in the room. People with diverse perspectives or who sit in different parts of the organization, so that when we do make a decision, we have all the information that is relevant to be able to make the best decision. So, I agree with inclusiveness, but the right inclusiveness. Not saying we need the entire organization or the entire unit, that we need everybody to come into the room. That could waste a lot of energy and still not help us to make a great decision.

Speaker:

Thank you for that. Yes, it's a great conversation. I would like to add diversity and inclusion. That doesn't mean that we include everyone in a meeting to be effective. It's a trend these days that we want to have everyone included in the decision-making, but truly this is not the right path for making a decision. We should have a platform for the subject matter experts. *Why I am in this meeting?* There should be a dialogue about that. *What do I take into the meeting? What's the business value of me being a part of the decision-making?* Because, without looking into those elements, you will probably have more people in the meeting, like a check box approach, which doesn't add any value to making the best decision. Good examples are the many decisions being made these days in NGOs. We see that they don't have good value when they implement in the field.

Patty:

One of the things that came up in our break-out group, that what was helpful to me, comes back to the notion of privilege. When I'm in a position of authority, when I'm president of the faculty and I can decide who's going to be in the room, I do tend to surround myself with people who, not necessarily will agree with me, but people who I know I can work with well. Perhaps there will be a better representation of the stakeholders needed if the person who's the ultimate decision maker is not the one who picks who should be in the room. So, invite somebody who is in less of a position of authority to decide whose voices need to be in there to make a good decision.

Speaker:

Thank you, Patty. What I was going to add is that the process that we use within the VADOC is the Working Dialogue. That has a first phase, which is called the Set-Up. In the set-up phase, we talk to the sponsor and we invite people who would have voices, responsibilities or expertise relevant to the topic. When we get all of these people in the room, it is regardless of rank. It may not be the departmental head; it may be another person who's within that particular area that comes into the discussion. In the setup phase, we make that decision as part of developing and planning a Working Dialogue process. When we meet, if we find ourselves talking about 'them' we know we need to include them too. So that's very beneficial to reaching a successful meeting and solution to the problem at hand.

Peter:

Thank you. I'm noticing we're getting close to time, and I want to give you a chance to say something, Mine. You are the only panel member who didn't say anything yet. Then Bill and I can finish off, handing it over to Jane before we close. Do you have a comment you would like to make, Mine?

Mine:

Only to say, thank you for inviting me. It's been really eye-opening, as always, to hear from so many different types of organizations, people and types of decisions. It's really refreshing. And Thomas, I have to say I was thinking you must have cameras around our organization somewhere because your point was so relevant – about inviting so many people into a room to make a decision so that nobody's really on the hook and nobody's accountable. It's very refreshing to know that it's not just where I work. That's something I see often. So, thank you.

Harold:

Peter, if I may make a quick comment, I would just like to say that not all meetings have the same purpose, and not all meetings are dialogic. Some meetings are just to seek information, some to share information, and some are dialogic and are therefore conducted differently. One thing that I've seen over time in the four different jurisdictions that I've worked in, is often people complain about having too many meetings, but what I have come to realise is that some of those same people are the ones that also complain about not knowing what's happening, and not having a voice. We could keep that in mind as we talk about meetings.

Peter:

Yes. I agree entirely. When you particularly need a dialogue meeting is when people have different ideas about what we're trying to do and how to do it. We must get a common context of understanding. Okay, this is what we're trying to do. You can't do that through only sharing information or through snap decisions. You must think it through together. A closing comment from you, Bill?

Bill:

I don't have anything particular in mind other than appreciating that this territory is bigger than I had previously thought. It's a huge intersection, and it's a way to make what we do much more accessible. Many of us are interested in this because people are struggling with trying to make decisions about stuff all the time. What's the methodology? What's the approach? Who does get included, and in what ways? But more important than that, in my mind, is the quality of the inclusion and the energy behind the motivation. That's the missing and often unspoken thing. If your motivation is right, that produces the kind of conversation that expands understanding without judgement.

Peter:

Good. We will all be here tomorrow. Over to you, Jane.

Jane:

If you take seriously the name and the intention of this conference, which is Your Organization Needs Dialogue, and you want to go further or start taking dialogue into your organization, then Harold described some of the things on offer. One part of what the Academy offers is a range of educational opportunities. The Academy is a non-profit educational charity registered in the UK. We have developed a curriculum, and we continue developing our curriculum.

The educational provision runs from how to bring dialogue into any room – whoever's in there, however many people, and however many different dissenting voices there are This accreditation program is called *A Different Way of Working*. How to bring dialogue into any room. Then we're currently developing the curriculum for *Dialogic Intervention* work, and in time we will provide education in *Whole-system Dialogue*. That is about how you take dialogue across a whole system and embed it there.

This conference is a bit different. Here we're trying to think together by hearing different case studies from panellists and learning together, and learning for ourselves, from them. But this is not education, with a set curriculum of the kind that you can access through the courses available from the Academy. We have courses in place for *Dialogic Engagement* where we look at different modes. There, as Peter mentioned on Monday, we distinguish between a more operational dialogue and a Generative Dialogue. We look at the difference between them, as well as the many other ways of engaging with people. We have the *Dialogic Engagement* course which looks at those different modes.

We also have a *Dialogic Decision-Making* course, which considers many of the things we've talked about today like, *Whose decision is it?* and, *What is involved in making a decision?* We explore the structure and the process and how you engage people in different ways to make decisions together. That's another one-day certificated course from the Academy.

We're laying out the course for *Working Dialogues*, which many of you will have heard about from VADOC staff who are here. And also, a course on the *Dialogic Practices*. Again, during the conference, people talked about voicing and listening, about respect and suspension. This course is a chance to really get into those in some depth together.

Of course, the big one is the accredited program. If you want to become an Accredited Professional Dialogue Practitioner, the online program lasts six months, and once accredited by the Academy you become part of the community of professional practitioners. Some participants here at the conference have the initials APDP after their name. They are in our community of accredited practitioners.

So that's a quick version of the education that is available. I'll put the link into the chat so that if you want to find out more, you can go there. I'll be back tomorrow with Harold. Bobby is going to play us out with some music from Iran, which was chosen by Faezeh, who is here with us. I believe it's an Iranian composer, and you'll see him here with his orchestra playing the piano, performing in Tehran.

Thank you all!

TWND! 6: Your Organization Needs Dialogue!

DAY FOUR

What is a Dialogic Culture?
Why Does Your Organization Need a Dialogic Culture?

We began the conference considering the nature of dialogue and why it is needed in organizations. During the following days, we explored dialogic leadership and dialogic decision-making. For dialogue to be sustained in an organization, a dialogic culture is necessary, and thus the fourth day of the conference was set aside to enquire into the nature of a dialogic culture and its impact on the successes and failures of an organization. The experienced co-hosts were Harold Clarke and Jane Ball, and the format of the day was similar to the previous days, involving a plenary session with a panel, then concurrent co-facilitated Participatory Dialogues followed by open conversation during the final plenary session.

DAY FOUR

What is a Dialogic Culture?

Why Does Your Organization Need a Dialogic Culture?

PART ONE

Plenary session with a panel of four practitioners

HOSTS

Harold Clarke (USA) – Academy of Professional Dialogue

Jane Ball APDP, APDPA, (UK) – Dialogue Associates and Academy of Professional Dialogue

PANEL

Lars- Åke Almqvist APDP (Sweden) – Alamanco

Leo Hylton (USA) – Colby College and Maine State Prison

Susan Williams APDP (USA) – Virginia Department of Corrections

Ben Wright (USA) – Abilis Solutions

Harold Clarke:

It's good to see your faces again this morning! Welcome to Day Four of our conference, Your Organization Needs Dialogue! In case you have forgotten who I am, I'm Harold Clarke, and with me this morning is Jane Ball. We will be serving today as your co-hosts.

Today's theme is 'What is a dialogic culture? And why does your organization need a dialogic culture?' I've been thinking about that. What is dialogic culture? And do we need it in our organization? You'll hear the panellists speak about their experiences. As I think of culture, I think culture is so powerful because, in my estimation, culture determines the degree to which you're going to be successful – because the culture holds the stories and all the storylines. And those storylines have a major impact on the culture, which is going to determine success. That's why I always say a leader, or anyone interested in the welfare of an organization, has to focus on the culture. If you don't, chances are you will not be successful in achieving your goals and objectives.

Jane will now give you a check-in, and perhaps some opening comments.

Jane Ball:

Thank you. Our check-in question is, *What's the culture we need to be successful?* As a starting point, I think that is quite a good question. First, think about your circumstances and the organization where you work. If you're a consultant or a coach, it may be the organization you work with or in. Think about the local culture, that part of the organization, the functional unit or the office where you are located, rather than talking about the whole organization, which may be huge. So, think about your local culture. The culture can be seen as the habitual ways that people behave and act all the time. What's something that happens in the organization close to you, that is typical of the culture? And what impact does that have on you and on others?

We are going to put you into trios to consider this. To repeat, what's something that happens in your organization that's typical of the culture, and what impact does that have? See you back here in 7 minutes.

Participants are in trios in break-out rooms for 7 minutes.

Jane:

Okay. Let's look back. It would be really nice to hear a couple of stories. Harold and I were sharing some stories about what we've seen happen that indicates the culture. Would anybody be willing to share what they said in their breakout?

Speaker:

How is it being within a company and working directly with people, having contact with people? The culture is more obvious when you're around someone. Being connected remotely is an obstacle to dialogue because it is harder to communicate. It interrupts the culture of dialogue when you're working remotely. I experienced that myself when I worked remotely for two or three years, and I felt left alone.

Jane:

A very interesting point. The impact that working remotely has on culture. You can feel it when you walk into an organization, and you pick up the culture very quickly in how people welcome you. Do they smile at you and make eye contact, or not? Do they use your first name, or call you Mister or Miss, or whatever? But if you're working remotely, it can be a very different experience. That's a great point.

Speaker:

Yes, in our health services at VADOC, we have worked to tackle just that because we have a lot of people that do work remotely. We've established a professional development day where in the morning we have no scheduled meetings so that people can catch up on all the little tasks that they need to get done, and then we'll have a professional development activity where folks will come together. It has done such a brilliant thing for our ability to connect and start relationships, and it has really helped with the experience of dialogue in health services.

Speaker:

I can share something that I think is prevalent in our government culture as well as private industry, that is not being able to provide constructive feedback at all. People push it to the side. People make up their own stories about what's happening in this case, and it's usually wrong. We typically are unable to have those hard conversations early on. It's very prevalent in our culture, as I said, and perhaps prevalent in the private sector as well.

Jane:

Do you want to say something, Harold? And then we can invite our panel to join us.

Harold:

I echo what Jane said in terms of how you can feel the culture as you walk into an organization. You get a feel for the culture just based on how folks communicate with you, what the environment looks like and so forth. It's not hard to see. It's something that is very powerful, and it can give you some lasting first impressions. As I said earlier, the culture determines the degree to which we're going to be able to achieve our objectives so we must mind that culture.

Now I would like to jump right into the panel conversation. We will have two rounds. First, who are you, where are you, and what is your role in your organization? Do give the simple answer. This doesn't have to be some existential sort of explanation. Leo let's begin with you.

Leo Hylton:

Sure. I am Leo and I am currently incarcerated in Maine State Prison. I consult with a number of different restorative justice organizations as a scholar and practitioner in the field. I am in Maine, in the USA. I work within the Maine Department of Corrections as an incarcerated person, within this prison. I also work for an alliance for higher education in prison. My role in each of these organizations tends to be that of facilitator or organizer, pulling people together and helping them to hear each other when they can't really seem to do so.

Harold:

Very good. Please tag one of your fellow panellists, Leo.

Leo:

I'd love to tag Susan because she's right next to me on my screen.

Susan Williams (now Susan Dandridge):

Hello, everyone! I'm Susan Williams. I am a psychologist in the Virginia Department of Corrections. I work at headquarters in Richmond, Virginia, and I do mental health work and mental health projects. I am one of the original Dialogue Practitioners here in VADOC, where we started with Dialogue Practitioners in 2012. I will tag Lars.

Lars-Åke Almqvist:

My name is Lars. I live in Sweden, in a small town called Knivsta, 50 kilometres north of Stockholm, the capital of Sweden. I'm the CEO of a consulting company called Alamanco and we work all over Sweden in organizations that provide care for elderly and disabled people. The second role I will talk about is when I was Vice President until 2009 of the largest trade union in Sweden. I started a dialogue project to change the trade union culture over a period of 12 years.

Ben Wright:

Good morning, good afternoon! I'm Ben Wright, Vice President of customer success for a company that builds software for correctional agencies. I'll talk a little bit about my current role, but also my previous role when I worked for the Virginia Department of Corrections for 18 years. Between those two, I was a college professor for five years, so multiple careers. I'll talk about my experiences within and without all that.

Harold:

Very good. Thank you all. Now a second round. Based on your experience, share with us what you believe to be a key characteristic of a dialogic culture. If you have a story that you can wrap that into, please do so. Lars, can we begin with you?

Lars-Åke:

Okay, I'll start with my first example. I started working for the biggest trade union in Sweden, the Municipal Workers Trade Union, in 1980. Workers and white-collar workers are organized to a large extent in Sweden, and 60 to 70% of the workforce is in unions. At the end of the 1980s, we realised some unprecedented, forward-looking, strategic thinking and changed the role of trade unions. Trade unions are different in different countries, of course, but they are mainly conflict-oriented, reactive, hierarchical and very defensive.

I started a consulting company, and I had the chance to join a dialogic leadership program (called Leadership for Collective Intelligence) with Bill Isaacs, Peter Garrett and David Kantor. Based on that, I created a three-day dialogic training program. Our headquarters was pressed by the districts who were asking, *Why should we have headquarters that give us orders all the time, but never listen to what we have to say about the reality for our members?* So, we started with the 200 people working at headquarters and they all attended our three-day dialogue training. The organization was very fragmented with each unit separate from the others, and lots of silos. In mixed teams of 10 to 12 people, each team leader presented different ideas about how to change the culture. Altogether there were 196 proposals presented to my colleagues in the management team, which resulted in a very exciting meeting for several hours. I've always regretted that I didn't have a video camera on my forehead to document the kind of conflict process we had! We reorganized the whole headquarters, and all 196 proposals were implemented. Then we started the dialogue training with local trade union representatives together with employees all around Sweden to create better working conditions for our members.

Harold:

Before you go to your other example, tell me briefly from that story, what would you say is the key dialogic characteristic?

Lars- Åke:

We had totally different communications within and across the organization, we had better collaborations, and we involved the districts and the local organizations. To a large extent, we reorganized the districts through a dialogic process, as a result of the work we had done in the headquarters, and that is something that could not have happened in an organization that was not dialogic.

Harold:

No. Trade unions are very top-down in all countries that I know about.

Lars- Åke:

They typically come with directives from the national board of the management team, saying, *Do this, do that, do it this way, don't think for yourself, just swallow and do what we tell you.* We were able, during these 12 years, to change to something totally different, involving our members in many controversial questions. About 25% of the members were working for private companies, and that was seen as a threat to people working in the public sector. We had a huge referendum with 26,000 members in a four-hour meeting thinking about how, as a trade union, we should deal with freedom of choice for the citizens – as well as the competition between the public and private sector, since they are all members in the same union. What kind of culture can we have so that people can see that they are equal members? We must listen and work in a different way.

Harold:

So, your next example?

Lars- Åke:

In my consulting company, we work in organizations that care for the elderly in what are very fragmented organizations. When we work in a municipality, we see different accountants, human resources people and the managers who work with direct care for the elderly. 80% to 90% of the budget is for staff costs. All these organizations have great difficulty keeping within their budget. So, we try to find ways to create an economic system that helps deal with staffing resources in a better way. We start a process together with the managers and the front-line teams to create a new idea about working in their organization. We ask, *What, how and why do you think about your work?* We use the dialogic actions (as we call them in the Academy) and dialogic practices to look at these questions and as a result, they plan their work in a different way. They now dialogue with the users and agree on a care plan that creates better continuity, quality, and care. Everyone who wants to have full-time work can do so. In one local project, we documented, we started in a community in West Bay where only 30% to 40% were working full-time. Today everyone works full-time. They are all organized in small work teams that they call 'bubbles'. We had a fantastic result during the pandemic, because of the continuity between staff and users.

Harold:

Very good, thank you, Lars. Who would like to follow? Susan?

Susan:

I can follow Lars because Lars made a couple of points about collaboration, reducing fragmentation, working in a different way and managing your budget and resources. For me, the key to a dialogic culture is thinking together, learning together and creating new meaning together in order to do those things that Lars just pointed out. I think a quick story would be helpful. When people think about prisons they usually just think about correctional officers and incarcerated individuals, or maybe about the warden. Actually, a prison is a whole community, like a city, and we have all the functions that you have in a city. One of those things is trash. If you have, say 25,000 incarcerated individuals and 13,000 employees, you're going to generate a lot of trash. In the old way, or I call it BD meaning Before Dialogue, you just threw out your trash. You had the trash collectors pick it up and haul it away. But when you have that much trash it's not free, and of course, it costs you to pay for the trash service. Now AD, or After Dialogue, we came together to think about how we might look at trash differently. We had a series of dialogues that included the collaboration of different departments including food service, trash service, agribusiness and vocational education. We came up with some new ways of handling food waste. We started to turn our food waste into compost, thereby reducing the cost of fertilizer for our agribusiness. We send less waste to the dump, which means that we save the environment, and it costs less to haul away less trash. It did not take any skills to set out the trash for the trashmen to pick up, but now we have developed careers for incarcerated individuals who are learning new skills in recycling. As a result, they can get jobs in recycling centres, in composting and in driving, because then they become drivers of the trucks to come to pick up some of the things and whatever. So overall, we have saved hundreds of thousands of dollars. maybe close to a million dollars, for the agency in how trash is managed. In a dialogic culture, we have been thinking differently, coming together and crossing those silos of different separated units, to think about how we might do business differently.

Harold:

Very good, Susan. Perhaps as well as BD (Before Dialogue) and AD (After Dialogue) you might have AC, meaning After Clarke! Who would like to follow Susan?

Ben:

I have a rather simple story that focuses on the concept of collective intelligence. What I've learned in both private industry and corrections is that you can have the most talented people in the world, but without the concept of collective intelligence, and allowing those individuals to have voices, you will lose a lot in terms of productivity and your ability to resolve issues. I had the fortunate opportunity to open up a brand-new prison as a warden, and 80% of the staff members that I hired had never worked inside a prison before. That's a unique experience, and it's hard to prepare for that kind of situation. After we had been open for about two months, we introduced learning teams and dialogue. That was even before we started getting our first group of residents into the facility. It was part of our initial culture, and it was different for a lot of the staff members who came from working in factories or other private industries. The concept was different.

About three months after we opened, we had an incident where a staff member made an ill-advised decision. That ill-advised decision could have led to a very serious incident at our facility. Luckily it did not. Historically, the way to handle this situation was to discipline the staff member – we would have addressed that individual, and that's where the incident would have ended. But with the concept of collective intelligence, you want to be able to learn from those situations, to learn how to make sure those situations don't arise again, and I was able to use the learning teams to do so. I introduced this incident to the learning teams and said, *Hey, you know these things don't happen in a vacuum.* Staff may make bad decisions, but it becomes part of our culture if the staff doesn't understand that the decision was a bad decision. I used the learning teams to talk about the incident, how it occurred and what we can do better to support staff to make sure that those kinds of decisions are different in the future. All the learning teams came together and provided feedback that was brought to me. It was about how to change the way we did certain things at the facility. I think the unique thing was that many of the great ideas came from non-security staff, even though it was a security incident. We had people from maintenance, medical and behavioural health, and they all provided feedback about how we can prevent what happened from happening in the future.

If you don't have that open feedback, you could become very siloed, where decisions are made in a vacuum without consideration of others. That can lead to personal conflicts, it can become very difficult. It can hinder the growth of an organization, and the growth of individuals as well.

Harold:

Thanks for the story, Ben, and take a moment to say a bit about learning teams, so that everybody understands what they are.

Ben:

Yeah, certainly. Learning teams are a concept we introduced in VADOC to help foster communication. It involved taking groups of individuals at a facility, or a location, and scheduling regular dialogue sessions. We purposely had these groups as mixed groups from different departments and different areas, so that they could have a shared experience as they listened to one another. The concept behind the learning teams was meeting regularly. We made sure that we allocated time for the individuals to be at those sessions. I know sometimes in businesses and organizations things can get in the way of that, so we made sure that learning teams were a focus. We made sure our staff had a regular interval to get together, to dialogue, to have those opportunities to talk to other people with different viewpoints. It made a tremendous impact operationally, and on how I handled situations as a leader. It was no longer like a paramilitary top-down approach. I was utilizing the learning teams to get information to me as a leader.

Harold:

Thanks for that. So, Leo. We now come to you. We don't have anyone else, so you're it.

Leo:

Before I share my story, I want to name, for those who work outside of dialogue, the sensitivity around the term culture. Outside of this space, I engage in activism and advocacy around politics, around racial justice. So, talking about culture within an organization can activate something for people who feel culture in their body tracing it back through lineage, as opposed to culture within the organization or corporation. I just want to name that for the purpose of this conference, I'll use the term culture, but for me, it's really better to call it organizational dynamics or interpersonal dynamics within a certain context. One of the things that I bring to this work is a focus on conflict, analysis and resolution.

I'm going to speak about the context that I've been working in, to help spearhead the creation of the Earned Living Unit in the Maine State prison, here. The prison used to be the supermax when I first came, and I was down there when it was. There are videos on YouTube about cell extractions that were taped down in that unit, and it was horrific. Now it is different. The smell is the first thing people notice now when they step in there. *Hey? It actually smells good!* And for those of you who work within departments of corrections, you will understand. For me, the key characteristic of dialogic culture is the ability to do the gritty work right. Then there is an absence of fear about giving and receiving feedback. No fear of giving or receiving feedback is necessary. Sometimes there is a focus on the top-down building of dialogue. Well, I'm about as bottom of the barrel as you want to get, as far as society is concerned. Right? I'm serving a 50-year bid for a violent crime that I committed as an 18-year-old. I have five weeks of lived experience as an adult outside of the carceral system. I was a foster kid before that from the age of 10 to 18. I have lived within the dictate of State supervision since I was 10 years old, except for five weeks.

Yet throughout my incarceration, I have received my associate bachelor's and master's degree in conflict, analysis and resolution, and I'm currently a PhD student. I bring all of that to the table. I am living within an organization with an administration that is willing to do things differently. Within this context, I hate to use the term expert, but my expertise is in the field of conflict and restorative justice. I was well into the Restorative Practice Steering Committee when the former Warden contracted with the Restorative Justice Institute in the State to look at how we might introduce restorative practices within our environment. My name kept coming up through all the listening circles, and then two years later I was invited by the Warden to give feedback and to do an analysis of what we were doing. Well, we were not doing so well, in fact, we were doing terribly if you compared Maine State Prison to Halden Prison in Norway. She asked me to read this 100-page article and give her some feedback – no pressure, just super informal. I said, *No, thank you, this is going to be formal.* So, I wrote short-term, medium-term and long-term goals, one of which was the creation of a self-governed unit that did not have direct staff supervision, and I showed how that was supported by policy. My warden then took it to the Chief Administrative Officers meeting that was being facilitated by the then Deputy Commissioner, and then after a few months, there was talk of the creation of a self-governed living unit.

I was in the second group that moved down into the old supermax, this place where I was extracted, this place where my memory is nothing but the smell of mice and blood, bodily fluids and faeces. You want to talk about gritty, then let's get gritty. That was the environment that I was moving back into. I participated in scrubbing it out and deciding how we were going to live together. When I moved down there, there were seven men. We gradually expanded to 11, to 15, to 18 and then to 21, all under indirect supervision. There was a central area from which the staff could see, and they would come through for their rounds, but there were no staff permanently on the unit. When it came to what decisions we were going to make, we talked about dialogic decision-making. We had to do it ourselves when it came to conflict, prevention, mitigation and resolution. We did that ourselves, and there was not a man there who was not in prison for a violent crime. Most of us were serving life or virtual life sentences.

What we were doing was not supposed to be possible, and yet we did it. We were running around with the sledgehammers and long steel bars and power sanders, and everything that is not supposed to be possible when you put violent people together. Even though to a man we had all committed a violent crime and caused violent harm, it did not mean that we were violent people. We worked together to create an environment of community within the prison, running right across the institution being historically adverse and oppositional to the building of communities. Throughout this process, we talked about the absence of fear in the giving and receiving of feedback. The work that we were doing with boots on the ground was in direct communication with the administration. It was a bottom-up groundswell of energy and a top-down support. It built a middle culture because we were able to welcome line staff and middle management into dialogue in the decision-making process. We were able to ask, *How do you think things are going?* Some staff members said they knew that I was down here when it was what it was, and they knew how hard that was. I have been able to have conversations with staff members about trauma, and about being able to suspend our positional power differences to deal with each other on a human-to-human level. That has made all the difference. I'll pause there.

Harold:

Very good. Well, Leo, thanks very much for your story – and thanks to all of you for sharing your stories as well. A couple of things sit with me. You've all spoken about, or shared elements that feed into a dialogic culture, and your stories revealed things that arguably led towards successful outcomes. The next question is, and it seems like a basic question, but I think it needs to be asked because not everyone believes that we should work towards creating dialogic cultures. You will find folks in large institutions and elsewhere that don't want to change. So, the question is, *Why is there a need for dialogic cultures?* You may have already shared it in your stories, but could you articulate it a little more? *Why is there a need for dialogic cultures?* And then, secondly, *What does it take to create a dialogic culture?* Jane, do you want to comment or add anything to that?

Jane:

I have too much that I want to say because those were really strong stories. With the last story, talk about symbolic change! Not just to create an end, but to take the segregation, and everything you said about that unit being so stuck, and to change not only the culture of that unit but to have a ripple effect that goes beyond that specific unit. I want to dive into all your stories! But I don't want to miss your question, Harold. Describing the care for the elderly, Lars, you said that from 30% to 40% of staff being full time it went up to 100%. But I also believe that in those care homes, there was a lower rate of morbidity and mortality during Covid, because of the quality of care. Basically, fewer old people in those care homes for the elderly were dying during Covid than in other homes, because of these bubbles of full-time staff, and the way that care could be provided. So that's a significant outcome amongst these remarkable stories.

Harold:

The positive outcomes from working dialogically, that was what I wanted to underline.

Lars-Åke:

We believe in dialogue, but if you stand back and see, for example, the problems that the organizations for care that everybody deals with in

Sweden, it's so complex. From the politicians down to the managers, there is fragmentation in every organization, and fragmentation at the very local level because the workforce is employed in such a bad way, being employed day by day. You can also see what is happening to culture in our whole country. There is a world value survey that measures how people think about life in different countries all over the world, and Sweden today is one of the most individualized thinking countries in the world, even though we pay more taxes than most other countries, we are more organized in unions, and we have built up this welfare system. Organizations cannot be changed in any other way than through dialogue. At the same time, this fragmentation is more and more evident in our society. In the organizations where we work, we see more desire for people to have something different, to have a better collaboration, and to be together with other people doing something meaningful. Besides this individualistic culture, which is more and more increasing in Sweden, there's also another desire among both managers and workers to have something different. And that's also why dialogue is needed. And the answer to your second question is, of course, management must believe in this. If they don't, it's not possible. The woman who is a care manager in West Bay had her first dialogue training in 2006, and we started the latest project in 2015. It takes time.

Jane:

I was thinking about this question of, *How do we get there?* We've had top-down, bottom-up, and sideways just in these few stories. There are different approaches to introducing a dialogic culture, and different outcomes. Maybe that's something we can come back to in the plenary after the Participatory Dialogues when people have had a bit more time to think. Why don't we open the chat just for five minutes to see what is moving with everyone?

Harold:

Sure. Let's see what people want to say or ask. Please add any thoughts, comments or questions, and you can also make recommendations in terms of why a dialogic culture is needed.

Speaker:

I wanted to focus on Mr. Hylton's story really quick, and how he's using dialogue within the institution to deal with behaviour in the community and with behaviour in the institution. He's using communication and dialogue to have individuals see a different way, a better way of processing how to work in an institution – and how we can use self-governing and teaching a skill set while people are serving time for their offenses, right? The whole goal is rehabilitation, and using dialogue in that way is very inspiring. Anybody can learn the terms, and anybody can utilize the skills – they just need the information. I wanted to highlight that, and that you're doing a really good job. Continue the good work!

Harold:

Thank you. Anyone else? Any questions or comments about a dialogic culture, the need for it, the benefits, and how we create it?

Jane:

I was saying to Peter that opening a new prison with inexperienced staff is one of the hardest jobs in the world. Ben is a remarkably talented man. I am impressed with how he used dialogue for fast and general staff learning. We worked on the opening of a large prison that at the time it opened was the largest prison in the UK, although here we have quite small prisons and only 2,000 people were incarcerated there. We used dialogue to help the opening of that prison as well, Ben, so it's special to hear of your good work.

I'm interested in your stories. All of you talked in different ways about people talking and thinking together in different groupings than they would do normally. Also, there was quite a lot there about the structure that held that in place. Maybe that's something we can come back to in the plenary, and perhaps it will come up in some of the Participatory Dialogues. *What's the structure?* The partnerships in the trade union, the 'bubbles' in the care for the elderly and the learning teams. Some of that will be interesting to explore.

Harold:

Very good. Any other thoughts or comments?

Speaker:

I have thoughts on having a dialogue or learning team that starts with small groups thinking about why it might be needed, otherwise you may not even be able to get through the first gate. Best to start with small groups in an organization, not because of buy-in but just to get some thoughts. My question was about an actual incident and there was a learning team to learn from it. Is it possible to have some perceived idea that you hear milling around in an organization about feeling helpless or low morale, or whatever, and having a dialogue or a learning team around a probable event, something that could happen? What would we do if it did happen? How would we collaborate?

Jane:

Susan or Ben? Do you want to pick on that from your learning team experience? Susan, you're still in a learning team, are you?

Susan:

I'm still in a learning team and I'm still the Subject Matter Specialist for the learning team. Yes.

Jane:

Do you want to respond to the question? I think it was about starting with the small groupings to talking about something that's real, or something that there's a risk might happen, and the value of talking it through in those smaller groupings.

Susan:

Well, here's an example, from my learning team. I worked for special services for health services during Covid, doing health service projects. We had two other health services management team members in my learning team, and we were talking about a particular issue. I can't even remember the exact nature of it, so many issues came up during Covid. We were generating ideas in our learning team, and then we took them to the nursing manager to discuss with the health services management team. Then it got taken to the whole system-wide nursing service. It all started with a generating conversation in the learning team.

Ben:

I didn't work in a prison during Covid, and I can only imagine what that was like. I did think about the people who had to work inside facilities during that time, and one of the things I thought about was the use of learning teams to deal with not just the work environment, but also with people's personal experiences during Covid. It dramatically changed their lives. especially people who are parents or had older people in their homes, and things of that nature. So, I think learning teams can be used not only for issues going on inside of your organization, but issues outside of your organization that affect people's personal lives. I've used dialogue in that vein before, because we've had tragedies happen, unfortunately, with Staff. How do people cope with those events? I think a learning team is a way for them to talk about those experiences, and to share those experiences. Also, as you asked, you can prepare for how we're going to deal with situations in the future, for sure.

Speaker:

As I listened to the experiences and the stories, it seemed that a dialogic culture is much more valued and recognized as important when things are very challenging. Leo's story, and other stories from within prison, made me reflect on our agency. Recently I looked at a five-year comparison of our employee survey data. In 2020 we had the highest percentage of our staff who felt that dialogue had noticeably impacted communication across the agency and increased meeting productivity, compared for example to this past year. It was interesting hearing that when things are going really well it's not thought about as much, and the dialogic culture may be taken for granted. But when things are challenging, that's when people really notice it.

Jane:

Then they recognize the value of it. Yeah. Harold, I think we are approaching the break?

Harold:

I think we are there.

Jane:

Thank you, Harold, for steering us through that. Thank you, Lars, Susan, Ben and Leo for your fascinating stories and for the amazing work that you've done. Good for you to come to tell us, and even better for the people who have benefited from the work that you've done.

DAY FOUR

What is a Dialogic Culture?

Why Does Your Organization Need a Dialogic Culture?

PART TWO

Five concurrent participatory dialogues

Thumbnail sketches

Thumbnail sketches to introduce the five Participatory Dialogues that follow:

Jon Steinman APDP (USA) and Peter Garrett APDP, APDPA (UK) asked why people might fear a dialogic culture at work. This seemingly negative question revealed that each dialogic benefit has implications that may test people's confidence to create a dialogic culture. A dialogic system with shared power and shared knowledge calls for open thinking, feeling and feedback – but sharing power requires active participation; more transparency means both good and poor behaviour are more visible; and the sense of common ownership means stepping forward to take responsibility.

Elisabeth Razesberger APDP (Belgium) and Qingmian Chen (China) had what they called a 'smooth' talk about dialogic culture. People found it to be, *a very rich conversation; authentic; very beneficial; really refreshing; a very good session; useful; and valuable.* Clearly, the tone was helpfully dialogic. To develop a dialogic culture at an organizational level, people felt that leadership, middle management and first-level staff all need to be willing. They heard accounts where middle managers were reluctant yet had no obvious forum to raise their concerns.

Carroll Macey APDP (UK) and Mary Morand APDP (USA) both work as team coaches, and they encouraged an enquiry into the initial emergence of a dialogic culture in a team. Culture feels big (how do you put your arms around it?), so some liked the idea of starting small by putting dialogue to work locally and having it become meaningful to people so that they want more of it - the ripple effect of 'start anywhere, and then go everywhere!' A cultural confusion about the phrase *white knuckling* came too late to be explored at the time, but value was clearly realised by later reflection.

Faezeh Tamimi APDP (Iran) and Sharon Burgess APDP (USA) had a room full of people who had all previously experienced dialogue as a mode of talking and thinking together. They felt this enhanced the quality of the exchange significantly. People spoke with curiosity; from first-hand experience, rather than quoting others; and they did not advise, teach or try to persuade one another. This kind of dialogic culture can openly address difficult issues about race, gender and transgender. In fact, in this spirit, even monologues can be done in a way that contributes to the dialogic culture.

Asma Beiranvand and Parvin Daeipour APDP (Iran) proposed an exploration into creativity and a dialogic culture. People found they needed time to understand each other's use of a simple word like 'structure'. It was not that they disagreed, but they had not previously taken the other person's perspective and meaning. Multiple meanings drawn from looking at the same thing from different angles encourages creativity, particularly if the speakers are at the same level and in the same dialogic playing field where nobody's formulation is judged to be better or worse.

Why might People Fear a Dialogic Culture at Work?

Jon Steinman, Peter Garrett

PRE-CONFERENCE DESCRIPTION

In many workplace cultures, it is an accepted norm that the role of leaders and supervisors is to tell people what to do, and that the role of others is to do what is asked of them. Whether talking with a prospective client or actively working within the workplace, introducing a dialogic culture can be met with resistance by some. Saying, *People don't like change*, is an inadequate description of the reasons people have for being cautious about being part of a dialogic culture, where you are encouraged to have a voice, and where what you have to say matters to those who are responsible for making the decision. There are concerns and fears that can affect any member of an organization, and there may be concerns and fears that depend on an individual's position within the organization. We would like to enquire into people's first-hand experiences in this regard and to expand our capability to anticipate and navigate any resistances to or fears of a dialogic culture.

CHECK-OUT

Peter Garrett:

> I'm just wondering, John, with the size of group that we have, and given we haven't heard from everybody during the time we've been talking, might we be wise to go into a check-out now? That that might ensure we can hear from everybody in the room.

Jon Steinman:

> Yeah, I think that's wise.

Peter:

> I'll say something and then maybe you can set it up? What we do is we record the check-out, and the idea is to try to get your best thinking. We've been together for nearly an hour talking and thinking. What's your best thinking from this time? We will transcribe the recording and use parts of it in the

publication that comes out a year later. It'll be a publication about dialogue in organizations, one part of that book will be about dialogic culture, and within that one piece will consider why people might be resistant to the introduction of a dialogic culture, or fearful of it.

Jon:

The check-out we came up with is a question that's a little more focused. Maybe I'll read the question, and then we can take a moment, twenty or thirty seconds, just to absorb it and consider it. Then, whenever anyone feels compelled, you can step in and lead the check-out, and then tag who's next. So, I'll read the question. Remember the question we posed, which was, *Why might people fear a dialogic culture at work?* The check-out question is, *How has the question we posed, in the dialogue we've just had, informed your own enquiry into what a dialogic culture is?* This is bringing it back to the theme of today in the conference. I'll read it once more. *How has the question we posed in the dialogue we've just had informed your own enquiry into what a dialogic culture is?* So, let's take half a minute to think about that. Anything you want to add, Peter?

Peter:

Just that if we can hear from everybody before our close at 20 minutes to the hour, we would be doing well.

Speaker:

I think that I've been discovering what a dialogic culture really is. It's an organization in which leaders release their power and empower their people so that their people can begin to help make decisions and become inclusive in the job they're trying to do. And they really work together. I think that it's the concept of knowledge is power, basically. When you have a dialogic organization, you release knowledge. It's a shared knowledge system. One person doesn't just keep the knowledge to themselves. They share their knowledge with others, and that is what empowers their people to become part of that organization and part of the decision-making process.

Speaker:

What really stood out for me is that a dialogic culture invites enquiry into who we are both individually and collectively, and that can be frightening at multiple levels. It raises the question, *How do we hold the space?* How do we all together hold and create a space of invitation? How does each one of us take responsibility for stepping into that space with each other?

Speaker:

Listening to all the comments, all the examples today, and looking at the creation of a dialogic culture, there will be a sense and concern of fear potentially for individuals who come into it because of what it asks of you. I thought a lot about our organization throughout this entire discussion and the challenges that we run into. The initial apprehension is a fear of giving up power. Then there are questions about how consistent are we going to be. Is this something that we are truly adopting? What are we going to move on to? What else is new, you know, a year from now? And that causes a level of resistance. What can we do to help facilitate and create what is really needed? What is coming up from a lot of the comments from folks, as far as fear and apprehension is concerned, is do we truly create a safe container for folks to trust, and that is something they can buy into? This is a true shift in understanding the value of people's thoughts and ideas, and it is really changing the thought process and the culture of our organization.

Peter:

I want to note the pace. We've heard from three people which is fine, but we have used half our time. So, we have 10 minutes left for everybody else. Let's pause for a moment and give you time to think about how you can share what you have to say in just one minute.

Speaker:

Okay. I'm probably the worst person for this, unless I write it down! I want to say that I'm pleased that I chose this dialogue and the considerations that I just heard. It really has furthered my interest in this particular topic.

Speaker:

Listening to everything that everyone said, I am going back to the beginning. What may people fear? I just say that I am thankful that I am a part of a team and an organization in the Department of Corrections that empowers me to be great. When there are hard conversations, I don't mind being one that's sitting in the circle to be able to help facilitate it or give a different perspective, because that's the purpose of a safe container and bringing everybody's voice into the room.

Speaker:

I think that one common denominator that everybody keeps on talking about is feeling. I think that with a dialogic culture comes a level of soft skills that people are not comfortable with. As someone said, they find it *crunchy*. So, I think that there's that fear of opening up a can of worms, and of being in touch with your own feelings as well as being open to listening to others and understanding other people's feelings. People aren't comfortable with that, so I think that there is a fear of feedback. I believe Jon mentioned the need to be innovative and creative. I think that is because of a certain level of fear of receiving feedback. So, enabling that requires innovation and creativity.

Speaker:

I think this dialogic culture welcomes questions more than answers, and that everybody is invited to be the whole person. We're arriving at a goal, and the goal is not as important as how you got there.

Speaker:

The answer that I'm coming away with is that when I see someone fearful of the changes that dialogue brings, I model being aware of my own feelings of being vulnerable. Listening to myself, being seen, and allowing my identity and who I say I am to feel threatened. If I can model that to others, maybe I can help them and calm their fears.

Speaker:

I think what I get out of this is that whether you talk about a person or a system, deep down there is a longing to develop, to develop ourselves. That asks me to dare to stand on the border of knowing and not knowing. By definition, that's challenging the status quo. So, this brings a fear of being exposed as a person to ourselves, to others and also as a system to ourselves and to others. I think there is great value to a culture where you have a deep shared awareness of that. You create a space that you foster, and you help people when they slip because we will slip if there's fear in the room. Also, a culture where we are compassionate to ourselves and to others.

Speaker:

I think leaders have not always released their power. Once they go into the dialogue and share their power, it gives people a sense of togetherness that you know as you walk into that room. You feel mutual or equal. We're not pushing being a Sergeant or a Captain level. We are all one kind of thing. That way it gives people an opportunity to expose themselves and show their true authentic voice.

Speaker:

if there are any leaders out there who think they've got all the answers, that would be wonderful, but I sense that is what some call wilfully blind.

Recognize that we don't have all the answers. It is really complex. That does make us all feel scared. I think that's okay. The reason why dialogue can create fear is that you have to bring your whole self into it. You can't half do it. But I've always been much prouder of the things that I have called, rather than the things that I didn't dare call. I love the phrase, *Keep your resignation letter in your pocket*. You've got to enter with that kind of spirit and frame the right invitation to people. What is it you're prepared to bring people together for? And it will definitely be much more powerful than any other means.

Speaker:

I'll be short. My point is to stay connected and trust the atmosphere. That allows us to be the best in our worst times.

Peter:

Thank you all. Jon? You or me?

Jon:

I'm happy to mostly echo what's being shared and maybe kind of reframe it. Through this dialogue I've received a lot more clarity about the question, *What is a dialogic culture?* One way I would articulate it now if someone were to ask me, is that it's a culture that is aware of how to create spaces that allow people to be seen. That really rings true to me. It's that it's aware of how it does that, it's self-aware. Then the last piece I'll share that I'm taking away from this time together is how important it is to be clear about what a dialogic culture is not. There's so much fear, it seems, as to what might happen if we engage in dialogue. It is something of a curiosity for me to get better at articulating and learning about how to talk about what dialogue isn't. I think there's some fear about creating some boundaries around what dialogue isn't, because I feel like people want dialogue to be boundless. I can sense some fear in me exploring that question.

Peter:

Thank you everybody for managing the time between us all so well. We're pretty well on our closing time. I found this to be a very enriching consideration. I think that if we looked at a transcript of this, we would find there's a lot of very good thinking about caution, resistance and fear about a dialogic culture. We could go on tomorrow and think about how to manage that. My own view is that the culture that we encounter is like it is for a good reason. The culture has its benefits. The culture we found in Virginia, where people didn't want to propose their thinking to their supervisor or leader was of benefit to them. They could laugh at the supervisor who was making silly decisions, and not be accountable themselves. Equally the leader not hearing from others gave him the benefit of not having to try to manage the complexity. So, I think for me, the key thing about a dialogic culture is that it is a coherent culture. The way to get into it is to notice the incoherencies. The things that are our habitual way of doing stuff that, overall, none of us get the best benefit from. We suffer from the incoherencies. This is a very interesting enquiry, and I wish we had longer to bring out more of the thinking that has been stimulated. Well . . .

Jon:

I'd like to submit a vote. I'd like to submit a vote, Peter, that next year the conference dedicates an entire day to this question!

POSTSCRIPT

Joint Reflections on the Process and Co-facilitation:

We felt comfortable going into the Participatory Dialogue together and had a good plan. On the day, we had 25 participants with very varied organizational contexts. Half were employed by one large dialogic organization, whilst the rest were individuals and consultants from different organizations, cultures, and countries. The check-in was designed to reveal this to everyone in the room, but it proved too time-consuming, and we had to abandon the process after six or seven people had checked in.

Peter's Reflections:

Typically, advocates for dialogue pose a more positive enquiry - perhaps about the attributes and advantages of establishing a dialogic culture at work. I was curious to see how people might respond to this more negative question about people's fears. Participants did well with this approach and raised a wide range of concerns whilst firmly believing in the value of dialogue. What later became apparent to me is that any assumed value has a shadow fear. For example:

- There is power in sharing knowledge with all, yet giving away knowledge may seem to reduce one's own power.
- Transparency and openness may be most helpful, but that can expose poor decisions for which people may then be held to account.
- Having a common sense of ownership and responsibility is ideal, yet it could erode the authority of those in leadership positions.
- Encouraging everyone to have a voice and to contribute their perspectives may be helpfully transformational, but it may also be complex and time consuming.

Predicting this and talking it through with people is a thoughtful and compassionate way to introduce a dialogic culture. Not being able to raise naive questions and concerns may create the most resistance to any cultural change.

Jon's Reflections

This session compels a consideration that a dialogic culture involves a consistent awareness and enquiry into how power resides in the organization, how it is used and perceived, and how it influences people.

Fear of losing power is real and is accompanied by a fear of people being more fully seen for who they are - an allowing of emotions and feelings. It could be said that dialogic spaces therefore rely on fewer boundaries, and this could be perceived as a loss of control. Such a culture allows individuals to be vulnerable and there are strong fears around vulnerability. This requires a set of soft skills for which many individuals are neither trained, nor have they developed them individually. This too brings up fears of not being adequately prepared for a dialogic culture.

As was evident in our dialogue, an enquiry into the fears of a dialogic culture is best accompanied by enquiring into the benefits of a *non*-dialogic culture. As one participant remarked, *The leader not hearing from others gave them the benefit of not having to try to manage the complexity.*

The richness of the enquiry compels me to propose dedicating a full day to this question at the 2024 conference.

Dialogic Culture: How Ready Are You?

Elisabeth Razesberger and Qingmian Chen

PRE-CONFERENCE DESCRIPTION

Raising a Dialogue Culture starts with the awareness of cultural differences wherever you are. Is there room for awareness of what cultures are present, at a personal and an organizational level? How do you facilitate skill building with the aim of generating effective communication? Once there is an overview of the challenge to deal with, are you willing to take the risk and work towards a common understanding? The exchange will look into what we perceive as cultural differences and how we manage to think together to move towards a common understanding.

CHECK-OUT

Qingmian Chen:

Our time is approaching the end, and we have ten minutes left.

I would like to check-out, if that's okay for all of you? I heard many reasons to take dialogue to people who are suffering, and where things are not working. People can feel isolated with all this suffering and feel like starting to dialogue. To start a dialogue in practice is difficult. The main problem is inclusiveness. Support from the middle managers and, of course, the expectations of management also matter. One thing I saw is that in situations where they trained the new staff directly in dialogue, it saved a lot of energy changing the culture. I think to create a dialogic culture takes years, and it might revert if we don't sustain it. It needs active support from top management, middle management and everyone involved. But again, as was said, it starts with an individual having one heart and one mind to start to affect others. That's my takeaway.

Speaker:

I think this has been a very rich conversation, and I really enjoyed how it was flowing like a dialogue – not just taking turns talking. One takeaway I have when it comes to growing a dialogue is the importance of an encouraging culture. Having a way to promote people to voice their concerns about the practice of dialogue. It can be hard, and if we all pretend that everything is working well, we don't really raise the concerns.

Speaker:

I enjoyed this! I think it was authentic, very authentic. There is a lot of work to sustain the culture and to continue growing the culture, and I think it's in constant change. I agree with what was said, that it does absolutely begin within. I know when I was deeply into dialogue, the person that grew the most was me, myself. And that's huge. You take it with you all the time, and you project your energy into the room, so it may not always work for everyone all the time, but I think that if we continue to believe in the process, we will effect change.

Speaker:

This has been so very beneficial. I've enjoyed the whole dialogue that we've had, and I learned a lot, being new to dialogue. I know that I have a lot more to learn. I'm just touching the basics. I do know that you will have people who are on board with it, and then you're going to have people that you are going to run into a brick wall with, because they have a mindset that they do things one way, and that's the only way. But you must keep your faith that you can make a difference, starting with yourself. That's where to start, with yourself, and be positive about it. Your reflection spreads to other people if you have a positive attitude about it. My philosophy is don't sweat that this is small stuff. Just keep making it grow bigger, and this small stuff can turn into great things. But patience is a part of it! If you truly believe in dialogue, then stick with it. It's just like a smile. We smile at someone, and they smile back. So, dialogue can be rewarding. And that's my take on today. I've been pleased to be part of this break-out today.

Speaker:

It has been really refreshing to share this space with you all. I am reminded that dialogue is a process, and it's something that didn't happen overnight. It's a process, and it takes time and patience. You must be patient with others. For me, it is just a matter of continuing to embrace the process and doing what I'm doing. I do feel like I can effect change and make a difference in the lives of people that I work with.

Speaker:

This was one of my better sessions and it was genuine dialogue. A couple of times Elisabeth asked if some of us had something to say, but it felt open I didn't feel forced to speak, the space was there if you wanted to, and it started with asking everybody to leave their microphones on, so we could just talk and dialogue. I appreciated that space. That's how I would like to see dialogue run, like an open space where you can come in when you want.

Elisabeth Razesberger:

Well, for me, that was a very . . . I can't think of the word in English, I'm sorry. Anyway, it was a very good session. We are always told in this kind of gathering that we should share success stories. I think it is so beneficial to hear the different perspectives and the different levels of experience about how the implementation of dialogue is working. It is working in the end, but it's just not always working at the same speed or in the same way. Sometimes it works better, sometimes it works less well, but it's still rolling. I really want to thank you for the insights you shared. They were very useful and valuable. There is the word I was looking for! *Valuable*. Thank you.

Qingmian:

Thank you everyone for your participation. I appreciate all your contributions, it was nice to meet you all, and I hope we'll see each other often again.

POSTSCRIPT

We had a smooth talk about a dialogic culture. It is still vivid for me now when I retrospect. One of our participants opened the dialogue by sharing a story about a dialogic implementation experience in her organization. Their top management had strong expectations for dialogue in the whole organization and many employees were willing to practice, especially the fresh employees. The dialogic training program went well. Everyone could bring dialogue into their work and assist the dialogic culture to expand. To build the capacity for dialogue, an individual needs awareness, willingness, and skills.

To build a dialogic culture in an organization, it needs strong support from top management. It needs the top management to have the right vision and expectations for the whole organization and to locate time and resources toward a dialogic culture. In other words, top management needs to plough the soil well for the (acorn) seeds to grow. In the story we heard, this was in place. Also, the dialogic training for new employees worked well. But some of the middle managers were not willing to adopt the approach.

For a dialogic culture to flourish in an organization, it does need one heart and one mind, but this was not in place with the middle managers. To adopt and implement a dialogic culture, middle management plays a critical role as they experience pressure from the top to accomplish projects and from the bottom to deliver daily performance. For them, building a dialogic culture means change and most people fear change. They might be scared of losing power or the status quo, etc, and therefore middle managers' adoption of new ways of working is the key. Our member's story illustrated that although they had good support from the top, and front-line employees were willing to practice dialogue, some of the middle managers didn't encourage dialogue. Rather, they did just the opposite. This negatively affected her passion for dialogue, and the dialogic culture implementation suffered.

Dialogue is a process that takes time and needs patience for yourself and for others. To emphasise one statement in the check-out:

> "*. . . patience is a part of it! If you truly believe in dialogue, then stick with it. It's just like a smile. We smile at someone, and they smile back.*"

How could a Group or Team Enable a Broader Dialogic Culture?

Carroll Macey, Mary Morand

PRE-CONFERENCE DESCRIPTION

What drives your enquiry? In teams and groups, there are more things that we have in common than the things that keep us separate. We are often drawn and separated by difference, at times even threatened by the discomfort that difference brings. Dialogic Culture enables us to think and talk together to build greater understanding and enhance a sense of belonging. What is the enquiry about? Sharing and exploring together the ways that teams and groups can or have used Dialogue in developing cultures where everyone has a voice and is heard. Why does it matter? Inclusive cultures are important for well-being, creativity, innovation, performance, reputation and so much more. By applying the principles of Dialogue, we can better explore different perspectives and make a positive difference in our workplaces and communities

CHECK-OUT

Carroll:

So, let's do a check-out. Just to remind you, this is the only part of the dialogue that we're transcribing. *What are you now thinking about dialogue, in relation to dialogic cultures?* In a couple of sentences. I am intrigued about where your thinking process has gone about the use of dialogue in dialogic cultures.

Speaker:

I've got loads of thoughts, but mostly I'm sitting with something about starting small. When I think about culture, it feels big and it feels like, *How do you get your arms around it?* But I think there's something about starting with baby steps and going slower now in order to be able, metaphorically, to go quicker later. Linked to that is: how do we model it? If a team has a positive experience of dialogue and that's their way of being and how they do things, then those teams are interacting with other teams within a system. Then the other teams notice, *Hey, this is different, and it is a helpful difference.* So, you get that organic mushrooming effect.

Speaker:

I'm going to build on what was said about starting small and modelling dialogue. What is also sitting with me is what I've heard on the call about a stealth approach that supports this starting small for me.

Speaker:

I'm sitting with an experience we had a couple of weeks ago with four teams. We brought dialogue into a highly fragmented business unit. We brought it in a very meaningful but simple way and just allowed it to unfold and find its legs, which is now opening the door for more of that to come with the broader team. So, I'm also sitting with start small, putting it to work and allowing the work to show up in a way that's meaningful for others so that they want to do more of it.

Speaker:

This idea about time is what I am thinking about. Someone mentioned a lot of anxiety, and then being able to slow down. It therefore feels important to look at how time influences how we answer this question. Being able to slow down and get the luxury of time – which is such a big piece of dialogue – and being able to let go of that anxiety because you do have the time. That is really neat.

Speaker:

Building a bit on what was said about finding a pocket of success, which can be anywhere. A phrase that that a lady some of us know often uses, *Start anywhere, and then go everywhere.* So, it doesn't matter where it comes from. In the very essence of it, you can build from there.

Speaker:

I'm imagining a ripple effect from a place of calm, with ripples of energy going up and down – and the ripple starts with a by-stand, an active by-stand that invites something organic to occur. I'm also still sitting with simplicity. Make this organic, not scientific.

Speaker:

I feel a little bit like the babysitter in the house as the parents leave. They go, but the back door doesn't lock. You're probably safe. That's a little bit of what I felt when we ended up talking about that fear. All of us saying, *Here's how you might manage it.* So, I have a huge question in my head that says, *Yes thank you for normalizing fear and I feel validated, but now, what am I supposed to do around what you've just reminded me of?*

Speaker:

I take away from this that we didn't wrestle with finding the balance between practice, theory and structure in creating a dialogic culture.

Speaker:

I'm like those professors who were mentioned who don't like not knowing something. This whole *white knuckling thing* I'm going to have to look into, as I'm not familiar with it. What is it? What is this thing? But I would say, where I am is having to know where their culture is, knowing where they want to be and bringing that awareness to them to get them into alignment, not where I want to take them, but where they want to be, and letting that unfold.

Speaker:

I'm struck with starting small. I had a moment where somebody said, *Well, it's learning together in relationships.* For me that resolved it. When I'm in any dialogue, if I'm not in the learning mode but in the teaching mode, then I'm not actively playing with my own fear and playing with people's spirit. When I am learning, there's something happening. It's experiential, not intellectual. I think that's my take-away. In any dialogue, I need to be experiencing, and that means it's new. I don't know what's going to happen, so I'm anxious but I'm present, and I'm in that learning mode.

Speaker:

I like the learning mode. It takes the pressure off the idea of answering the phone. You don't have the answer because you going to be learning from everybody. I feel like I can come at it by starting small and setting some of the expectations – for example, if we're going to free float and make a decision later. Just set the expectations, recognize that it's just a small start and let things float through us. A ripple. Then, *Oh look! A big wave is coming! Let's, whoa . . . okay, we're going to get through it.* I just envision it playing out in this undulating, unstructured way. Then all the fear goes away. So yeah, it's good. I just love everything I've heard today. Really fantastic! Thank you so much.

Mary:

I am sitting with many things. My couple of sentences are probably also around the balance of who we are, what we do and how we're showing up to balance the theory, the structure and the practice. Particularly as team coaches, we do a lot of practice with teams. So, letting the practice be the teaching, letting the practice be the space for learning and the use of self. There's something to be said for me personally to let go of the idea of role, and to recognize that in doing this work, particularly in the beginning of integrating it, there's a huge opportunity to put myself into the learning with the team. Just as the leader is part of the team, I am part of the team for the purposes of learning together. I'll keep thinking about that. How about you, Carroll?

Carroll:

I'm still carrying the white-knuckle metaphor, and I think I'm going to use it next time with the team because I think it's a good use of humour to dissipate the fear that stops people from talking. And it's invitational, isn't it? That combined with the question, *How do you get people into the room?* We've got 70 min together, or whatever, so I will probably use some kind of mindfulness practice to get people into the room, and then they might notice the white-knuckle moments as we go along. I'm going to play with that.

Speaker:

Would you mind defining that for me, so I don't have to look it up afterward and only then find out what everybody was talking about? Like, what does that mean?

Speaker:

When you white-knuckle, you're grabbing something really tight.

Carroll:

If you've ever been on a roller coaster ride and you're holding onto the bar. Yeah, that's white knuckling.

Speaker:

It's a cultural thing. I've never heard of that. And my knuckles don't turn white so . . .

Carroll:

Well, thank you, everybody. It's been a pleasure having this dialogue with you, and I've learned a lot of things that I'm going to take away and reflect on. So yeah, hope you enjoy the rest of the conference today.

POSTSCRIPT

The enquiry driving our Participatory Dialogue was, *How could teams or groups enable a broader dialogic culture?* Inclusive cultures are important for well-being, creativity, innovation, performance, reputation and so much more. By applying the principles of Dialogue, we can better explore different perspectives and make a positive difference in our workplaces and communities.

The dialogue raised some interesting perspectives. There was reference to culture feeling big and that it needs to be approached in baby steps, perhaps starting with a team that can role model using dialogue and allowing this to ripple through the organization. This was referred to as a stealth approach – start small, put it to work and allow it to show up meaningfully to others so that they want to do more of it.

The ripple effect was linked to the practice of active by-standing and the process being organic. This is an important aspect of how to introduce dialogue into organizations. It doesn't need to be approached with heavy theory and structure. It can be held lightly and shared through role modelling and authentic voice. The stance of the practitioner is important for the process to be effective. Presence, intention and coherence need to be part of the practice. One comment made was, *It's learning together in relationships.* To develop a culture of dialogue there needs to be experiential learning, and the container must hold a learning mode. Otherwise, fear may rise because of an expectation that a change in culture will happen rigidly. It feels more accepting to place the intention and expectation within the metaphor of a ripple effect. It starts as a ripple and then small waves build as the change gains energy and undulates throughout the organization, unfolding and emerging naturally, finding its own rhythm.

As facilitators, Mary and I were left with the following reflections following the dialogue:

The importance of balancing who we are, what we do and how we're showing up with theory, structure, and practice. This is especially important for those of us who are team coaches and do a lot of practice with teams. Our practice is the teaching, and a space for learning. We are present first with self to then be present with the team. When we are mindful of what the container can hold, our use of self helps the team explore its development edges. There's something to be said for letting go of the idea of role and recognizing that in doing this work, particularly in the beginning of integrating it, there's a huge opportunity to put oneself into learning with the team. Just as the leader is part of the team, we are part of the team for the purpose of learning together.

We could also use mindfulness to dissipate the fear of introducing dialogue into a culture. For example, we can help people come into the space and notice what's rising in them. This may minimize our embodied fight, flight and freeze responses.

The comment in the check-out about ‚white knuckling' was particularly relevant to our Dialogue. We had described feeling threatened by the discomfort of difference, and how we can use dialogue to create an inclusive culture. This takes time, of course, and the comment being raised at the close of the meeting meant we did not all have enough time to go into the cultural differences inadvertently highlighted by using a metaphor like ‚white knuckling' in a mixed-race grouping. It stimulated a reaction in others and then us. This, of course, is why we need dialogue! We have certainly reflected on it since the dialogue and value the learning it has provided.

What is Dialogic Culture?
And How Does It Affect the Efficiency of Teams in an Organization?

Faezeh Tamimi, Sharon Burgess,

PRE-CONFERENCE DESCRIPTION

Dialogic Culture plays a significant role in building effective teams within organizations. Teams in a Dialogic Culture are likely to be more cohesive and perform better as members feel valued and heard. Respect, listening and finding voice are fundamental. They create an environment where everyone feels safe to express their ideas and opinions. High-performing teams often start with a culture of shared values. Such teams also comprise individuals with diverse talents, experiences and perspectives, which lead to innovative solutions. These teams thrive when executives invest in supporting social relationships and demonstrate collaborative behavior. Building a Dialogic Culture of Teamwork provides the organization with a unifying focus and approach to work. In our time together we will think together about the following questions:

- What influences the efficiency and effectiveness of teamwork?
- How do different organizational cultures affect the efficiency of teamwork?
- What impact does Dialogic Culture have on team performance?
- What is the role of Dialogic Culture in building high-performance teams in an organization?

CHECK-OUT

Faezeh Tamimi:

Before the check-out, and I know you will have heard this in previous days, but I have to say it again, this dialogue is private, but the check-out may be transcribed and used in publications. If it is published, the comments will be shared anonymously apart from the names of the co-facilitators. Okay? So, for our check-out, please share one thing that you will take back from this room to your workplace to enhance its dialogic culture.

Speaker:

I want to start and say that I've learned a little bit about several organizations. I offer a different method of work, retraining. Sometimes we have a lot of people being promoted in a short time frame, and I need to remember the practices and the actions and how they could change the communication that I need to have.

Speaker:

I like the example that was shared. It was like a shot in the arm. What worries me the whole time is that when we talk about dialogue, we talk about how wonderful it is. We talk about bringing people into the room but are we really hearing their authentic voice? Do people really feel comfortable enough and included enough to offer what they really think? I believe there's a lot of work to do there. Not just the practical steps of doing a dialogue, but what really goes on in the room. And how do we lead the dialogue? How do we each use our leadership skills to lead that conversation? That is what really resonated with me. I really appreciate that reality.

Speaker:

What the two of you just said has been really eye-opening. I'm still new enough to the agency and to dialogue that I'm more in a listening mode. I want to hear what people are doing and how they're using dialogue. So, I hope my earlier question did not come across as aggressive. I just want the perspective. I also feel like I've learned a lot about three organizations, and what people are grappling with when it comes to dialogue. This, to me, is the most authentic conversation that I've heard throughout this whole week. I want to thank you both, Faezeh and Sharon, as leaders, for allowing this to happen.

Speaker:

I have a couple of things on my mind. I was thinking about culture rather than voicing. I think it's really important because I bet that you'll find that those two staff members who didn't find their voice will find their voice in other situations. There's something about the dynamic with that person, and them not finding their voice. So, for me, it's trying to understand the culture. What are the particular dynamics that are dominant at any time? Is it seniority, or what is it? The other thing is the question, *How do you change culture?* You can't just do a training or run a dialogue and then expect the culture to have changed. You must do a lot of things. For those who know the model, it is about the mode. We talk in lots of different ways, not just in dialogue circles. It's how you speak when you are using monologue, when you do a speech as a leader. How do you do that? How can you do that in a way that changes the culture? How can you bring a bit of yourself, your whole self, not just the official line? There are lots of different elements, and we need a process to change the culture. I am thinking about Patty Hawk's description in the panel conversation, about her work on campus where they are addressing some difficult race, gender and transgender issues. It's an open process. Anyone can come. You don't know who's going to come through the door, but they're managing to talk about some of those undiscussable things. For me, changing the culture requires a bit of all of these different things in it. I really have appreciated and enjoyed this dive into this subject.

Speaker:

I'm glad you mentioned that towards the end of what you said. The culture is going to require some collaboration with the rule makers, and I'll leave it at that.

Speaker:

Well, this one takeaway has a lot to do with what I just heard said. How and where we use different components of dialogue to influence the culture, and the influence that it has on the culture. It is important to think about it, and even how you might do a monologue. I get to do a lot of monologues in my role. So, that's important to me. How do you go about doing it? Looking at the impact it has on the culture, is it moving it the way you want to go, keeping it the same or making it worse? I appreciate that part of the conversation.

Speaker:

I have colleagues here from my institution, and I take them back with me, so that's a huge piece. I am young, but not as young as people think I am. For a while, I was the youngest on my team, which I find to be ironic, but we just got some new staff, and so there's one person who just came in who happens to be younger than me. But my clinical director often says that I'm one of the more mature ones. I'm just excited to see what I can take back. What I've said may sound more like complaints, but it's more to put out things that I am experiencing to see what it is I can take back. What I'm hearing from you guys brings a line staff perspective to some of the things I have been saying.

Oh! Is that your dog that just came in?

Sharon Burgess:
Yes, he's a part of the dialogic circle, and I've got a smaller dog as well!

What's sitting with me is that while we at the Department of Corrections are a dialogical organization, our conversation today was about the culture and what makes an effective team. What I am sitting with now is the lack of my voice, and the desire to move forward and to make better use of those opportunities to by-stand, to speak to the situation, and to help our staff and our teams become a dialogical culture. That will ensure that they feel safe using their voices, in a respectful manner because that is what is really going to strengthen those teams.

Faezeh:

Thanks to all of you. Something that resonates with me is about diversity. I wonder how diversity can create opportunities, or on the other hand, enrich a culture. Diversity without restrictions, or diversity with restrictions? Diversity without dialogue, or diversity with dialogue? How can these help or hinder us? I really appreciate this great conversation. While I followed and listened to you, I was remembering my first experiences at work, because of the cultural norms there, and how some of my colleagues treated me. At that time, I was just starting to become familiar with dialogue and I tried to bring dialogue there. I remember the feedback I received, *This is like a game or a joke.* I tried to explain the benefits of the approach, and I tried to listen to them and give them space. Then something started to change. They started to listen, and so did I. Thank you to all of you in this room. We are from different cultures and countries here, and I see and feel the safety. This is because of the application of dialogue; we can share our experiences here without judgment. I'm really thankful to all of you for this opportunity.

Sharon:

Thank you for sharing your story, Faezeh. Thanks, everyone for coming in today for this wonderful conversation. We appreciate you. We appreciate your final words, and you have a few minutes to get in some breathing exercises before we meet on the hour!

POSTSCRIPT

In the room, we had people from different countries and cultures, people with different experiences, and people who had worked in different organizations and teams. But we had one common feature, that is dialogue. Some of us had previously studied dialogue or had experienced it in practice. Others had a lot of experience and had been practicing dialogue for years. Some had recently become accredited practitioners whilst others were learning. In my opinion, this feature gave our conversation a different quality compared to a grouping of individuals in a room who do not know the difference between dialogue and other forms of engagement and have not heard anything about the dialogue practices.

A further feature of this room was that we talked about our personal experiences, not quoting books or articles, and we did not refer to statistics. We tried not to advise or persuade each other or impose our beliefs and experiences. This behaviour revealed that a safe space had been created in the container, especially when people shared their unpleasant experiences. Before starting the dialogue, I decided that if people talked more than usual about articles and statistics, I would pay attention and ask them to talk about their personal experiences. But in this room, I realized that it was better to listen well, abandon the preconceived plan in my mind and stay with the processes as they happened. This led me to understand the flow that had taken place in the room. It reminded me of a time when I was in a team and paid attention to the planning obsessively. But one day I tried instead to stay present in the moment, pay special attention to the processes unfolding, and to understand my role and the whole system that was in play. It was quite a different experience.

Something I noticed about the individuals in this room was that despite being from different cultures, we were able to dialogue with each other. In my opinion, this room became much like a small team that had only recently formed in an organization. When a team is newly formed or a new member is added, it takes some time for people to understand each other and to reshape the team culture. When forming a team or adding a new person to the team, if they knew dialogue, I think this familiarity and synchronization time would be shorter.

Although we were from different cultures in this room, we were familiar with dialogue. I guess if we did not know dialogue, we would not have had such deep listening and deep respecting of others during the conversation. It was that living practice in the room that gave each person the courage to find their own voice, talk about their experiences and understand each other. These are necessary for a better quality of dialogue, and importantly also for a better quality of teamwork.

A closing point is that the questions asked for the check-out enquiry came from a place of curiosity and called for thinking and not just thoughts. This is one of the important things we are looking for in dialogue.

Individual or Team Creativity in the Organization by Applying Dialogic Culture

Asma Beiranvand, Parvin Daeipour

PRE-CONFERENCE DESCRIPTION

Structure easily recalls words like power, control, limitation and a lack of freedom and creativity. It is apparent that organizational structure can influence creativity, by facilitating or hindering communication and collaboration. Organizational creativity refers to the process of generating and implementing new ideas, products, services, or processes within an organization, and it is an essential component of organizational growth and success in today's competitive environment. Dialogic Culture plays a significant role in fostering creativity. A Dialogic Culture values creativity and encourages collaboration because people respect and listen to each other, which creates a safe environment. That, in turn, allows people to find their voice and is therefore more likely to produce innovative ideas.

These are the questions that we would like to think and talk about together. *Why is creativity important? What promotes creativity in an organization? How does Dialogic Culture influence creativity? How are Dialogic Culture and creativity connected?*

CHECK-OUT

Parvin Daeipour:

> We have almost 15 minutes, and I would like to invite you to answer this question, *What would you want to share with others, or what do you take away from this conversation and our time together?* Please, someone who's ready start, and after you finish, call on someone else.

Speaker:

> One thing I found during this conversation and dialogue is that we can say a word and people see it completely differently. For example, the word, *structure*. Before I answered the question raised, I asked, *What did you mean by structure?* The answer

started with a completely different meaning than the way I perceived the word *structure*. How he answered it and what he said made sense, but that was not what I was thinking of. So, I didn't respond to what he was saying, which I agree with. I almost felt like we were answering two different questions, or we were finding two different answers to the meaning we each gave to the same question. But we were still having a dialogue. It reminds me that no matter how intentional we are about listening closely and participating in the conversation, we can still process things differently – unless we have the time to process with someone and take the time to go back and forth until we end up on the same page. That can be time-consuming, which is why I think a lot of people don't use dialogue. We're just in a hurry to make a decision. When we are in these situations, we need to create the time and space not to rush conversations, and to maybe focus on one thing only rather than just rushing to try to just make decisions.

Speaker:

Yeah, it's amazing how you can have different opinions from those held by somebody else. When I feel somebody speaking from the heart, authentically, how much I resonate with what they're saying. Then, I think it's exactly how you said it. It's probably because we approached it slightly differently. It is not quick working it out, right? I absolutely agree that we need to give ourselves time to see how we are each thinking. My idea might be different from yours. I think we do want to meet and connect. We want to communicate and create something together. That is the beauty of it, but I think it does need some structure in that sense to help guide the process, but not in the sense of oppressing it or putting it down. I want to say that I have a lot of gratitude for listening to the different things that have been said. It's been very enriching.

Speaker:

I have the impression that we all basically think in similar ways because we are all familiar with dialogue. We all have had our experiences with it, and so the *structure question*, to me, is a superficial question. Of course, dialogue needs a setting and a structure, but basically, we all follow a very similar concept. I think we all want to get in as many views as possible. I always think about very heterogeneous groups where the top people and the people from the bottom of different parts of an organizational come together. I think this approach gives new ideas to everybody if they are on more equal terms, and I think that is really worthwhile.

Parvin:

Although we are a small group, I have really enjoyed our conversation. I take away lots of things to think about. I liked some of the sentences spoken, and

I wrote them down. Like, *Dialogue is a creative process*, and *Thinking together is a creative process*. Someone talked about using dialogue with her team, but at a higher level, something else might happen. It is interesting to me that sometimes it's good to poke the leadership, so that you reach the same feeling, and you understand each other. So, it is wonderful. Although I'm not sure if I understand the concept of creativity through dialogue, I could understand a lot about the dialogic culture and thank you to all of you.

Speaker:

I take away acknowledging. We talk about organizational structure and bringing in dialogue when we want and hope to have support from the top. There are ways, I believe, that you can introduce dialogue going upwards. In other words, managing upwards to get them on board if they are not already. I think a great light was thrown on that topic.

Speaker:

One of the things I love about coming to this conference is all the different perspectives that come to the table. All our experiences bring a different perspective. Like you mentioned, we're looking at the same question but maybe from a different angle or in a different way. Our ideas about a question are different, depending on where we're coming from. It's just all a matter of our experiences, and that's just one of the things that I love about the conference. I thought about something else while you guys were speaking. It is that having a dialogue puts everyone on the same playing field, everyone is at the same level. Even if I have the director sitting with me, and my line staff along with my Probation Officer, when we're in that room at that time we're all on the same level. We bring in our ideas at the same level. Nobody's idea is better or worse, or higher or lower than anyone else's. It's where we're all, at that moment, on the same level.

Speaker:

I was surprised to learn that there are 42 Probation and Parole Districts in Virginia. I didn't know that. My God, the agency is big! When someone talked about poking the leadership, I thought what he was saying was poking the bear, but it's about really questioning. Dialogue is an invitation. It's not about convincing you to also think the way I'm thinking about something. It's about allowing you to self-develop, to want to be a part of this and to want to share. You are curious, and that has more to do with an internal motivation than an external one. That was my takeaway, looking at the different generations, looking with leadership and really questioning. This is something I want to do. I think it will put a lot of agencies in a position to really start looking at creative ways to do things differently. Otherwise, if we are not interested in other things and other areas we're going to lose people.

Asma Beiranvand:

I'm thinking about leadership, and that we should start dialogue with leadership and then go from the top down. It is possible then that leadership, all the teams and all the organization can become familiar with dialogue and a dialogic culture. Then creativity will grow in an organization. That's what I'm thinking about it. And thank you for your participation in this conversation.

POSTSCRIPT

Thinking about the questions we chose for this Participatory Dialogue like *How does Dialogic Culture influence creativity?* and *How are Dialogic Culture and creativity connected?* I was surprised by the curiosity and the many questions by the participants. They asked about creativity, creativity barriers, organization structure and even the role of leadership in creativity and dialogic culture. I thought the concepts of creativity and dialogic culture were deep issues with many aspects. Maybe holding only one session on this issue was insufficient, given the limited time.

During the session, I was happy that we had chosen a topic for dialogue that engaged the participants and raised their interest. I could see that were there more time, each sentence spoken, especially the participant's questions, could have been inquired into more deeply and a common collective meaning could have formed. This point is relevant to determining the topic of future Participatory Dialogues and will be more prominent for me when I am not already familiar with the participants in the room, and I do not know their experience with dialogue and the topic I might choose. In this case, a few of the people in the room had no previous knowledge of professional dialogue, but most of them observed the practices (especially listening and respecting) to a significant extent and they made good inquiries. This was interesting to me. During the dialogue, I was thinking that deep down people love dialogue and are somehow familiar with it and seek it.

What happened in the room was like a skilful conversation. Participants engaged with the topic. They spoke, listened and inquired about it, and they left the room with a sense of respect for everyone, a passion for the topic and some good questions. During the dialogue, sentences were spoken and heard about dialogue. Thinking together in a creative process, these sentences did not encounter opposition and were well worth considering. Since dialogue itself is a creative process, a dialogic culture in the organization will have a positive effect on the emergence of creativity.

I will continue to think about this Participatory Dialogue that we had at the conference. I would like to give my appreciation and thanks to Peter, Jane and all my colleagues at the Academy of Professional Dialogue for their efforts, and for the opportunity they created for me to be a co-facilitator in one of the conference rooms this year.

DAY FOUR

What is a Dialogic Culture?

Why Does Your Organization Need a Dialogic Culture?

PART THREE

Co-hosted plenary session

HOSTS

Harold Clarke (USA) – Academy of Professional Dialogue

Jane Ball APDP, APDPA (UK) – Dialogue Associates and Academy of Professional Dialogue

Jane Ball:

We now have the opportunity to hear what's coming up for everybody. There may be some learning, or perhaps a question or an enquiry that you would like to raise. You can just speak up when you are ready, or you could raise your hand because sometimes it can be hard to get your voice in, particularly if English isn't your first language. If you're more of an introvert and you don't like shouting out, take more time over these things and use the hand-raising function as well.

Speaker:

This is my first conference as a practitioner. I am learning every time I get into a group of practitioners. I'm learning more and more about myself and the practice of dialogue. I've been kind of laid back, watching and listening a lot. I have intentions to take this forward as a training tool to help my staff. I have a small staff, but I want everybody to become aware of and engage with dialogue and the dialogic practices. I've noticed that you're listening and coming forward in our plenary session beautifully, and I really appreciate it. That's what I do. I sit back and I just watch and listen, and then I feel that I can bring something to the table. I just don't want to open my mouth, I want what I add to have relevance. Thank you.

Harold Clarke:

Our topic today is dialogic culture. What resonated with you, in the breakout session or at any point today, as we considered dialogic culture? What sits with you?

Leo:

I want to name a personal learning. I've spent most of my life feeling outside and disconnected from the communities I lived in, and feeling like I didn't have a voice, whether in the foster system or later in the prison system. Over the past couple of years, I have had a voice and I have used it very powerfully to advocate for people who don't have a voice. What became apparent to me today is exactly why I need to be so intentional about being fully inclusive of people's voices. Today, I caused harm by making someone feel like their voice was not fully included. In the same way that I navigate racial justice spaces, needing to include white people when we're talking about inclusion, right? We can't be inclusive to the exclusion of whiteness. Today, in my effort to uplift people who are not from VADOC, I made somebody who is within VADOC feel like their voice wasn't welcome. So, as we engage in the dialogic practice of building a dialogic culture, it's important to hold grace for ourselves. We're never going to be a perfect practitioner, and it's also important to name harm if we cause it and to own it. That's my personal learning here.

Jon:

I'd like to build on that because it connects to the curiosity I have about the theme of the day, *What is a dialogic culture?* There has been a theme throughout the week regarding how integral all voices in a room are to the dialogue. That seems really clear to me and unwavering. There's another aspect, however, that seems unclear, and this is where my curiosity now emerges. What does a dialogic culture look like that creates the space for all those voices, and is also clear about what we're doing with those voices? When everyone is understood or is understanding in the same way, what happens next? What's the value of having all the voices in the room? That's a new curiosity for me that I've taken out of today and the previous days.

Jane:

Inclusion and purpose. They kind of go alongside each other.

Jon:

I would just add that it partly came out of the Participatory Dialogue I was co-hosting with Peter that asked, *Why might people fear a dialogic culture at work?* There were themes that came up about fear of those in positions of power and therefore feeling a sense of responsibility to do something with the space and those voices. Perhaps it's just getting clear about what it looks like, and what it isn't. That is what is emerging for me.

Peter:

I was in a similar kind of enquiry thinking about any culture and about a shared dialogic culture. A culture is a way of doing things and thinking that everybody subscribes to, or expects of each other. When you go into a new culture, you may find that it's not particularly coherent. People say, *We must do this*, but then they do something which isn't that at all. You start to notice that most cultures are incoherent. It seems to me they're hiding problems underneath as part of the way of doing things. Perhaps in the past when they had a terrible director, they did certain things that weren't very clever and so on. It's an easier story to say it was all because of the director, but when you look you see everyone has been involved in what's been happening. So, often there are incoherent cultures. I was wondering whether we should really be talking about a dialogic culture as a coherent culture. That logic implies all sorts of skills may be needed for a coherent culture. It seems to me that would meet the kind of thinking just presented by Jon. We all know what we're trying to do here, and we have a common understanding of the way forward, and so on. We've all got voices. These voices are all apparent in a coherent culture. In an incoherent one, on the other hand, I can't find my voice, or I can't get my voice in, or I don't know what my contribution is.

Lars-Åke:

I was in a dialogue about how a group or team could enable a broader dialogue culture, co-facilitated by Carroll Macey and Mary Morand. We had a very good dialogue about how a team can create and promote a dialogical culture. How could that be done? My conclusion is that what we were doing during that dialogue was wrestling with the need for practice, making it possible to dialogue with colleagues in everyday work. Having a theory that helps you to understand what is happening, like the dialogic actions and dialogue practices helps. I tried to describe during the panel that a dialogical culture must, to some extent and very basically, be built in small teams where people are able to develop dialogue together. If people are not able to have dialogue in a small team with their closest colleagues, then it's difficult for them to understand the whole picture. We also concluded that by-standing is important to create a dialogue culture. If we don't have active bystanders to help with that, we don't see the whole system. I also had a good conversation in the breakout about how to restart this process after the pandemic. This is not a quick fix. It takes endurance and courage. We talked about the dialogue as facilitators, and we must be able to deal with our own fear about not being able to lead a process forward.

Harold:

Lars, I hear you talking about sustainability, and about structure for the dialogue, and those things are very key. We have done some things deliberately within the VADOC to cause those things to occur. I would like to ask Whitney Barton to take a couple of minutes to tell us what was done to create sustainability by putting some structure around dialogue in an effort to nurture it.

Whitney Barton:

Thank you. I raised my zoom hand so hopefully you can see me? As Lars was talking, I was thinking that exact thing. A few things came to mind for me that have been recurrent themes I've heard throughout the week. One is intentional structures. Structures are important. Another is taking the small wins that enable a culture to change over time. It made me reflect on our journey in the

Virginia Department of Corrections. Often across the agency, you will hear people talk very generally about dialogue, that we have dialogue and that we're doing dialogue. But for it be to as comprehensive a business practice as it is, we have really been intentional about growing and developing the practice of dialogue. One of the first things we did, and one of our first small wins, was just to train people, to train everyone across the agency about what dialogue skills are. It helped us to introduce a common language across the agency, and some shared expectations that this is how we talk with one another in the agency. From the very beginning, our employees are oriented that this is important, valued, and the expectation for how we communicate. We also train supervisors and managers about how to coach people and how to deal with accountability in a manner that first prioritises dialogue and coaching as opposed to first holding people accountable or disciplining them. Over time, we've also built an employee development program. We have a Dialogue Practitioner Development Program. It is in our leadership skills training curriculum. Across the agency, we've developed over 300 dialogue practitioners who are committed to doing this work and carrying it forward. It's how we interact day to day as well, you know. We use the modes. We engage in debate when it's necessary, we use monologue and we bring in dialogue where it's useful. It's part of our decision-making process. We collaboratively developed a structured process for how we make decisions, called a Working Dialogue, which you may have heard about during the week. I could go on, but these are the structures that we have put in place based on the principles of dialogue that, over time, have become embedded in how we do business in corrections in Virginia. It's not something that is just going to go away, you know. These structures help us sustain and will continue to help us sustain the practice of everyday dialogue.

Jane:

Very nice. Thank you. I appreciate your clear words. I was thinking about Leo saying that you will never be the perfect dialogue practitioner. That's the same with the organizational culture, isn't it? You have all the training, and you have the structures in place, but in the Participatory Dialogue I was in, we were talking about the work you have to keep doing to ensure that it's coherent in the way Peter said. As individuals, and collectively as organizations, we keep working on building that infrastructure and also on everything that is possible from the bottom up.

Leo:

That's right. I didn't have access to a Working Dialogue framework and so on, but what I did have was leadership that was willing to support the creation of the space for our ingenuity. I had support to be able to have my friend order a dozen books on crucial conversations so that I could start a reading and discussion group. I put it out to all who were interested, and then I held a semi-formal reading and discussion group for 13 weeks. There was enough interest at the end of that to build collective capacity to address issues as they came up. We developed the shared language that there is in dialogue and in Working Dialogue in particular. We used crucial conversations to develop that shared language. And then there was interest in, *What's next?* Well, the next book in the series was crucial accountability. I had support to be able to purchase those books and we did a further ten-week reading and discussion group. We were getting feedback on a regular basis from the guys who would come back from work and be like, *Hey, you'd be so proud of me. I did this thing here about it right? I was able to do the things that we've been reading and talking about.* If you take one thing out of a training or out of this discussion and implement it, you will see the benefit in your immediate surroundings.

Sometimes it can be really important for agency building to celebrate those little successes. When you're able to be successful, you're able to be a successful practitioner of this work, right? Stepping back, we may not be making the major change that I want to see in this whole area that I'm working on right now, but I'm able to celebrate this victory right here in the small group of people – or even in this one interaction with this one other person. That can make all the difference in building the agency necessary for sustainability. We had the structure of a physical unit that we all moved into as well, which is as material as you can get. We built the social infrastructure grounded in dialogue and restorative justice practice. We had Monday night meetings on the end living unit where everybody (30 guys now, built up from seven all the way to 30) was holding the space by rotating the leadership of who facilitates the meeting each week. We have a general structure for talking through creating space for shared gratitude and the uplifting of good work that other people have done. We talk through whatever issues come up throughout the week, and anyone in the community has the power to call for an impromptu meeting at our set time in the day. At five o'clock anyone can call an impromptu meeting if they have something pressing. We had emergency house meetings when it felt like things were going to explode if we didn't all come together to talk through it. But the structure remained the same, and everyone was empowered to call for a meeting.

Jane Ball:

Nice. We would like to see some of your colleagues from the end living unit at the conference next year. Maybe. Let's see what we can do.

Lars-Åke:

In our dialogue, we talked about the fear we have as a dialogue practitioner when we're leading a process in the team. But one day I realized that I don't need to have any fear about making mistakes as a facilitator or practitioner. I will do the best job I can, and we must also allow ourselves to make mistakes. To be honest, the best learnings have come through my mistakes, not my successes.

Speaker:

Reflecting on the dialogue that we had in our group, I'm really conscious of what you were saying. We found the language that you use is so important. Fragmentation can happen within an instant if you don't use the right language. There was one instance where we didn't use the right language, and this reminded me of the need to continually practice being a dialogue practitioner. We talked about sitting in the fire and making mistakes. You're always going to make some mistakes because we're all human beings, but it's by-standing yourself and having the courage to address a mistake in the moment, or soon after, that makes the difference. Apologies to anybody who was offended in the dialogue earlier. It was a huge learning curve for me, and I know for a few others, that will always stay with me. That's what I want to say.

Harold:

That may be one advantage, amongst others, that we have as an institution or organization that is implementing dialogue it is easier to develop a common language. There are things that you can do when you have developed a common language. You can evolve. One of the things we did within the VADOC was to develop a reading list. There are now 28 books in what we call the Director's Reading List. Yes, Bill, your book is on that list! Supervisors and all others have those books, and they also pass them down through the headquarters to the prison institutions and the probation and parole districts. That common understanding, knowledge and language takes us a long way to our success, I believe.

Speaker:

I want to piggyback a little bit on that because I agree with you, Harold, that a common language gives you a structure to create a common understanding, and there's still this other part, our own individual journey or lack thereof. The individual journey is the journey of the self. The learning from our dialogue today is very personal to us, I think, for those who participated. The learning that is surfacing with me is really sticking, and there's a lot of self-reflection along the lines of being able to by-stand oneself. The implementation of a dialogic culture within an organization is also dependent on each of us as individuals because it is the individuals may make up the whole

Bill:

Something that's very striking to me is the long list of tactics that enable a new culture to be present. We can focus on attitudes and internal development, and all this really does matter. Also, there are tactics that are essential for how to bring about the culture at any kind of scale. Perhaps we need a compendium of cultural dialogue tactics that could be quite worth assembling. In Virginia, you've already got a long list, but I'm sure others have things to add. The distinction here is that it's not just any set of stuff, it comes out of the intention to build a different kind of pattern.

Jane:

Something relevant here is what Peter will talk about later, from the publication of last year's conference, Dialogue as Story. What happened in Virginia was shared as a story, because the story shows how all the different tactics are held together to take you into the culture that you want to create.

Bill:

There are lists, and people talk about tools in their toolkit — a phrase that I personally don't like because it's how you weave dialogue into the transformation that you're creating that is the point. The innovation here is showing the relationship between the story and the tactic. There are endless lists of tactics up in the world, right? Everybody's got them. But there is the issue of making them accessible. I could see an annotated list of things with the tactic, the story, and the feedback loop. It would be informative as a pattern language about how to create a deeper, richer picture here.

Peter:

In addition to that, it shouldn't be overlooked that a prison is a container. We talk about creating containers and what we do in a container. A prison is a container. It contains people for an extended period of time. The real shift here in the Virginia Department of Corrections is using that container for healing. That's a very high-level shift within which the tactics we are talking about are necessary, and so the story unfolds. If we ignore the fact that a prison is a container, we miss the extraordinary value of the Virginia story.

Bill:

That is an interesting insight. That the prison is a container used to hold people separate is the conventional understanding of prisons — not to create a healing context. That's all the way out there, like radical! The interesting question is, *What's the moral equivalent in other businesses, or containers that now make value for shareholders?* You need something very different for it to be moving in the direction we're talking about now.

Bernhard:

I want to share something from the heart, and it is that I am a little bit allergic to this technical wording because for me it's further away from authenticity than the dialogue needs. But that's my personal feeling about it. If you talk about coherence, I resonate with what Lars was sharing. One very important value is that if you slip, you can repair and allow another to repair, to come back. And you can allow yourself to come back and repair. That's not a tactic, that's a deeply felt value. The moment it becomes a tactic, then it's too 'mind-ey'. People stop believing me because I'm then talking from the head and not from the heart. I think dialogue is from the heart. That's what I wanted to say, thank you.

Susan:

One of the participants in our group helped us to reshape that thought also, the one about tactics and tools in the toolbox. They talked about skills for embodying the practices through reflection and, more simply, by-stands to bring awareness to people just to help them see where they are. It's less of a tool. It's less of a tactic. It's more of an experience that helps to shape the dialogic culture.

Speaker:

One of the words or images that came up for me when the word tactic was used is the image of a map, and that's what I've been trying to draw on my paper here. If you were to draw a dialogic culture adjoining a non-dialogue culture. What would it look like on a map? A map that says here's the direction but like most maps from Google gives you multiple directions to go. That's how I'm imagining the word tactic. That's my interpretation of it. But I'm not going to take on the assignment just yet, Bill.

Speaker:

It is a great insight, I think, that the prison is a container already. That's quite profound. Every organization is a container as Bill was saying, so I think what we're talking about here is the challenge of implementation coming from the heart. I think we have to be experiencing. That was my learning, today. Whenever I'm in a dialogue, I have to be in the learning mode, not the teaching mode. I have to be experiencing the dialogue and be in touch with myself. But to sustain dialogue, which is what I think the VADOC have done, they went much further with implementation. They brought in coaches. It wasn't the train and pray method, which is what we usually do – we train, and we pray something is going to be different. There's more needed. Fidelity questions because you can use dialogue to beat people up by saying we're doing dialogue and you're not being dialogical. Then you are judging people. You're using the words, but you're out of it. How would we bring this sustainability? That's a big question.

Lars- Åke:

Talking about language, and containers, we could translate the word container into Swedish to mean that which we throw garbage into. So, we must be thoughtful with words. I think Bill is right, we need to understand the different structures and cultures in different organizations to be successful in creating a dialogic culture.

Jane:

Although I don't like the term toolkit, as I said, I don't think the two things are mutually exclusive. I think I work from the heart, and I have strategies and skills and a whole range of different things that altogether are helpful within a clear intention about what I'm trying to do.

Speaker:

One of the things that came up in our break-out group was fear. It was such a lovely break-out, and I really liked it when they started talking about fear. Everybody seemed to have something to add about fear, except me. What I gathered from the conversation is that in order to be good as a participant or a facilitator, you have to be humble. You must be willing to make yourself vulnerable if you're asking everybody to make themselves vulnerable. When something comes up that challenges what you're doing, that goes to your identity – and if you're really invested in what comes up and it does go to your identity, then say, *Okay, that hurt, and I need to process that. I also need to be prepared to say, thank you for that, because I wouldn't have gotten there on my own.*

Jane:

We only have three or four minutes left, so if you've got something you are burning to say, or that you feel would be a real gift to other people here, now's the time.

Speaker:

In VADOC it is not just the prisons, it's also the probation and parole districts. They are a much larger container than all the prisons. These people, for the most part, are going home. The inmates are going to go home and they're going to be back in their communities. So, as Laura brought out, it's also about their families. It really is much larger than just the prisons. The idea everywhere, I think, was that we had been an organization of command and control and we could move away from that and still be safe.

Harold:

Jane, I just want to say that success is individual, and how we treat ourselves, how we process things, how we hold ourselves to account and how we make ourselves vulnerable is key. If you make yourself vulnerable, you have to be able to do something constructive with it and to learn from it.

Jane:

Tomorrow we will be looking at the multi-stakeholder work that happens in the communities around the probation and parole districts in Virginia, as case studies. So, I think we'll highlight exactly what was said about the districts. It's about how to create a container within a multi-stakeholder situation. That requires something else. Good. Should we transition to hand over to Peter?

Harold:

Yes, that's what I'm thinking, given the time.

Jane:

Peter. Over to you.

Peter:

I very much enjoyed working with John Steinman on our Participatory Dialogue. It was partly a dialogue and partly a skilful conversation, I would say. We were interested in the concerns people might have about the introduction of dialogue or being part of a dialogue culture. There was a lot of good thinking there. It's hard to remember it all but fortunately, we do record and transcribe check-outs to help us. Each year we publish a book from the previous year's conference. I have the chance to be involved in the editing of them, and I'm always surprised how much more happened than I remembered. I don't think our lead editor, Cliff Penwell, is here right now. You can tell by his name, Penwell, that he's an editor and he is a very good editor, and a good colleague. Each year the conference theme has been The World Needs Dialogue, and there has been a sub-title. The first one was Gathering the Field, then Setting the Bearings, Shaping the Profession, and Putting Dialogue to Work. All these volumes are available if you want to look them up and get hold of them.

The one we are publishing today is sub-titled Dialogue as Story. The interesting thing here is sense-making. When we hear things and read or see things, to make sense of them we make them into a little story. You might say no, we make assumptions like I assume this or that, but the assumption takes the form of a story. From what I heard here and there, this must be what happened. Perhaps I assumed we had enough money, and my story was that we can be quite liberal with our spending, and therefore I acted in a particular way. This automatic formation of a story to make sense of different information happens faster than we notice. There is a story there, and I may not realise I was the author of that story. Instead, it seems to be an obvious description of what happened.

This process of sense-making through story is very closely related to the whole matter of dialogue and of a dialogic culture. If we have a coherent story across the whole organization, we have a coherent culture. If we have competing stories we might have a lively culture – but if we have stories that are contradictory, we have a problematic and fragmented culture. Here's the cover of the book, showing a man surrounded by floating books and letters, since he's online. We all have this kind of challenge every day, faced with a flood of disconnected information. How do we make sense of all these things that we're hearing and being told?

If you choose to have a look at the book, you will find that there's something about our personal first-hand experience that we can use to make better sense of the information that's coming from so many disruptive sources. Whether we draw on our first-hand experience or not, we will find we have a story about the situation, about what has happened, is happening now and will happen. That story determines how we decide to act in the moment. I recommend this, our fifth volume. It's blue because we're going through the colours of the rainbow, and the earlier volumes were red, orange, yellow and green. Now we're on blue, so next year we'll find out what indigo is like. The current book is available on Amazon or any good bookseller. The cheaper way is to buy the eBook, which may be around $20, but the hardback is, of course, what you really want. If you are a collector, get them now whilst they are available. Thank you, Jane and Harold, for giving me a few minutes to talk about our latest publication, and our growing archive full of rich material.

Jane:

Thank you, Peter. Thank you everyone for your attentiveness and contribution throughout the day today, and we look forward to seeing you tomorrow morning.

I was reminded earlier of Matt Burgess, who many of you from the Virginia Department of Corrections knew. He passed away after the last conference and before this book was published. I will just read a couple of lines from the foreword to the book, which I wrote, that makes a special mention of him. I wrote, *I'd like to make a special mention of Matt Burgess, whose session is included. Matt was a dedicated dialogue practitioner at the Virginia Department of Corrections from 2014 onwards, and sadly passed away in December 2022. So, there's no postscript from Matt's session, but his enquiry into the impact of the unforgiving storylines that communities hold about offenders was characteristically courageous of him.* I would like you to note that, and have a thought for Matt. He was a great practical, courageous and loyal guy. Thank you.

Having read that, it feels a bit odd to put on some music, but anyway I know Matt would not mind. He really wouldn't. We've done a lot of thinking and a lot of talking. We've spent a lot of time in our heads over the last couple of days, and maybe a little bit, as Bernhard would say, in our hearts, but now we're going to play something that gives us an opportunity to get into our bodies. If you want to, but you don't have to, it's your choice how you handle this. This piece of music was chosen by Susan Williams, who's been one of our panellists. It shows people dancing together. We've had people singing together across the world. This is people dancing together. If you want to stand up and join me, I'll be dancing. If you want to sit down, you can do this in your chair. Or if you just want to sit back and watch, laugh and listen, or whatever please do. But it's an opportunity to kind of bring another part of ourselves into this conference. Join me if you'd like to!

A lively piece of music followed, and many participants chose to dance.

TWND! 6: Your Organization Needs Dialogue!

DAY FIVE

What are Multi-Stakeholder Dialogues?
Why Does Your Organization Need Multi-Stakeholder Dialogues?

The final day of the conference concentrated on multi-stakeholder dialogues. Although every dialogue could be considered to have multiple stakeholders, this becomes far more complex when the participants come from different organizations rather than all coming from the same one. The challenge is that although the organizations and participants may be interdependent for the success of their work, they are directed by different leadership strategies and measured by different criteria.

The panel on this closing day was drawn from two Virginia Department of Corrections Re-entry Councils. These Re-entry Councils each have around 30 or 40 participating members representing local organizations that are actively helping justice-involved individuals through their re-entry and re-settlement back in the community. In this case the collaboration between the many stakeholders who provide enforcement, treatment and support services enables them to be collectively far more efficient and effective than if they acted in isolation from one another. That they are particularly effective is indicated by the statistics – they have the lowest or second lowest rate of recidivism of any state in the USA over the past seven years.

During the Participatory Dialogues and closing plenary session the conversation broadened to explore the relevance of multi-stakeholder dialogues in commercial, educational and other settings.

DAY FIVE

What are Multi-Stakeholder Dialogues?
Why Does Your Organization Need Multi-Stakeholder Dialogues?

PART ONE

Plenary session with a panel of six practitioners

HOSTS

Jane Ball APDP, APDPA (UK) – Dialogue Associates and Academy of Professional Dialogue

Peter Garrett APDP, APDPA (UK) – Dialogue Associates and Academy of Professional Dialogue

PANEL

Deidre Bailey (USA) – Child Support Enforcement Division

Antoinette Bennett (USA) – Virginia Department of Corrections

Sara Dimick (USA) – OAR (Opportunity, Alliance and Re-entry) Richmond

Alan Dorrough (USA) – Virginia Department of Corrections

Kathryn Hall (USA) – Virginia Department of Corrections

Karen Wilson (USA) – Virginia Department of Corrections

Peter:

Good morning. Welcome to the fifth and final day of our conference. I was a big advocate for playing that piece of music. The younger boy is nine years old. The older one looks like he might be in his twenties, although I don't know exactly how old he is, and the piano they're playing is in a shopping arcade. The two of them have never met before. He said, *Would you like to play?* and the young boy comes up and they play a piece of music they both know. They really do play well together. It was quite a beautiful duet, I think.

Did they have a container? I think they did have a container. *Did they have a working relationship?* I think they did. *How long did it take to make that?* One minute? *How long does it take to make a container and form a working relationship?* Not that long if we are practicing doing it all the time.

Jane Ball:

I think so too.

Peter:

Day five, and Jane and I are hosts for today. What are multi-stakeholder dialogues? And why does your organization need multi-stakeholder dialogues? That's our focus. We touched on multi-stakeholder dialogues a bit yesterday with Susan Williams' impressive story about dealing with trash, or rubbish as we call it here in the UK. That was a multi-stakeholder situation, with a lot of different groupings collaborating to get a better result. We'd like now to look at some external multi-stakeholder dialogues, and we have two panels if the panel members are ready to join us.

Jane:

We're doing things slightly differently this time. Maybe we should start with a simple introduction from each member of our panel. Then I'm going to call on Kathy and Karen to say a little bit more about the multi-stakeholder work that they are involved in. First, can we hear your names, role, organization and geographic location? Let's go alphabetically and start with Alan.

Alan Dorrough:

Good morning. I am Alan Dorrough. My role is the workforce development specialist for Indian Creek Correctional Centre here in Virginia, and my purpose is working with everybody as they get ready to go home – getting any kind of relationships that we can build and getting all the resources we can so that they hopefully are less likely to come back into jail or prison.

Antoinette Bennett:

> My name is Antoinette Bennett. I am a senior parole officer in Richmond City, which is in the central area of the State of Virginia. In my role, I oversee an assigned prison and work with the inmates who are returning to the community. I try to make connections with all our stakeholders.

Deidre Bailey:

> Morning! My name is Deidre Bailey, and I am a family engagement case manager for the Division of Child Support Enforcement. I am a Statewide family engagement worker. Although I am based in Norfolk, we handle cases throughout the State. My job is to work with individuals who have barriers to paying for support. Most likely they are people who have been incarcerated. Once they are released, we work with them to try to get employment. We try to work with them to modify their child support orders, to get them on their feet and just get them out from beneath that debt.

Sara Dimick:

> I'm the executive director of the Richmond OAR. We're in Richmond, and OAR stands for opportunity, alliance and re-entry. We are the area's oldest and largest re-entry non-profit organization. We worked with over 5,000 individuals last year, coming home from local, state and Federal facilities.

Jane:

> Kathy, can I encourage you to introduce yourself, but maybe say a little bit about your re-entry council in your area at the same time? So, do go beyond yourself in your role.

Kathryn Hall:

> Good morning, I'm Kathy Hall, the chief probation officer in Norfolk, Virginia. Our area is towards the coast of Virginia, but it is a large urban area with five cities squashed into this corner of the State. Because of our proximity, we all work together. Norfolk Re-entry Council is a consortium of stakeholders who work together for a more positive reintegration of justice-involved individuals back into the community.

Jane:

> Would you say more, Kathy, about who is on your re-entry council? Which agencies are involved?

Kathryn:

Well, my co-convener is from the Department of Human Services here in the city of Norfolk. You can see, Dee Bailey with child support enforcement, and they've been a partner forever. Alan is with our divisional facilities. Although he is in the Virginia Department of Corrections, we cover different areas and work collaboratively together. Then we have representatives from the court, we have treatment providers, employers, justice-involved individuals, and various resource providers who share information and we work with them to provide the best resources for people to be successful when they're re-entering.

Peter:

Okay. How many different agencies do you think you have in your re-entry council Kathy?

Kathryn:

I'd say Between 35 and 40.

Peter:

This is a big group!

Karen Wilson:

My name is Karen Wilson. I am the chief probation officer for Richmond Probation and Parole District One. I work with Ms. Bennett. We are located in Central Virginia, right in the middle. A little bit about our council. Miss Dimick's organization and my organization together co-convene the re-entry council and all the stakeholders that are involved. The treatment providers, criminal justice-involved individuals, local law enforcement and a plethora of folks who are engaged in our re-entry efforts. Our council works as a network to enhance services, remove barriers, strengthen collaboration and promote family integration and community engagement for criminal justice-involved individuals. So that's the focus of our council.

Jane:

This isn't a competition, but how many agencies are involved in your re-entry council?

Karen:

It fluctuates. Sometimes we have more individuals, but I would say, like Chief Hall, we probably have about 35 to 40 folks as well that are consistently engaged in our council.

Jane:

Right. Thank you. So, you are here as individuals with a role, a job that you do. You're also part of your own agency, and part of this larger multi-stakeholder grouping called the re-entry council, where people work together for the benefit of those people who are justice-involved.

Peter:

We have two teams here. Kathy, who are your colleagues here?

Kathryn:

My colleagues are Dee Bailey and Alan Dorrough.

Peter:

Okay. Therefore, Karen, yours must be Antoinette and Sarah.

Karen:

That is correct.

Peter:

So, we are talking about criminal justice, talking about the Virginia Department of Corrections, and talking about people coming out of prison. That's what you refer to as re-entry into the community, and presumably re-settlement as well. As we said yesterday, most people in the care of the Virginia Department of Corrections never go into a prison. We're not ignoring that – we will come to a little bit later in the day – but at this point, we're looking at the re-entry councils you have.

Jane:

Yes, and we're looking at multi-stakeholder dialogue. At this point, we would like to put all of our audience, our participants, into breakout rooms to think a little bit about multi-stakeholder dialogues. The question that we'd like you to think about is this, *What do you think are the three biggest challenges of getting the best value from multi-stakeholder dialogues?* You will be in breakouts, with three of you together to answer that question.

Participants went into break-out rooms for eight minutes.

Jane:

We've been having a good conversation here. Let's hear what you came up with, and then our panel can share some of their experiences.

Speaker:

One challenge is to connect people given their personalities, hierarchy and all the power issues. Then to connect interests given that everyone's doing different things. And thirdly, to connect the organizational structures that are sometimes very different. Lastly, to have the willingness to invest a lot of time to do all that.

Jane:

Very good. Thank you. These are real challenges.

Speaker:

We actually came up with eight, but I'm going to try to consolidate them. Check-ins and check-outs would have to be very short, else with 40 people in the room, it might be difficult. Also building and establishing a safe container, by building the confidence of those in the room, with people who maybe don't trust the process. Establishing a safe container and making sure that everyone's voice is heard. One of the biggest ones we thought would be people being able to suspend, because everybody comes in with their own concepts about what they do, and what is needed. They would have a difficult time, maybe, suspending.

Peter:

Thanks – I think you did well!

Jane:

Could we hear a couple more people?

Speaker:

Morning everybody. We came up with two major things. Getting everybody together at the same time, because everybody has their own job that they're trying to do. You've got someone at this end of the building, someone at that end of the building, someone who's in security and others who do non-security things. So, getting them all together at the same time. The second one was, *What's their purpose?* When they come to the table, everybody wants to know, *Why am I here?* When you've got security and non-security together. non-security always wants to know, *Why am I here?* Someone who's in medical wants to know the same thing. If you've got someone that's in receiving, what's their purpose of being at the table? That's a big challenge.

Jane:

OK. We've got time for another.

Speaker:

Hello, everyone. Our group had a consensus as well. We agreed purpose is very important. If we can agree on the purpose, then we can focus on what we need to accomplish, and from there we need to take a moment to acknowledge that everybody present has something important to contribute to make this purpose happen. Taking your ego out of it, *How can we bring together and mesh to do what we need to accomplish?* Mentally, if we can mesh and remove our ego, that will definitely help to accomplish a goal and a purpose.

Jane:

Thank you. Right, let's hear from our panel. I'll let you say whatever you would to say, but maybe it would be interesting to hear if you've had some of those challenges, and how you've tackled them. Then we'd love to hear some outcomes of doing that. Is it worth this investment of time to get it right? What difference does it make? Richmond?

Antoinette:

I'll start. I was writing down some of the comments that individuals were sharing, and I think we may be getting a little off track. I'm hearing, you know, about safe containers, and we want to focus on the re-entry council itself. Multiple stakeholders within a prison facility are already within a group or a single organization. I have to agree that sometimes when it comes to the investment of time, we have found that it was difficult. But I feel that a lot of our stakeholders have now bought into what our re-entry council stands for and what we are here to accomplish, and so I'm seeing more participation. We have found though that we have to give notice way ahead of time. Instead of just saying, *We've got to have a re-entry council meeting next week* and sending out an invite. Currently, we have our meeting every other month, and we remind people by sending notifications of the things we need. I go into the prison institutions, and when I am there, I communicate with the counsellors and ask them, *What is going on with your inmates? Is there anything that they need? Give me a summary of people with an identified need.* They give me a summary of what's going on and needed, and after I review that and look at everything in our system, I filter that out to the re-entry council. The re-entry council jumps on saying, *Okay, I can help them with this, if you can get that.* Then individuals are connected with those resources prior to their release. We even have individuals go to an institution to pick a person up on release just to get them onto their visitation list in order to help them with those services. We have individuals meeting at the district office to help individuals with services. So that's one of the things that we do. If people don't have time for this or that, we hold them accountable. We put it up there. If you want to be a part of this re-entry council, this is what our need is, and this is what needs to be done.

Karen:

I want to follow that. It's very important when bringing internal and external stakeholders together that you are clear about why. You must be very clear about what the mission is, and what the goals are, and why. That's the starting point. It's very important for us to understand why we are here. We are meeting with a purpose, not just meeting because that's what we were told to do.

Sara:

I'll add from the Richmond standpoint that we used to be a regional re-entry Council. We did some strategy around that. We looked at who was coming and what we needed to look like, and we ended up splitting our councils into various counties and cities so that we were able to best serve folks. So, that has been important. Did you know that there's no money attached to re-entry councils? People show up thinking we have money and we're going to be able to put money out, but that's not the case. Our purpose is solely to come together as a community to provide the services and things that our returning citizens need. Defining that purpose, that *why*, has been huge, and it helps us to be successful. The other thing is not meeting just to meet. That's why we meet every other month. We make sure we have a good agenda and that our time together is well spent. Those things have allowed us to grow, and to be successful.

Jane:

We're going to come, Kathy, to you in Norfolk, and let's similarly hear some of the challenges you've overcome. Then I'd like to do a round where we hear some of the outcomes and what have you achieved as a result of these multi-stakeholder dialogues. First, can we hear from Norfolk about how you've gone about things, herding the 35 to 40 cats in your re-entry council? Alan, do you want to start from a Norfolk perspective?

Alan:

Well, I know from the Norfolk perspective that one of the big things is that we have seven cities that are connected within 10 miles. We are also regional, and a lot of our stakeholders are not just in Norfolk, but primarily we are servicing those folks who are living in Norfolk. One of the challenges is having everybody become vested in the council. I like the term shared vision or shared mission and helping people to understand what we're trying to do. *This is where we're trying to go — what are you bringing to the table?* And if you are bringing things to the table, please bring your whole toolbox because we need it.

Deidre:

Well, at the beginning of this panel, you all had two individuals playing the piano. You said that the older guy invited the youngster to play, and they played well together. That's how I think of our re-entry council. I think that we all play well together. The invite is put out, we come in, we do what we have to do. We have a common interest. We're not just there because we have to be there. We're there because we want to be there and because we want to be there, we put our best foot forward. We do what needs to be done for the justice involved. What I also like about re-entry councils, anywhere, is that they bring the brochures and pamphlets to light. What does that mean? Rather than saying, *This is someone from probation and parole and here's a pamphlet,* people speak for themselves about their work, and then like Antoinette said, you can hold them accountable. If I'm there to talk about child support enforcement and you send someone to me but I don't do what I'm supposed to do, then you can hold me accountable because of what I said to the Council. Our council is just so vested in what's going on around in our area. That's what I love about the re-entry council.

Kathryn:

Someone brought up power as a challenge in the breakout rooms. As was said about Norfolk, we leave our egos at the door. We work collaboratively. No one person can do this alone. We recognized early on that we had to work together. We can't say, *Well, I provide substance abuse services, so there shouldn't be someone else on the Council who does that as well.* We need everyone's services. Money was brought up and people thought, *I can get business there,* but those people don't come to the Council for very long. It's because they see that we work collaboratively. We are not business-oriented, we are service-oriented.

Karen:

That's awesome. I follow that — that's good.

Peter:

The first thing I heard was that it sounds as if the Council's not an event but an ongoing process. It sounds like you're interacting right through between meetings, and the meetings are a particular juncture in that collaboration. The other thing that I'm interested in is holding people to account. Within an organization, you can do that, but between multiple organizations it is different. Without a council, how would you address holding people to account? One on one? Having a collective group, discussing it all together and holding each other to account is such an important part, isn't it? And then, clearly understand what resources are available. What do you bring to the table? What have we got, and how can we best use what we have?

Jane:

The other thing you've all been talking about is the common purpose. *We're here to support people who have been incarcerated and who are being released, and to support them on that journey.* And that's where the focus is. I think that gives you a common purpose. So, what did you achieve as a result of this work? It'd be good to hear about some outcomes since we are talking about multi-stakeholder dialogues and why your organization needs them. Presumably, the outcomes are part of why we need them. Let's go back the same way. Antoinette?

Antoinette:

I feel that the work that we've put in has led to us being very successful. We have a re-entry council, but we also have businesses, and they all understand business. I can call on any of my stakeholders, and I say, *Hey you're on my council, and I noticed that this is one of the services that you give. I haven't heard you or seen you for a while, but this is what I need.* This is how I hold them accountable. When we have our re-entry council meeting, if someone has done something helpful, I'll send a massive email about the individuals who stepped up and describe one of the biggest successes that we've had, one of many. When the State had earned sentence credit for individuals being released, we sat down, and we had a dialogue on, *How can we help these individuals?* In the State of Virginia, we had a mass release of individuals due to the new State code, and these individuals were not afforded an opportunity to connect to our resources because of the length of time suddenly being cut. So we got together, and we had a dialogue. One of the things that we did before the releases, for example, was that the re-entry council members, myself, and some of my partners went into the institutions to talk with people and say, *What is the need? What are you hearing? Link us up with these individuals.* We had to get buy-in from our stakeholders so we invited individuals from headquarters and administration to come to speak at one of our meetings so that everybody knew what was going to happen. This is what we foresee in the future. And with that being explained, our council was all over it. I was so excited to see who was doing what. We decided, well, we can all do more. We ended up holding a multi-district Resource Fair. We invited our own district and had major resources from the other districts as well. We put in for a grant through collaboration and seeing the needs, and we ended up with 55 resource providers in one area. Over 160 individuals came through the doors to take advantage of those resources. They were individuals coming out of the institutions with nothing. We had housing, mental health support, clothing, substance abuse treatment and job resources. Everyone was in the room.

Jane:

Can I just check something, Antoinette? There was a change in law that meant you had a lot of incarcerated people released quite suddenly in your area, about 160.

Antoinette:

160 participated in the Resource Fair. I don't know the exact number of people who were released, but just coming through the doors of the Resource Fair we had over 160 people take advantage of our resources.

Peter:

Without the council being there, that would have been very difficult to achieve . . .

Antoinette:

It wouldn't have happened. There's no way.

Karen:

I was just going to follow what Peter and Jane said. If we hadn't had our re-entry council up, running, engaged and involved when that legislation occurred here in the Commonwealth of Virginia. we would have had some major issues. Let's say you have one resource provider in the city of Richmond. All these people are released and everybody's going to this one person, right? They're not going to be able to keep up with providing a service to those folks. But with the council, we have multiple people that can do multiple things. We have ten providers that do substance abuse services, or ten providers that can help with mental health issues or skills building, things like that. Without our council, we would have had some challenges with our re-entry efforts. I'm very pleased, very, very proud, and very happy for everyone that was able to help during that time.

Sara:

I would like to come in with a separate story, that Officer Bennett and I were talking about yesterday. I have a lot of proud moments that have come out of collaboration with the council. Here's just one. We worked with one gentleman who had been incarcerated for 25 years. He had been adopted as a young child. When he had been incarcerated, a lot of work had been done to get his birth certificate. It turns out his name had been changed several times, and we were able to work together collaboratively with the Department of Health to eventually find this man's birth certificate and get him his identity documents. We have a picture of him hanging in our office where he was standing in front of the office showing his papers. It took us three years working together to figure it out. I don't know how many phone calls and many emails, but we did it. That wouldn't have happened without the right people at the table having the right conversations. It was a big thing, but it's also a small thing – like a part of the whole behind-the-scenes work that didn't happen at one council meeting but over time.

Jane:

And a massive thing for that man. A huge thing!

Sara:

Oh yes.

Jane:

Before I come to Norfolk, Sara, your organization is a third-sector not-for-profit organization. In different countries that is called different things, but you are not a governmental organization. Here in the UK, where we are, the culture within non-profits is very different from government organizations, particularly in corrections, which is largely command-and-control. I wonder if you have any reflections on the kind of relationship that you have with all the other agencies, but especially with the Department of Corrections, given that difference? I'm just interested in how that has developed over the years.

Sara:

Oh, that's a good question. I would say we have developed trust and respect, and that has come through our conversations and learning together, as you said, we are very different. As a non-profit, we operate from a social work perspective and that is a part of our core tenets. I think what happens in the Department of Corrections is the respect of the individual. But on our side, we don't operate from a security standpoint. That's not our perspective. I think sometimes Miss Bennett will tell me I'm too easy on people, but sometimes I tell her she's too hard on people! And then we'll just talk through it and come to an understanding together because we trust each other. We know that we both have good intentions and that our heart is in this. I think without that trust and that dialogue, we would not see eye to eye. I think there are days that she probably does not want to talk to Sara one more time today, and there are days, you know when she's shaking her head. I think we talk almost every day, or at least weekly, to help folks and to make sure that we're doing the work together. She couldn't do this without us, and I certainly couldn't do this work without her. I think that that's why we keep doing it. But you brought up a very good point. We do see things differently, but without talking and listening we would have problems.

Jane:

I think it's easy to say we all get together and do this stuff, but it's in working those differences where the really hard work is done, isn't it? That's where the grit is, I would say. Thank you. We may come back to that point, let's see, but now let's come over to Norfolk and hear a bit about the kind of outcomes that you've achieved as a result of your re-entry council.

Kathryn:

Well, we've had a lot of outcomes. I'd like to give Dee and Alan a chance to share about their relationship and how the interconnectedness between our facilities and our resources, fairs and child support services have changed.

Deidre:

Alan, let me go first because I want to talk about Alan, too. You know what you know, and you don't know what you don't know, because there is so much going on in the re-entry council. I just love all the providers that are there. One of the things that I liked when I started going to the council is that it gave me the opportunity to talk about child support. Usually when you hear about child support enforcement, when somebody invites me to a resource fair, I am the only person there that they see as taking from them. All the other providers give, give, give. So, I need to be able to change the narrative about child support enforcement. That is one of the reasons why I want to talk about Alan and the prisons. He used to invite me into the prison, and I only got that invite because I met him on the council. No one would choose to come to talk to me, they would bypass my table. So, I had to get out and talk about child support. And the more I talked about child support and all the good things that we do, and that we do have services to help individuals, the more the information got filtered to a lot of different people. Then they started to invite me to more and more events because I wasn't seen as the bad person anymore. I'm glad I was there on the council to dispel some of those myths about child support. We have a lot of services to help individuals. It's not just about taking, taking, taking.

Peter:

Can I ask, because I'm naïve and I know nothing about this, *Was the narrative about you that you take children away from families?*

Deidre:

No, not take children away from families, a lot of the time. They just think that child support means you are going to put them in jail, or we are going to take their money. That's all you hear.

Jane:

They think you are after their money, that you're trying to get money off parents to pay for their children.

Deidre:

Correct. But child support has services too, and we help individuals to find employment. I go to different job fairs to help people to find employment. I can provide bus tickets to people who need transportation. We can provide work uniforms if they have a job that needs a uniform, but people don't know about that. So, me being on the council means I can always talk about that information, and then they take it to their people. It spreads out that you need to talk to your Child Support Worker. I love it with probation and parole that whenever someone comes to talk to them, and that person has a child support issue, they have my name, and they have a face that they can relay that person to. So, it's not just that code here called 'child support'. It's a warm handoff now because they don't see child support as the bad guy because we have services to help the whole family, not just the person who is receiving support. We want to help those people who need help as well.

Jane:

So, the re-entry council helps you to do your job better, because you know people, and they are helping your cause, your role, to make sure that people take on their responsibilities.

Deidre:

And another thing is I listen to people saying something in the check-in or the check-out about what they are about. Everyone can hear, who's in the room at that time when they give a little snippet about their business.

Alan:

I had no problems deferring today because Deidre is awesome. When I used to invite the different agencies into the prison a lot of my inmates would question it, *You're only bringing them in so they can get my money, so they can get my stuff.* It took a lot of education but now I cannot hold an event without my guys telling me, *You better make sure and have Child Support here.* They see that benefit. That's awesome. Now, following up on Sarah's comment earlier, a big part of the re-entry councils is that it helped us with the collaborations that set us up for success. One was when the enhanced sentencing credit came in and many were released at once because we already had those relationships in place to move forward together. Another that was huge was coming into Covid, because with Covid everything shut down. That collaboration set us up for virtual presentations and virtual resource networking because we already knew the folks and they understood what we were trying to do. They were there ready, willing and asking, *What do I need to do to ensure the success of our guys coming out?*

Jane:

I want to ask you a question, Alan, just because you're in Indian Creek, which is a prison. Anyone who's ever worked in or visited a prison has found it's quite hard work just to get in if you are not located in a town. You have to drive, find the place, park your car, present your ID, go through security measures to get in and wait to be escorted somewhere. That can sometimes, in my experience, make relationships with community organizations really difficult, because it's so hard to get through the gate. I wondered if you had any thoughts about it from inside a prison, and about the culture there of engaging with people in the community. *What have you found in terms of those different cultures?*

Alan:

Well, there's definitely a difference between when an individual is going into OAR (Offender Aid and Restoration, a non-profit) and when they're going into Probation and Parole. They may have some security checkpoints, but it's definitely easier to get in there than it is to get in here. I have found that going to the re-entry councils and maintaining those solid relationships helps the folks outside. It helps my organizations and my stakeholders be more apt to go through the security checkpoint process knowing that the guys are really looking forward to hearing from them and working with them. Dee and I have had some conversations about things that may need to change to make it easier to get her in through the front door. She has always been ready and willing to make that happen. So that's that relationship-building.

Jane:

Unless you've done it, it is a bigger thing than people realize, I think.

Alan:

Correct, correct.

Diedre:

Could I add, that one of the things that he and I had to go through was getting rejected from going into the prison because of my hairdo? I had too many bobby pins in my hair. I told Alan I was so determined to come because there was a need, so I had to completely change all of my hairdo before I went out to the prison. I wasn't going to take my bobby pins out and I knew the requirement in the prison, so I changed my hairdo so that I could get in.

Alan:

Yep. Relationships count.

Peter:

Kathryn, any comment you would like to add because we are nearly out of time.

Kathryn:

I think, changing your hairstyle so you can get into a prison pretty well sums it up. People will do whatever it takes to get in and provide the services! Covid gave us all challenges and we had to find different ways to work together. For example, for years annually we have had Town Halls. We had planned to have our Town Hall with all the resource providers coming in and providing information in a Town Hall fashion to the folks at the prisons. Well, we couldn't do that once Covid hit. Instead, we had our resource providers all make short videos, on Child Support, signing up for Medicaid and ASAP services. That was a way to still share information and reach the people that needed the resources. Were those relationships not already built that would not have happened.

Peter:

Kathy, I'm wondering if you have any advice for other re-entry councils right across Virginia. We met you when we first arrived in Virginia a decade ago, so I guess at some point you'll probably retire. What words of wisdom do you have for the other re-entry councils, some of whom are probably listening right now?

Kathryn:

Well, my partner Madonna Flores and I have spoken with a number of re-entry councils who want to know, *How do you do it?* The one thing we say is that you've got to leave your ego at the door. You have got to work together. You cannot stand on that positional power, and you cannot isolate yourself. No one can work successfully in a silo. By building those relationships, building those partnerships, you can get your work done better and you can help others better. So that's the important piece, to build those relationships and partnerships.

Peter:

Thank you, Kathy, we're about to close. I want to point out that the Virginia Department of Corrections has prisons and community Probation and Parole offices, but it is only a part of the criminal justice system. It's a very large system, the criminal justice system. The problem we identified early on is that we've got something wrong in our thinking when we imagine we're independent and only need to concentrate on our bit when actually, we're interdependent. The re-entry council is a good example of how all the services have been working together because recidivism, which is the measure of success in your corrections business in Virginia, is incredibly good. Over the last seven years, I believe you've either had the lowest or the second lowest recidivism rate in all states across the USA. Well, that's not just VADOC, it's the whole system, and this symbolizes cooperation across the whole system. It definitely pays. You started your re-entry council, I think, back in 2010, and it's paid off.

Jane:

We going to open up the chat, as we've done on other occasions for people to put in comments or questions, and then maybe hear a few from the floor. I can some have their hands raised already.

Speaker:

Mine is really short. What is that word you just used, Peter, that began with an R and ended in ism? I don't know what the word is. Is it like reoffending?

Peter:

Yes, Recidivism.

Speaker:

Okay, that's a big word.

Jane:

We should have a glossary of terms.

Harold:

Recidivism is the rate at which individuals return to prison during a three-year period after release, and for the last seven years, Virginia has had the lowest rate of return in the United States for four of the years and the second lowest for three of the years. Peter, I'm glad to hear you speak about interdependence. It's something we speak about a lot within VADOC. We speak about independence as a value, but interdependence has a greater value. If we were not aware that we are interdependent, we would never have been able to achieve the things that we have been able to achieve. I just wanted to say thank you to the panel members and all the staff.

Peter:

You must feel very proud of how it's all worked out.

Harold:

Well, you know, we have a good team. and I give all the credit to the team.

Bernhard:

I really appreciate the conversation about multi-stakeholder dialogues around prisons, and I would like to bring in another perspective, a broader perspective. I've been working quite a lot with large projects like installing wind turbines, and other projects with many stakeholders, and the complexity is that they don't automatically have the same agenda. There can be neighbours that are environmentalists, and city councils who are contrary to their ideas or have very different ideas. There can be contractors who have different agendas during the contract. This is another field where multi-stakeholder dialogues between them all are very, very useful. I do recognize some complications that you sketched out and also the importance that you call the two tiers, where you have a dialogue with people in the more day-to-day field, and you have to get the boards of the other organizations on board also. That is quite often a struggle. I'm hoping to learn a little bit about that here.

Peter:

Do you find you can establish a common purpose or intention?

Bernhard:

Well, I agree with what someone mentioned earlier, that it takes time, especially when you have people who are afraid about their environment and about their neighbourhood – Not In My Back Yard – and things like that. It really takes time to connect with them and it pays to do that in the very early stages. I even had a project about heightening the dykes around the Ijsselmeer, which is a very big sea in the Netherlands, and there happened to be a lot of celebrities living in one village there who had direct contact with the politicians so they could halt this project for three years. That was highly complex.

Peter:

Yes. You know when we got involved with prisons, we found criminal justice went wider and wider. We included the courts and the police, and so on directly. We found people had very different agendas and different ideas about what was needed. It was when we took it right back to public safety that we all met. The police wanted public safety. The courts wanted public safety. The community wanted public safety. It was all the way through. Then we could start to bring things together. It was a challenge initially to step back far enough to find what everyone needed. Having found that common need, when you get that, then you can move together.

Bernhard:

Exactly. Find a transcending perspective that we all want. That is what I'm always looking for. I've met some situations where it was really difficult to reach that.

Jane:

Yeah. I think the first thing is if you can enable those people to stay in the room together without arguing and debating with each other. That's the first step, isn't it? So that we listen and try to understand. Then maybe together we can find that integrating purpose. But as you know, the tendency is to go in to argue and debate to win over the other. So that is the first step. I think. We've got the Participatory Dialogues next, and I'm sure we'll go further with some of these inquiries. I just want to let two people at least name their thoughts, and then I think we're going to stop for a break.

Speaker:

I used to work in the Norfolk Re-entry Council. They had a subgroup that came up with resource pamphlets for four different over-arching things. They were instrumental for me because I could pass them on to my guys saying, *Have you seen these pamphlets? You can get help with that.* And they were like, *Wow!* It was amazing.

Jane:

Whitney, a brief comment, and then we're going to have our break.

Whitney:

My enquiry was around something that came up in the break-out, and again just now. *How do you bring stakeholders to the table to engage in dialogue who have no clue what dialogue is, or the foundational skill set? How do you get those folks to engage? Do you set some rules of engagement, about how we're going to interact together?* That seems important with multiple stakeholders and a real challenge.

Jane:

We will leave it there. This may have been materially helpful because you are members of a re-entry council somewhere in VADOC. For others, like Bernhard, you may be trying to take the lessons into other multistakeholder situations. Luckily, we have a couple more hours. Next, we have the Participatory Dialogues and then we come back together for a plenary session at the end of the day.

Peter:

Thank you, Karen, Kathy, Antoinette, Sarah, Alan and Deirdre. Very helpful, and much appreciated.

DAY FIVE

What are Multi-Stakeholder Dialogues?

Why Does Your Organization Need Multi-Stakeholder Dialogues?

PART TWO

Five concurrent participatory dialogues

Thumbnail sketches

Thumbnail sketches to introduce the seven Participatory Dialogues that follow:

Ali English APDP (UK) and Jane Ball APDP, APDPA (UK) raised the value of early engagement with stakeholders to influence strategy. Different stakeholders talking together, and admitting what they don't know, can fill in gaps and naturally lead to innovation. Participants thought that people in multi-stakeholder situations should ponder together to formulate the right question, before embarking on finding a solution. This can lead to creating what they do want, rather than identifying fixes for what they don't want. Early engagement builds trust and understanding – but it's also never too late!

John McKay APDP (USA and Canada) and Mary Morand APDP (USA) explored the implications of exclusion from a multi-stakeholder dialogue. they cited the Grimm fairytale about *The 13th Fairy* who, on being excluded from the blessing ceremony, arrived unannounced and cursed the princess. Implicitly, the common view was to include all for a fully generative outcome. Some felt we might exclude others because we don't want what someone brings, or perhaps a fear of losing our voice in the larger mix – others that it can happen unintentionally. Many felt the 13th fairy could refer to a part of oneself.

Bernhard Holtrop (Sweden) and Jennie Amison APDP (USA) explored the benefits of multi-stakeholder dialogues and the challenges of realising them. One participant pointed out that every dialogue is inherently a multi-stakeholder dialogue, and indeed in this session, there were members of Re-entry Councils who now felt better equipped for the role, others new to the approach and some even suspicious of it. Mainly felt a common need was essential, and all effected should be included. One noted, *Why waste a crisis? It could be the start of a much-needed multi-stakeholder dialogue!*

Elisabeth Razesberger APDP (Belgium) had a small group that considered what is at stake in starting a dialogue in your organization. One issue was whether first to use literal terms to teach dialogue, or to learn by experience which could seem manipulative. The resolution was that either could work, depending on the situation. Of course, you are not being manipulative if you are transparent about what you are doing. If you consider dialogue as a process, rather than an event, then the choice may depend on which approach would allow a more sustained ongoing experience.

Troy Adams APDP (USA) and Eric Fling APDP (USA) asked how dialogue can build better professional relationships. People described positive communication towards a common goal, and a prison officer wanted all officers to learn dialogue given the impact on security. Others referred to the confidence people gain from dialogue as they achieve better results, leading one participant to commit to introducing dialogue into their Re-entry Council. Another stressed the importance of being authentic and seeing from another's perspective, whether or not you know all the dialogue vocabulary.

How Does Early Engagement with Stakeholders Influence Organizational Strategy and Innovation?

Ali English and Jane Ball

PRE-CONFERENCE DESCRIPTION

In a global environment, where change is accelerating, the challenge of developing sound business strategy is complex, multifaceted, and requires an open and adaptable mindset. Assefa Hizkias, a founding member of the Center for Justice and Peacebuilding in Virginia, states that regardless of how complicated problems might appear, it is possible to work through them and find solutions that are mutually satisfactory to every stakeholder. We contend that an early dialogic approach, which progressively engages with multiple perspectives, holds the power to maximise awareness and systemic thinking. That is critical to informing the strategic thinking and innovation that is the lifeblood of every successful organization.

CHECK-OUT

Ali English:

Let's move on to a check-out. Let's think, let's adapt in the moment. We have slightly less time than we might, so let's have maybe a couple of sentences from each person about what's sticking with you from our dialogue today. It might be just one sentence, but not a paragraph. What's sticking with you from our dialogue today? Let me give you a moment to think that out.

Speaker:

The importance of space and time.

Speaker:

I think what I go away with is to try to be open for them to evolve.

Speaker:

What's sticking with me is just that there is hope. This was one of the loveliest experiences of my week! I'm grateful.

Speaker:

It's critical to return to the 'why'. Why are we doing this? What outcomes do we want? Keep in mind the big picture, and if we can all focus on that, we have a chance of getting that.

Speaker:

I kind of follow that. Actually, it's the why and the purpose. Those two are the main things that are really sticking with me through this dialogue as well.

Speaker:

I'm less on the theory and more on the practical list. What's sticking with me? I'm thinking about not just having the multiple stakeholders there to carry out the decision, but to ponder the question before the decision is made.

Speaker:

We need not to be afraid to admit what we don't know, and work with other people to fill in those gaps.

Speaker:

Purpose. When people come together, be really clear about the purpose. The other bit that I'm still mulling links to what was said earlier. There's something going around in my head about where there is similarity, even though it might not be recognized. The word that came to mind for me, for both groups described was that possibly fear is present in each of them, but the fear is for different reasons. There's something about this similarity, even though it shows up differently.

Speaker:

What was said about the slow speed of change in dialogue, and its effect, it's good effect. And then our process and the consideration of Generative Dialogue was very nice for me.

Jane Ball:

A couple of things. One is that you get some innovation simply by having different stakeholders together, it inevitably leads to innovation. Then there is something about a truly generative process that you can enter together, where in an organizational setting I think you do need time and confidence to allow that. Then I'm left with the question asked at the beginning, *Is it ever too early?* I'm thinking we need to keep in mind that it's never too late. If you realise you need to go back to it, and you've got the authority and the potential to do that, you say, *Okay, let's just stop now before we buy any more trains*, and go back to see whether this is going to be helpful or not.

Speaker:

I have this really funny image of stakeholders as people holding stakes or holding puzzle pieces. There is something around the mechanical nature of the words and the way that there's usually a problem like trains that need to be bought, which is a predefined problem. Then I thought of some other initiatives where we really trying to do something generative together. We don't have specific stakeholders because we're not addressing a problem. We want to create a learning environment together. So, we want a specific kind of people, but they don't represent part of the system. That is quite different. That's the way that we eventually start building a world that's not so broken up into problems where we've got to get all the stakeholders in to fix it together.

Speaker:

One thing is that deep listening to each of the stakeholders within your organization and out of your organization is important for making a shared vision. Also, having the same picture and seeing the whole picture. Another thing is that slowing down the thinking is very important for innovation.

Speaker:

I frame my thoughts like my early engagement with my wife. because it was the early engagement that built trust, support and understanding of unmet needs. That's why my early engagement was so important. I like the idea that it's never too late.

Speaker:

I've been writing all your thoughts down. Mine are connection, and the hashtag 'got your back'. The hashtag 'got your back' is from when we ran a very big change program where lots of stakeholders were trying to do experimentation on a big scale in the Standard Chartered Bank. They came back to us with this hashtag 'got your back' because if you feel someone's got your back, it makes a huge difference. I feel like you've all had my back today. Thank you very much — it's very special.

Ali:

> There are two things for me. There's space, the importance of space, and to be able to take the time to say, *I wonder what I've missed. I wonder what else there is out there, that if I just take a little bit of time, or I look under this stone that I've been ignoring for however long, there might be something really beautiful under there.* The other one, for me, is just the innovation that often comes from the ability to adapt. I know that adaptation is not a strength of mine, and every time I do it, I'm always surprised by it. The learning for me is adaptation can be such a gift.
>
> The universe is speaking to us, and it is time for us to close. But first I want to remind you, as we've done every other day, that the recording here will only cover the check-out, and apart from me and Jane, you will just be identified as 'speaker'. Thanks, and bye!

POSTSCRIPT

During our dialogue we wanted to explore the group's experience of stakeholder engagement and the value for organizational strategy and innovation. What follows is a summary of what emerged and what we learnt.

In addressing the powerful impact of early engagement, the group highlighted the profound importance of defining purpose. The emphasis on the purpose and the 'why' underscores the power that clarity and intentionality bring to including stakeholders, and guiding actions and decisions. The value of purpose may be commonly known but we explored beyond that ideal to the practicality of working with stakeholders around a core purpose. Our enquiry raised the necessity both of defining and then iteratively returning to the 'why' and hence coming to understand the deeper motivations and desired outcomes behind our actions. The practice of reflective questioning was considered crucial to encouraging a focus on the bigger picture and fostering a collective effort toward achieving meaningful goals. Also, to achieve meaningful engagement that has the power to influence strategy and innovation, we thought it is essential to make space, invest time and foster meaningful connections as well as generating ideas.

Taking this a little deeper, we saw that meaningful stakeholder engagement asks of us to recognise our limitations and not be afraid to admit what we do not know. We need to work with others to fill those gaps, in service of tapping into the strength found in including different perspectives in collaborative problem-solving. Displaying vulnerability during stakeholder engagement and recognizing underlying similarities, such as common fears, can foster empathy and unity even among seemingly disparate, fragmented groups. In fact, one of the participants did just that, raising a real and immediate issue they were facing that was troubling them. The resulting collaborative problem-solving led participants to notice the stronger sense of connection and fulfilment that such vulnerability fosters, and the benefits that it can bring to collective thinking in the group.

Deep listening was considered essential for developing a shared vision. Listening to understand rather than simply to respond was seen as being pivotal in incorporating diverse perspectives to achieve a holistic view. Similarly, the value of slowing down our thought processes, to notice them and include other perspectives, was acknowledged as crucial for fostering innovation and thoughtful engagement. Early stakeholder engagement not only enriches the decision-making process but also ensures a more inclusive and generative conclusion and outcome. It recognizes the importance of diverse perspectives and expertise in influencing strategy and innovation.

Finally, the dialogue circled back to the themes of space and adaptation, recognizing the potential for discovery and innovation in taking the time to explore uncharted territories and the transformative power of adaptability. The conversation, and the diversion that the group uncovered and welcomed, served as a reminder of the beauty that lies in openness to change, evolution of ideas and the unexpected gifts that adaptation can bring.

Sitting With the Thirteenth Fairy

John McKay and Mary Morand

PRE-CONFERENCE DESCRIPTION

What drives your enquiry? When we think of stakeholders who do we think of first? Who do we bypass in Dialogue? What are the consequences? What is the enquiry about? What is it we don't think about when considering the stakeholders to be invited into a Dialogue and what are the biases, blocks and perceptions that we hold? Why does it matter? What are the consequences? All voices add richness, depth of understanding and power to the dialogic interchange. If we expand the depth and breadth of stakeholder inclusion what will the impact be?

CHECK-OUT

Mary Morand:

I like what you said. If we can't avoid it let's just embrace the journey like we embrace the thirteenth spirit. We're at the point in time where we need to check out. Our check-out is really simple: *What's shifted in you? What has shifted in you as it relates to our dialogue about the thirteenth fairy?*

Speaker:

What has shifted in me is the awareness of possibility and an expansion of awareness. And I have some questions to reflect on, which is enriching.

Speaker:

I feel like there's something that has shifted, but I might not be able to name it just yet. Certainly, a piece of it is wanting to bring more awareness to setting up containers and opening up dialogues with this new awareness and consideration of the exiled voices, the exiled parts of ourselves. That's a new exploration that I really appreciate from this dialogue. There are parts of ourselves that we are pushing away, that we might not want to look at or we might not want in the room. Some parts within the system, within us, are positive, bring joy and are successes. What about the parts that get exiled because we get oriented toward a problem, thereby exiling the recognition of what's already here? That's something that is starting to become more alive for me.

Speaker:

I echo that. What is sitting with me is that the thirteenth fairy is a condition or factor that needs to be thought about and considered.

Speaker:

First, I just want to say, Mary, I think you should read books because you have such a good voice for it! Second, I feel like suspension is what is needed. A lot of times the thirteenth area gets left out because we don't suspend our judgment or believe and what they are going to bring. That was that was what I took away from today.

Speaker:

Someone spoke earlier about the thirteenth fairy being a part of themselves that they didn't allow to come to the table or come to the party. That struck me because we always hold something from being a little introverted. There's always some part of me that's held back something that I have to work on professionally and personally.

Speaker:

What stands out for me the most is how not just the Department of Corrections, but other people that work in other fields and companies, have dealt with that thirteenth fairy. Once people found out what the thirteenth fairy was, it was important to recognize how they might bring it back in. That's what has stuck with me the most.

Speaker:

My thinking about the thirteenth fairy is that it is not somebody we intentionally want to leave out. The word exile was used a lot, and I want to make the point that it's not that we are going to intentionally leave someone out. If somebody gets left out it's not because we thought they were inconvenient, a pain or going to be disruptive, or whatever. You never really want to leave anybody out intentionally. And as a side note, I've got to look into that fairy tale because my daughter's name is Aurora, so we're very much attached to that story.

Peter:

Years ago, I ran a community dialogue in the city of Cambridge. Half the people were offenders who had come out of prison and were under supervision in the community, and they were trying to settle back into the community. The other half were ordinary people in the community, a fireman, a secretary, a housewife, whatever. There were about 20 people in the room every week for a dialogue. Then I proposed inviting a magistrate, who sits in a court and makes decisions about imprisoning people. Most of those under supervision said that they wouldn't come to the meeting if the magistrate came. I suggested we talk about it again the following week. Then, they eventually agreed they would come to the meeting, but they wouldn't talk. The week after that the magistrate came. Of course, it was a brilliant conversation between all of them. The magistrate was explaining that I don't know how to make a sentencing decision if you don't tell me what you need me to know, and so on. What they realised was that they were interdependent. The person they never communicated with, they needed to communicate with much more. They learnt a lot from each other. He carried on in the group and they were very appreciative. What I draw from that first-hand, explicit story is that I think they thought they would lose their voice. I think they voted against the magistrate being there in the dialogue because they wouldn't be able to express themselves. I think that is probably the generic fear about why we would exclude some people. I know that in these annual Academy conferences, when I first advocated inviting prisoners, inmates, to come into the conference, many correctional staff said they would not be able to talk openly if inmates were there. But last year we inmates in the conference, a lot of them, and a few this year, and it all works just fine. So, I think it's the imagined suppression of one's own voice that is probably the key factor in it all.

Speaker:

I just want start by saying thank you to John and Mary. You guys are very capable. I was very appreciative of that in several ways. Your set up in the first place, the holding of the space and the moves you made. A lot of things to appreciate. I don't think there are too many concentrated capacity building efforts to do what we were talking about – the aim to include factors that don't normally get included and to figure out how to do that live and in front of other human beings. I think there are individuals here and there doing it, but I don't think it's a particularly concentrated thing, yet I think it's absolutely essential to get anything significant to happen. This is showing up here, and there's more than just a handful of people involved. I'm really excited about that. I think there's a lot to do, but I think it's showing up which is pretty good.

Speaker:

I just want to really thank everyone for the exciting topic.

John Mckay:

Mary, what's popping up for you?

Mary:

A couple of things. I'll go back to a horizontal and a vertical continuum. For me, the horizontal is that I'm a person who has spent a lot of years working to be right. That comes from a well-learned family system conditioning. Right? So, I love letting go of that and recognizing, and continuing to shift into, the concept of a continuum. And then the vertical continuum is that I think all this work starts with self and feeling empowered around that. I liked the contributions of this group and the openness with and the encouragement of each other. I appreciate that with gratitude. John?

John:

Well, I'm chuckling, because of what you said about always being right. I said to myself, well, I grew up always being wrong. So, what am I going to do with that? I think this conversation today on the concept of the thirteenth fairy continues to pull on my curiosity and my wonderment about what's out there that I'm not hearing and seeing, and that I need to hear and see.

Mary:

Lovely. This was a wonderful experience. I appreciate all of you, your contributions, and your presence. Thank you.

POSTSCRIPT

The Thirteenth fairy is the uninvited, unwanted or forgotten guest. Resenting her exclusion, the thirteenth fairy in Grimm's tale arrives uninvited and casts a spell on the princess. In our dialogue, we opened to what might get in our way of recognizing and embracing this *inconvenient guest* who holds power and promise.

Consider that the thirteenth fairy can be friend or foe, and an inconvenient guest all the same. Perhaps she is inconvenient because we simply forgot to include her, or inconvenient because she is "trouble", or inconvenient because he "gets in the way." And like the thirteenth fairy, if excluded, she can make her presence known! And without the inconvenient guest, our dialogic work is not whole.

So, how can we identify the thirteenth fairy within our dialogic process? How might we open ourselves to receive him or her? In the dialogue we saw the thirteenth fairy in organizational, in group and in individual form. Each of these lenses serves to identify stakeholders and perspectives so that we can invite them all to the party.

Upon further reflection, we submit that a thirteenth fairy resides in each of us. For example, it could be one's conditioned tendency to pull away that keeps one from sharing one's voice during controversy. How would the dialogue change if one were able to bring that part of oneself forward? What part of our own self have we exiled or denied? What if we were able to bring that part of us to the dialogue? And further, what don't I know about myself that I haven't let go of yet?

We all have something at play fears, hopes, biases, aspirations-all parts of the human experience. With self-awareness, we can notice ourselves and skilfully choose how we listen, voice, respect and suspend during dialogue. Our best presence creates the opening in us that enables our extension to others, including any "inconvenient guests". The whole will always be better.

All of this brings us into reflection about the containers we co-create. We bring ourselves and our tendencies; we bring others and their tendencies; we bring organizational history and certainly organizational culture. All fellow travellers in Dialogue creating together what's possible.

What are the Benefits of Multi-Stakeholder Dialogues – and the Challenges to Realising Them?

Bernhard Holtrop and Jennie Amison

PRE-CONFERENCE DESCRIPTION

Every organization, and every human, derives its relevance from being and functioning in contact with its surroundings. For an organization this entails employees, clients, customers, suppliers, partners, etc. To be relevant and effective both as organization, as well as ‚chain‘ of organizations, attunement (of processes, logistics) and trust (between people) are essential. How can multi-stakeholder Dialogues contribute to this? What could they look like? What concrete benefits do we envision with Multi-stakeholder Dialogues? What challenges and potential pitfalls do we see?

CHECK-OUT

Jennie Amison:

Now we want to move to the check-out. We have a closing statement, and then we move into the check-out so that people have enough time. The check-out is going to be recorded and transcribed because it‘s going to be a part of a publication, but your names or will not be included – just those of the co-facilitators. So, we have 15 minutes.

Speaker:

You know if it is recorded, they are going to recognize my voice, and yours. So, I‘m going to keep it short. Listening to the other voices in the room, I‘m wondering if Peter and Jane might want to consider some parameters for this multi-stakeholder dialogue. I‘m hearing that using the term stakeholder has some connotations in and of itself. It doesn‘t sound like any of our regular dialogues, but I don‘t know. They are always open to new dialogic paths, like, for example, the Resettlement Journey, and Working Dialogues. And there‘s probably a bunch more that I don‘t know about. So, I‘m going to reserve any great love for the term multistakeholder dialogue, until I understand who decides in a situation like that, who picks the stakeholders? Because the person that picks the stakeholders suddenly has a lot of power. If we're trying to find a location for a transition home for females, people might show up just because they can make some money off this, you know. It really does have a business connotation. So that's my sense. I appreciate everything, everybody said, and I am proud of myself for listening.

Speaker:

I have really enjoyed this dialogue with you. For me, it is going into unknown territory. I've really been listening and appreciating all the different perspectives. This was very useful. Thank you all.

Speaker:

I learned a lot about different perspectives that I didn't get the chance to share. I felt that the pace was but a bit fast for me. I would like to share my understanding about dialogue. I think dialogue is, itself, always involved with different stakeholders. I feel it is, itself, a modest multi-stakeholder dialogue. When I relate to a company, for example, a team, they might have dialogue within the team. And the whole project might have dialogues with different departments that are involved. If we say multi-stakeholder dialogue it points, for example, to the idea that the project might bring benefits to another project or an upcoming project. Might we invite the other project people to join this dialogue so that they might learn from it and avoid some more mistakes in their project? Or in similar projects that could extend into other projects, or even across organizations. You cannot always pick, you can only invite others to see if they have the interest or willingness to join. I think that's my understanding of multi-stakeholder dialogues.

Speaker:

I have enjoyed the conversation, and it's been really enlightening. When we did a multi-stakeholder dialogue, we didn't label it multi-stakeholder because we didn't even know about dialogue. They learnt the language in the dialogue, and I really like to point out the unknown here. So that was a real, *Aha*, moment for me. I've enjoyed all of you today.

Speaker:

I hope one of the things that will come out of this is, *How are we going to put this approach into practice?* I look forward to conversations about sharing new ideas and new ways of accomplishing our goals.

Speaker:

It was interesting to observe the process, especially in the later phase when we were all trying to make meaning of the words 'multi-stakeholder dialogue'. That made me think, *How do dialogues work?* What if there is information missing and the person who came up with the expression in the first place is not here to tell us? So, we were constructively trying to make meaning of it, and we've come up with so many ideas.

Speaker:

I want to offer a by-stand as a check-out. I was originally scheduled for a different Participatory Dialogue, but it was cancelled right beforehand for lack of subscription. They opted to reallocate people, and I chose this group because it had the most diverse international participation. I want to point that out because I think it's interesting that despite the broad commonality here, we're all interested in this idea of multi-stakeholder dialogue. We are not sure what it is, but we're all interested in it.

Speaker:

I came here for Bernhard, I wanted to hang out with him a little bit, and to make his life difficult, so I check off that box! I do like to have a sense of what I'm doing, and I've not used the word before, so like others said, multi-stakeholder dialogue was new territory for me. They are words that get thrown around a lot. I thought it was important to get an understanding of it because I've even been asked to do multi-stakeholder dialogue in corporations. I thought, *Okay, it's good to know what I'm doing if somebody's asking me to do it.* The sense that I now make is that it seems worthwhile to do when there's clearly something at stake. For example, if there is a shared waterhole, and the water is drying out, and a lot of people are affected, including lodges and industry and so on, then it makes sense to me. If there's a clear agenda and centre to it, and the people all have stakes in it. That's the most sense I could make of it today. It is nice to listen to people and their different views. I like diversity. I thoroughly enjoyed myself today.

Speaker:

I will take with me the need to establish shared meaning.

Speaker:

I'll be carrying with me greater clarity on how many different people are involved in the work that needs to be done in the near future. How important it is to be intentional in inviting all voices, especially being acutely aware and careful to remain vigilant for the voices who haven't been heard.

Jennie:

Well, I want to thank you all. Firstly, for participating in this dialogue. It really opened my eyes to some things about the use of language and how important that is. People can easily misinterpret what is meant. This has been very rewarding for me. It has helped me because I sit on a re-entry council in Harrisonburg, Virginia, and I see some things that now, having heard your voices, I will go into differently. Thank you for that. I appreciate it.

Bernhard Holtrop:

I take away three things. Be sure that the persons at the end of the line, those who are really affected by it, are involved. Then the process, the theory, the structure, the thing, the challenge of how to do it. The idea of a fractal was coming up, starting dialogically to decide what the dialogue should be about, and who should be in there. Then let it grow. Allow it to grow, and then get into the dialogue. It is a recurring fractal process that I see for such a multi-stakeholder dialogue. And I agree with the comment made that a multi-stakeholder dialogue is very good for never wasting a crisis. When the shit hits the fan, that's a good opportunity for having a multi-stakeholder dialogue. Thanks very much, y'all!

POSTSCRIPT

Multi-stakeholder dialogues have some challenges. People and/or organizations most probably will make their own voluntary choice to join. Since, as the word explains, it is a dialogue between people who hold different 'stakes', and so they may be coming from different organizations and backgrounds, and with different agendas.

When someone makes a call to convene people to talk, it is important to address the shared concern, issue or opportunity. A good starting moment for a multi-stakeholder dialogue therefore is when a clear crisis or opportunity arises. This brings the participants more easily around the table.

Then there is the question of who is doing the call, and who is to be invited. We realised that initiating things brings you into a powerful position. Too powerful for a true dialogue, perhaps? It is therefore good even to overthink the ignition – process, and the challenge of how to set this process in motion and how to spread engagement and co-ownership from the beginning. The idea of a fractal pattern came up, starting with a dialogue in a small group, in which the wording around the 'why' of the shared concern and opportunity can evolve. Then the same with the 'who' to invite, where this thinking fractal process could be repeated, gradually enlarging the group and sharpening the 'why'. Allow it to grow, considering both the group to be involved and the subject to be explored. Of course, we need to be sure that the persons at the end of the line, those who are really affected by it, are invited and involved. There may come a time when the group will have to limit itself to those already invited, and to the 'why' already defined. We recognise that inevitably some people will not feel involved. After this fractal beginning, the actual dialogue can start around the content.

A few thoughts about applications, both inside and outside an organization. When starting inside, for example, perhaps allow a project that other people can join, think and learn along with everyone else. This might seed future projects or bring benefits to an upcoming project. Might we invite people from other projects to join this dialogue so that they might learn from it, and perhaps avoid mistakes and recognise opportunities in their own project? We could work across similar projects, or even across different organizations. Again here, you cannot pick, you can only invite, to see if they have the interest or willingness to join.

Overall, we see the enormous need and potential for this kind of dialogue. Since no organization is standing in solitude in its surroundings and in the world. The art of connecting purposes, in service of a higher goal than our own, will be more and more a challenge and an enormous potential in the future to come.

Starting a Dialogue in Your Organization: What is at Stake?

Elisabeth Razesberger

PRE-CONFERENCE DESCRIPTION

We can all bring Dialogue into our work environments. What might end as successfully bringing all stakeholders together, starts with many questions and challenges. Are we ready to hear all the stakeholders? Is there an agreement about what should be achieved? Getting ready for a Stakeholder Dialogue means connecting people, interests, and structures. How can this work in either a very large organization or in a very small one?

CHECK-OUT

Elisabeth Razesberger:

> We are approaching the last ten minutes of this session, and we have heard a few scenarios about how we approach introducing dialogue amongst different stakeholders. We have also discussed how to create dialogue experiences. I would now like to hear what you're taking away from this session. Have you learned anything?

Speaker:

> I guess I'm taking away people's enthusiasm. I really liked the idea of calling it a process or an approach versus calling it a dialogue. We talked about functional leadership, and while I have my own team and can set the frame there, I'm also part of a leadership team and the rest of my leadership team is a hot mess. I cannot get through to them, and we meet a lot. They say to me, *I want my team to look like your team*, but I just can't bring everyone together. A lot of it has to do with schedules. We just put out fires, and we don't have time collectively to make changes within the organization, although we all know it's bad. So that's something for me to think about for the future. I'm going to be buying them all some new literature and we're going to get this to work. I am going to get them on the same page with me because I think

that there's something that is missing. This session was really, really good. I've learned a lot. I like knowing that you don't necessarily have to use the terms and you can use dialogue without having that foundation. Everyone doesn't have to have that foundation.

Speaker:

My takeaway is that sometimes you don't really have to use the literal terms. You just call it a process, or not call it anything. Just meet and internally realize that we are kind of following those practices in our head, without necessarily communicating that we are doing that, and in order to achieve the outcome, sometimes we may need to keep things to ourselves and not communicate so much. Just find a common ground and try to work through that.

Speaker:

I have had lots of Aha! moments. I believe that there are lots of ways to reach dialogue. I am aware that I don't have to use all the terms. I just need to transfer the concepts by teaching people about the terms and asking, *What is suspension, finding your voice*, and things like that? I felt like a person who probably didn't know where they were going. Now I can see other ways, which is fantastic, and I find it very suitable and useful for my society. So, thank you very much.

Elisabeth:

What makes sense to you now following our dialogue? Is there something that you can take away?

Speaker:

Realistically, it seems like there were two groups that were saying the direct opposite of each other, although there was also some merging together. What I took from one group is more about educating individuals about the dialogic practices. Meanwhile, the others were saying they didn't want to use those words. What is coming to my mind is that may be more about addressing the manipulation piece, where you try to get people to experience dialogue without teaching it. But I think that in some sense, you are still educating someone about something that they are not aware of or familiar with.

During this whole conference, I've been trying to get a grip or an idea about how to use everything that I've learned. About how to align the staff perspective so that I can take it back to my director for it to be utilised. From my standpoint, my voice isn't loud enough yet. Because it's not loud enough, nothing moves. Nothing gets done. So, the dialogic leadership day was really a very heavy day for me. A lot of you are in leadership roles, so your voice is automatically heard – naturally – because of the title that you hold. But when your title doesn't hold much weight, it is difficult to be heard. I plan to speak in the big group, which I've been nervous about all week. I think that I've learned so much that I think I should say something. So yes, thank you all.

Speaker:

If I may just clarify something. What you heard from one group versus the other group is not opposing, they're more situational. What we were saying is that in some instances you set out to educate and to teach dialogue but sometimes you are not in a position to educate and to teach, so you practice it without naming it and without telling them what it is. You just do it – and you can sometimes get the same results – as opposed to spending time teaching as well. It's all situational and about moving people towards common ground, regardless of the approach that you take. And one piece of advice is never to underestimate your voice. Never underestimate your voice. Most of the changes that we have made in the Virginia Department of Corrections in the last 13 years came from dialogic sessions that began at the lowest levels in the districts and institutions. We have records to show all of the dialogues that led to the changes. So don't underestimate your voice!

Elisabeth:

In conclusion, I would like to make one remark about manipulating people. It's not manipulation if you're transparent about what you're doing. If I say I want to hear you, I am clear about my intentions. If I say to the group, *Let's look at this from an outside perspective'* it's also clear what we're doing. I personally believe more in learning through experience than learning through teaching, and therefore I prefer facilitating dialogue programmes through experiences rather than through teaching concepts in a more academic manner. Thank you all for your presence.

POSTSCRIPT

On the last day of the conference, formal introductions were no longer necessary. Many people had met in one way or another – either through dialogues or through having been introduced as speakers. This was therefore an opportunity to have a more informal, personal introduction round to set the tone and make connections. At the beginning of the session, we shared stories about what we looked forward to doing during the upcoming weekend. It turned out most of us were looking forward to clearing leaves from the garden or driveway. This could be taken only as an indication of the timing of the conference, in autumn, but with further enquiry it also revealed a variety of different tools and preferences on how people preferred to address a task. Working methods ranged from an ecofriendly rechargeable state-of-the-art leaf blower to a simple rake. The dialogue provided a lovely short glimpse into our choices and habits, and to a certain extent our different ways of working.

The session was attended by a small number of people, which allowed space for participants to describe individual scenarios as well as the challenges of bringing together stakeholders and their different ways of working for a dialogue. The participants' practice fields covered many levels of experience and very diverse organizational backgrounds. Some of them were just starting to get a grip on what dialogue can change in an organization, others were halfway there in bringing dialogue into practice, and there were participants who had already seen the benefits of introducing a dialogic culture into an organization.

One of the issues raised was the identification of the stakeholders. It is essential to clarify the situation you are looking at from the very beginning. This can be less obvious than one would assume as it involves shedding light on who is pulling the strings. Dialogue meetings can be used to help recognise who needs to be included to bring about change.

Another point of concern was how to engage stakeholders in dialogue and how to create open-minded attitudes for cooperation. For example, how do you start a process in a context where the stakeholders are not committed to collaborating? In a context of high tension or hostility, it can help to introduce elements of dialogue in existing meetings without using any references to theory or the jargon used by many dialogue practitioners or consultants. The same is applicable to contexts where the stakeholders are not (yet) open to declaring that they want to learn together. That way, stakeholders can move slowly without fear of rocking the boat too much.

The comments made during the closure of the session reveal the richness of this short meeting. To me, the smallness of the group within the context of a big gathering was an unexpected gift. I dare to suggest the other participants shared that feeling.

How Dialogue Can Build Professional Relationships

Troy Adams, Eric Fling

PRE-CONFERENCE DESCRIPTION

Organizations need positive relationships with many stakeholders to be successful. Creating good first impressions is crucial when building relationships with stakeholders. Dialogic check-ins can help organizational leaders introduce themselves in a positive way to potential new stakeholders. Once rapport has been created, successful working relationships can be built using formal Dialogues. Longevity is the key factor for both the organization and the stakeholders to become and remain profitable. Fragmentation between organizations and stakeholders is the cause of many problems that lead to the loss of profits. However, functional working relationships can be maintained through dialogic communication. Dialogic practices such as Intervention Dialogue and Working Dialogue can help solve most problems that could hinder successful relationships. Dialogue promotes unity, and unity creates power, which in turn leads to success.

CHECK-OUT

Troy Adams:

> I think it's time to move into a check-out. Eric, do you have a check-out ready?
>
> **Eric Fling:** The check-out question is 'As a result of today's discussion, what are your thoughts about the use of dialogue to build professional relationships?'

Speaker:

> I think it can only help to support better professional relationships. For me, the tenets of dialogue help to foster not only positive communication but also move people towards a shared, common goal. I think if you use those tenets in any way, in any relationship that you may have, it's always going to be positive and successful.

Speaker:

My thoughts about the use of dialogue to build professional relationships are that I feel it's great to use, it is knowledgeable, and it is something that I didn't really know to look into when I started. I'm with the Department of Corrections. When I started, someone who was incarcerated came to me and told me that I was using dialogue without me even knowing it. That made me want to know more about dialogue because I was told I was using something that I had no knowledge of. It helped me get information when speaking to people, and to grab resources. It built my confidence. It built a lot of things. So, my thought is that it's been very useful for me in building professional relationships.

Speaker:

What I'm thinking is that the perfect communication is very important. It depends on how I'm using dialogue, regardless of whether other people are familiar with the skills or not. If I am trying to use them it seems to work. If someone doesn't know about dialogue or the strategies I am using, it can still help the other person to communicate well.

Speaker:

I have two takeaways. First, I believe that the more I try to conduct communication using dialogue the better the outcomes I receive. The second take-away, given the story we heard, is that I will try to find a dentist who is familiar with dialogue!

Speaker:

I think that my main thought is not to focus so much on the roles, and more on the purpose of dialogue. The purpose of dialogue is for us to be able to have effective communication. We know the rules, we use them and the more we do use them with those that don't necessarily know the rules the more it will serve its purpose of creating effective communication.

Speaker:

I think dialogue is so important, and just like you said, it works even without knowing what you're doing with all the different model names and everything. I think we get caught up with them. It is about being authentic and being honest in any relationship, whether it is business or personal. As long as you apply those personal tools, like treating people how you want to be treated, and all of those other things, you will be processing and applying those dialogic tools helpfully.

Speaker:

Well, everybody said what I was going to say, and every idea that I was going to put into the check-out. Very well done by everybody. I would say, because it just really didn't really dawn on me until now, that it is different for me because I'm still transitioning into my new role in the community. I've been there since February and being in all these Re-entry Council meetings makes me think maybe I need to look into potentially adding dialogue into that structure a little bit. They are already using some of the dialogue methods, but maybe I'll put more definition to it for them. It might make things a little more productive.

Troy:

I appreciate what I've learned today. I've been doing dialogue for a few years now, yet I learn so much every single time that I listen to other people. What Eric said got me to tune in and listen a lot. You have all really made me think about how I define dialogue in some situations, and maybe sometimes we need to use some of the other skills without really worrying too much about the process. So instead of always saying that we've got to use certain skills, there may be times that we need to just use more suspension and listening. Maybe just have a conversation, and not move into a dialogue all the time. It also made me think that I've got lots of different skills, and not to use the same skill for every situation. There may be more times that I'm going to use the practice of suspension, and then in other situations, I may need to move into a different mode, maybe even a monologue. A monologue might be more helpful than a dialogue in some situations. What you guys said has really made me think a lot about using other aspects of dialogue.

Eric:

I agree. You hit the nail on the head about how we can get caught up with the names of the actions, the practices and the whole vocabulary of dialogue. While they are important, my personal opinion is that it's much more important to be genuine, authentic and honest. Be true to yourself – whilst also allowing yourself to see another person's perspective, their point of view. Try to understand why they have that perspective, why they see the world the way they do. When you're able to let down your guard and suspend, you open yourself up to a world of knowledge that you probably have never encountered before, right? Now you are becoming more worldly. It sounds like a cliche, but it's true. There are many forms of dialogue. Many forms. We heard about common ground, we heard about integrity and honesty, and being true to yourself. Non-verbal communication and communicating as a whole. Eddie has a great point as well. He and I have both been through many years of dialogue. When I went into the accreditation program at the beginning of last year, after being a regional facilitator and a regional lead for many years, I didn't know how much more there was to learn about dialogue. Suddenly, in this program, I felt like, *Oh, my gosh! I know nothing about dialogue!* That's the beauty of it. Regardless of how much you study and learn about dialogue, there's always more to learn. It's not that that I have my dialogue degree – there's really no such thing – but because there's always continuous learning.

Speaker:

I agree with everyone about dialogue. As far as working relationships are concerned, it is more important than people realize. A lot of people in my field have the mindset that they just want to go to work, do their job and go home. But in our line of work, there's a lot more to it than that because we are trying to make sure that security comes first. We're also working with re-entry. You must be able to communicate with people. That is the most important thing for us as officers. Whenever the inmates see that we are not of one accord, they can play on that. When you have those officers who really talk too much, and to the wrong people, they cause trouble. A lot of the information that inmates get, they get from officers and other staff members. You must know when to communicate, how to communicate, what to communicate and who to communicate with. That is huge in my line of work. It would do the working environment a whole lot of good, in my opinion, if a lot more officers and staff members learned dialogue. Then they would understand what it really means to use dialogue and utilize the tools that dialogue comes with.

POSTSCRIPT

Organizations must create and maintain many positive relationships to be successful. The best way to develop this rapport with important stakeholders is through using dialogue. However, it is important to not only consider dialogue as a mode of conversation but also as a set of skills to promote crucial conversation. When used properly by organizational leaders, dialogic skills can be beneficial even with stakeholders who do not have a knowledge or understanding of dialogue.

The purpose of dialogue is to promote effective communication. Often it may be better for organizational leaders not only to focus on their roles but rather on the purpose of a dialogue. When organizational leaders are proficient with dialogue and use it with those who do not necessarily know the rules, a dialogue will still serve its purpose of providing effective communication. Stakeholders will usually pick up on the dialogic structure surprisingly quickly and they may begin to use the skills without even recognizing they are doing so.

The appropriate use of dialogue is especially important in institutional settings such as prisons and correctional facilities. Correctional employees have responsibilities that reach far beyond punching a time clock, completing a task and clocking out. The security and safety of the facility and people's futures are all at stake in such environments. Therefore, the appropriate use of dialogue and a show of unity by staff are crucial factors, which are related directly to people's success upon re-entry into society. When the wrong people get the wrong information, or when classified information is compromised it can cause big problems. Correctional employees must know when to communicate, how to communicate, what to communicate and who to communicate with. For this reason, staff in these settings need a knowledge of what it really means to use dialogue appropriately and how to best utilize the dialogic tools.

Skilful dialogic conversation includes many tools that help make business conservations successful. Organizational leaders should use strong relevant check-ins to create good first impressions with new stakeholders. The mode of monologue may be useful when introducing one's organization and its mission to new cliental. Subsequently, the conversation may be moved into the mode of dialogue to take the conversation into a deeper level of understanding between the organizational leaders and the stakeholders.

During conversations with stakeholders, suspension and listening may be the most valuable tools that organizational leaders could use. These skills allow others' voices to be heard, which may bring new ideas, perspectives and points of view into the conversation. This in turn may introduce a wealth of knowledge that organizational leaders may have never considered otherwise.

Once prosperous relationships have been developed, longevity is the key for both the organization and the stakeholders to remain profitable. Fragmentation is the cause of most problems that lead to loss of profits for both the organization and the stakeholders. Dialogue encourages the process's honesty and authenticity. If you apply respectful personal tools, such as valuing another's genuine voice and treating people the way you want to be treated, you will be applying the tools usefully. Dialogue helps to foster positive communication. It also encourages people to continue to move forward toward a shared goal, which in turn promotes successful lasting relationships.

DAY FIVE

What are Multi-Stakeholder Dialogues?
and Why Does Your Organization Need Multi-stakeholder Dialogues?

PART THREE

Co-hosted plenary session

HOSTS

Jane Ball APDP, APDPA (UK) – Dialogue Associates and Academy of Professional Dialogue

Peter Garrett APDP, APDPA (UK) – Dialogue Associates and Academy of Professional Dialogue

Jane Ball:

Welcome back! I had an interesting time in the Participatory Dialogue with Ali and others. I hope yours went well. I want to give you a few minutes, maybe two or three, to journal before we move into our final hour of the conference. This is a chance to capture whatever is landing for you right now about multi-stakeholder dialogue work. We will take a couple of minutes quietly.

The participants journalled for two minutes quietly.

Jane Ball:

Please could you finish off, because we are going to change direction?

Speaker:

Mr Clarke! It's so good to see you this week at the conference.

Harold Clarke:

Thank you. It's good to be here to be educated.

Peter Garrett:

You may not be aware that Harold Clarke retired recently from his role as Director of the Virginia Department of Corrections. He did not have the chance to speak with all the 13,000 staff members there before he left, unsurprisingly, so I think he's enjoying seeing some of the faces now, and people are enjoying acknowledging him. That's what that little sequence was.

Speaker:

It really is a treat for us, because I didn't expect to see him. I did see his name on a couple of sessions, but to have him be a part of the whole week is amazing! I sent a text to my manager. I said, *I got a real treat this week.*

Peter:

Okay? Good. We would still like to be reflective, and now we want to think back on the whole five days. To do so, Jane and I will tell a story that covers all five aspects of the conference. I invite you to write on your page, or type on your screen, the themes of the five days of the conference, with space to add your thoughts. They are: *1. What is Dialogue? 2. What is Dialogic Leadership? 3. What is Dialogic Decision-Making? 4. What is Dialogue Culture? 5. What are Multi-stakeholder Dialogues?* The conference will finish soon, and in a day or two you might want to look back and say, there is something about that theme that I want to reflect on further, but I can't remember what it was. So, this can serve as a note to remind yourself. Jane and I will tell a short story, a true story, and the idea of the story is to evoke your memory in all these different areas. After our story, we want to place you in break-out rooms of five people for perhaps 15 minutes to digest things, and then we'll be all together in a plenary session for the remaining time. You are welcome to follow our story, and you are welcome to be distracted and write down what you're thinking about or what you are interested in. We will cover all five themes, that's our plan anyway, and we have a tough timekeeper!

Harold:

I am confirming that you have 15 min for your story.

Peter:

Thank you, sir. We want to acknowledge a friend called Steve Holland. I first met Steve when he was in the senior leadership team of an English prison. If you are not from corrections, you might prefer to think of it as the senior leadership team of a business. I liked him a lot. It was not that he was the most intelligent or the most talented individual, but his strength was that he was good and solid. At the time I was running a dialogue in his high-security prison, and I thought he might be interested. So, I said, *Why don't you come and see what we're doing?* In the dialogue group at that time we had inmates, members of uniformed security staff, treatment and other people all talking and thinking together. It was a real mixture. After the dialogue, he came up to me and said, *That was amazing!* He had come and participated well, and he saw what it was about. He said, *I could do my work in the prison in a completely different way!* He got it. He tried a little bit, and his bosses didn't much like it, but after a year or so he was given his own prison where he was now in charge.

Jane:

The prison he was now in charge of was what we in this country call a failing prison, or a failing business. There were 136 prisons in England and Wales at the time, and in the performance table it was right near the bottom, at number 135. It was pretty bad all around. It had a history of bad union relationships. It had issues around security. There was what the inspectors called a complacent staff. This was Steve's first job in charge of a prison, and he was taking on quite a difficult situation. He is very much a relationship-based leader, so he started off with building relationships with people. He quickly found that his leadership team really wasn't up to scratch. A quick example. The first time

I visited the prison one of his leadership team members showed me around the prison. When incarcerated men asked him questions, he said, *Don't ask me – I'm the chaplain.* (The chaplain is like a religious vicar within the prison.) He was so convincing that I thought he was the chaplain, and I only found out later he was really a leader in the prison, and this was his way of avoiding having to answer prisoners' questions.

Peter:

We said to Steve, *You have got to get the right people at the top. This is a tough job, and if you don't have the right group at the top, you're not going to make it.* We didn't see him for maybe nine months until he had found the right people for his senior leadership team. Then we invited his team of seven or eight to come to our offices and worked with them on the recent history of that prison. We asked, *What had happened throughout their time in that prison?* We chaptered it according to the various governors (or wardens) in charge and worked out what it was like in each chapter. It began as a Victorian prison. When was that? When did it begin?

Jane:

1880.

Peter:

It was rundown into a mess. But it wasn't a mess by chance, it was a mess because particular things had happened, chapter by chapter. So, we walked through the chapters together. *Why did we do that with them?* Because that leadership team needed to have one common understanding of their organization. When they engaged the staff members, they needed to know the whole story because staff members had lived through it. The staff held the history, and that history could not be overruled or overlooked. It needed to be understood and incorporated.

Jane:

And meanwhile, the pressure was on. Because it was a so-called failing prison, there was a threat that it would be privatized, and taken out of government management. So, it was taken into a government-led performance improvement process. That put an awful lot of pressure on the place because nobody who works for the government wants to go and work for the private corrections sector in the UK. The other thing we were doing at the same time as the top-down work was bottom-up work. Steve knew we wanted to end up including the incarcerated men in dialogues, so we started to use the opportunities that we had to get some of those dialogues moving. They were doing a consultation with prisoners around education, so we introduced a dialogic process for that and did some dialogues there. Also, Steve started some dialogues between himself and his staff as a way of building up his rapport and understanding of the culture from the staff's point of view.

Peter:

They had no strategy. They were really very good in a few areas, and really seriously bad in others. Whenever he said, we've got to improve in some area, staff said, *No, we don't*, and pointed to something they did well. So, we worked with them for a couple of days on their strategy. In the end, we condensed their wordy version down to a sequence of four words. That was a good move. The bottom word was, *comply*. If we are non-compliant, we are not going to survive, and the government will privatize the prison. So, in all these areas, we need to comply with requirements. The second word was, *perform*. Once you are complying, do so on a regular and reliable basis. The third word was, *serve*. Do what you do on a regular and reliable basis and do it in a way that helps others do what they are trying to do. And the last was *shine*. Shine means, keep improving until you are the best in the country! Those four words *comply, perform, serve,* and *shine* were used to define the next step in every area of the prison. It was a simple way of saying what to aim for next. It was surprisingly helpful. Steve physically put those four words onto the four steps the staff members walked up as they entered the prison every day! Every member of staff walked up the strategy every day to get into the prison. It was clear as a bell what he was asking them to do.

Jane:

Steve was also really keen on delegating the decision-making authority. That meant involving people in making a decision, as we've been talking about this week, but it also meant handing off the decision so that people could be generative and innovative within their particular area. He put quite a low-level management supervisor in charge of the segregation unit, and gave him the kind of authority to ask, *How can this be made into a very, very different place within the prison?* Lots of innovative things started to happen as a result. So how did it go? The auditors came back after we had been working with them for about 18 months, and the prison went from being 135th out of 136 to now being 35th in the performance table, So, it had leapt up a hundred places. What's more, that is the highest it could go for the type of prison it was. It was the best-performing prison of its type across all measures, including security, and in the quality of prison life, it was the second highest-scoring prison of any kind. All the measures went up. It was absurdly successful.

Peter:

We held a staff party to celebrate after getting the results. 85% of the staff came to that party. There was dancing, and everyone had to buy their own drinks and so on. They wanted to celebrate! 85% of them came. Others were still running the night shift in the prison. It was a victory that they had all earned themselves and they were proud of it.

Harold:

Jane, Peter, you have 5 min to conclude.

Jane:

Okay, thanks. We should go into the prison engagement, then. This was a men's prison. Men were incarcerated there. Steve wanted engagement between his staff and the men incarcerated in the prison and was very careful about how he might introduce it. Then one day, there was meant to be a dialogue between staff and the leadership within the prison. The prison was understaffed that day, and so we were told, *There is no way, we can't do it*, the meeting would have to be postponed. So, we said, *Well, why don't we bring some of the imprisoned men in instead?* And Steve, with one of his other leadership team members, could come and talk to some of the men who are incarcerated there. So, we did that. Then, as we were sitting talking, two officers managed to free themselves up and walked into the room. They looked very concerned because that grouping wasn't what they were expecting. We all felt it was a bit of a mistake. They sat down with us looking very uncomfortable all the way through. At the end of the session, they came up to me and the colleague I was with, and we thought there are going to let us know they are quite upset. But no! They said, *Man, that was amazing! I can't believe it. I've never heard any of our guys talk like that before.* So, despite being dumped into it, really, the dialogue had the same impact on them as it had done with Steve all those years before.

Peter:

You can hear Jane's careful involvement with everyone involved. We found there were many of what we called 'high repeat offenders. They were not long enough in or out of jail, to get any sustained treatment, yet they caused a lot of expensive damage. What we did was to track them into the community. We already had dialogues in prison for them, and then we set up dialogues in the community, which may echo some of your re-entry process in Virginia. So, there were regular dialogues in prison every week, and then we had them in the community. First it was for men now living in hostels, getting accommodation for one night at a time. Then we began one for ex-prisoners in sheltered accommodation and finally for when they had their own accommodation. Into those dialogues, we drew the police, who were seriously interested in connecting with the men they were regularly arresting. We drew in the local Council, who provided accommodation, treatment, and so on, and Probation. We not only drew them into the dialogues, but we involved them. We got representatives of the different agencies to come into the prison and taught them how to facilitate dialogues in the prison. We had police officers in uniform coming in as facilitators to facilitate the dialogues in the prison. They found it really valuable as a part of their regular day's work. They benefitted from coming in and meeting the people that they were arresting, getting to know and understand them and their families. It was a remarkable process.

Jane:

It is important to say that we established a Governance Board that managed that whole process. We had the chief officer level from prisons, police, housing and drug treatment running the board. Then we had an Operational Management Group, and the operational managers gave permission to act on the feedback they received in order to improve their own service. And then at the third level, we had the Facilitation Group, who are the people sitting with the men in the prison dialogues, and with them in the community dialogues, thinking about their re-entry, and how to make that successful.

Peter:

Resettlement was significant to these agencies. The big thing was that the police and other agencies believed it was their 'day job' to be involved. If dialogue was an extra, it would fail in the end. You can't do your job and, in addition, do the dialogue. It won't survive. You've got to actually produce results from the dialogues on a regular basis. And they found results through this work – significant improvements in their measures. If, when Steve Holland first came into the dialogue and recognised that he could do his work quite differently, we had proposed where we would end up, he would not have believed it. We wouldn't have believed it either! It's just step by step, step by step. We've described how dialogue works, and how it worked in this situation. It can work anywhere! It works if the culture becomes one that has a dialogic decision-making process, and people come to hold a common story. So, the question is, *What's your next step?* Don't aim for the moon – aim for the right next step, and lo and behold, the step after that will reveal itself.

Harold:

Concluding statement, Jane.

Jane:

Yeah. So, we are inviting you to think about your next step. You will be in a break-out room with five people, and you'll have a chance to talk for 20 minutes and reflect on that together. Thank you, Harold.

Participants went into break-out rooms for 20 minutes.

Peter:

So welcome back. From the sound of people coming back, it seems those were good conversations to have. We have just under a quarter of an hour now to close the conference. The invitation is for those that want to speak up, to close by saying a few final words to all the participants. We will keep aside three or four minutes at the end for us, the co-hosts, and Harold and Bill to say goodbye. Now we're going to open the floor and anyone who'd like to may say something about their experience of the conference, or about the next steps that they have in mind. Please speak up or raise your Zoom hand if that's going to help you to come in.

Speaker:

I just want to say that I'm so grateful to the Virginia Department of Corrections for allowing me to come to the conference, and I am grateful to all the presenters. It was just very, very enlightening.

Speaker:

I would like to say that I've really appreciated being able to network with everyone this week. I learned a lot from different agencies. I've learned a lot from our agency. We're such a large agency that we can't know everyone. This was very impactful, especially since there were people that have never been able to attend the conference before. And the new colleagues, the individuals from CSOSA, I really appreciate all of the things that you have shared with us. We have found an opportunity for us to network in the future and share some different challenges and struggles, and to be able to work together collaboratively, especially with our community partnerships. Here's my email address in the chat so that we can stay connected.

Speaker:

I just would like to repeat what was said about your story, Peter and Jane. It was amazing. I could do my work differently too. I take away lots of different things from today that I can speak about.

Speaker:

I'll go after that and say the same thing that everyone has just said about this whole conference. I am thankful to the Department of Corrections as well as my contractor, for letting me have the space to step away from the institution for a week, to really indulge myself in this conference. Jane and Peter, that story was spectacular. I mean truly, to hear how it works. To see how it works. You guys put it in front of us to really see it.

My biggest takeaway from the conference is to create the space for some of you to come into the facility and speak with the contractor that I work with — to introduce, educate and give the experience of what dialogue really looks like, what it feels like and how healthy it is for a company to have it. I've been so empowered by this conference. I know that I am a stakeholder and that my voice really holds weight, it carries weight. Mr Clarke said to never underestimate my voice. That that means a whole lot to me, to keep going although right now I'm a line staff, but to know that I'm not just boots on the ground, not just a line staff. My voice needs to be heard. So, I'm gonna keep at that. I'm excited about that.

Speaker:

I'll say, thank you all for using your voices. Your expertise is what makes the conference a success. I'm glad to be a part of a learning organization and to know how dialogue works, and the stories that you tell are evidence that it works for other people who don't understand it yet.

Speaker:

I'll add my two cents' worth real quick. I do want to say thank you to Peter and Jane and thank you, Mr. Clarke, for bringing them in and seeing the opportunity that it has brought for our organization. It's really helpful. I did learn a lot throughout this week, and I hope to continue learning. Thank you very much for the opportunity.

Leo:

Just a whole lot of gratitude for this space and for the support to be able to have a voice. I have spent most of my life not having one, so to be able to be here and not just have the space to have a voice, but to be welcomed and encouraged and affirmed through it! And to hear that I was able to inspire some people — that always feels good. I leave carrying with me the importance of voice, and the intentionality of care and inviting people. For everyone in a space to know that their voice is honoured in that place. One thing that I started today with was a stakeholder map. I'm getting ready to go into a big year next year. It is going to be a heavy lift to bring a whole bunch of disparate voices together toward the commonality that I see but that we somehow continue to allow to keep us separated. That is a tangible thing I'm taking with me. One thing I noticed this week was the absence of incarcerated folk from Virginia because last year it was amazing. I want to use this opportunity to invite VADOC to maybe next year bring back some inside folks to have some other voices. And I'll close with just a word of appreciation. Over the last couple of days, I've heard people talk of incarcerated people, incarcerated individuals, as opposed to inmates or prisoners. For those of you who spoke that way, I really thank you for that. I try to be the same way with people who work within institutions. The humanization of people means a lot. So, thank you.

Speaker:

I would just like to say thank you very much for this conference. It has been amazing. I'm so glad to be a part of it and that I was able to meet and network with other people. And I realized that there are some tools that I need to take with me and apply in my journey, in my daily path. I thank Jane and Peter, as well as Mr. Clarke. I'm thankful for the surprise that I got this week by seeing him. But I'm just so grateful for dialogue because it opens up communication, breaks down barriers and knocks down walls so that we can step in and be our individual selves with our own personality.

Speaker:

This is the first time that I have attended the conference. I really appreciate everyone, and I really enjoyed the way the conference kept moving on. I totally feel that I'm in the ring. There are too many things I have learnt to say them all, but I do want to thank everyone, and Peter and Jane also. For the future? I'm thinking that maybe I don't know whether we can manage the technology changes. Now, most people are engaging with the different tools in the technology, and how we can connect through dialogue, given the technology?

Speaker:

I really appreciate this conference. I want to thank all of you for working in these very novel and challenging areas, you have made so much progress with dialogue. I know that Jane and Peter have been working in areas like this for quite a while, and Harold, you created the space. But thank you to all of you for what you do every day. It would be incredible if you could take dialogue into all of the world's incarcerated areas. Please do and improve it and change it. If I can help, I will do so.

Speaker:

I want to say how appreciative I am of the internationality that's here. I have never met a person from Iran ever, and I love that. I have met some Iranian people, and I have seen a face of America that I had never before encountered. I see more now. All we normally see is what the press chooses to show us. I am so pleased to meet people from other parts of Europe and from South Africa, and if there are people here whose countries I have missed then I'm sorry. It has been a real joy for me, as someone who works in a very closed national system, to be with people from other different places. It's been wonderful.

Jane:

Can I invite Harold, Bill and Bobby to raise their hands so that everyone else can see you? I'm going to start by thanking Bobby. We've been going to Bobby all week. Bobby is the person who makes all of this happen. I've said all week that I have the Bat Phone to her at all times! Bobby, you have done a wonderful job in the run-up to the conference, and then in these five days, you have made everything so smooth and seamless. Thank you so very much.

Bobby:

Yeah, thank you, Jane. It is always a bit stressful running up to the conference, but when I get here, I always feel like all the hard work has paid off. This last session is the one I enjoy the most because I hear all these wonderful comments from everyone about the things they have appreciated and are taking away with them. Thank you everybody.

Peter:

I want to add my comment of appreciation to Bobby. She is a remarkable young woman, and I have a lot of affection for her and for what she's doing. I'm going to be brief because I would like to give more time to Harold at the end. For you, Harold, it is a special conference, I think, so we will let you finish. As a Trustee and an ex-director of the Virginia Department of Corrections, you have a lot of interest in this. On my side, there is always a next step. I have a step that I need to take tomorrow. I will take that step, and the next one will appear, and the next, and the next. If we each have a part to play, a contribution to make, and we do it as we go forward, we'll be amazed at where we end up. It is just a matter of taking each step deliberately. Bill, would you like to come in next?

Bill:

I'll be brief and leave the last word for Harold. Transformational magic happens in special containers. This is one of them. If you're here, you can't really miss it.

I think the challenge is to figure out how to let it expand. There's a wonderful old environmental professor of mine called Kenneth Boulding. who said, *If it exists, it's possible.* You know it exists, it's obvious. So, it's possible. I think we have to figure out how to let it go further. Thank you all for having me here, Harold, over to you.

Harold:

Thanks, Bill. First, I want to say thanks to all of you for choosing to be a part of this conference. I've attended every one of the six conferences, and I've enjoyed every one of them. I walk away with more learning every time. They are a chance for us to come together, to talk together, to think together, to learn together and to be able to create new things together, new realities. That's what it's all about. That is the opportunity that dialogue presents to all of us, as you all know.

I retired about six and a half weeks ago from the Virginia Department of Corrections and I did not get a chance to say goodbye to the 13,000 staff in person, so I will take this opportunity to say goodbye to those of you who are on the screen now. Thank you for your loyalty. Thank you for your service to the department, which is actually your service to the people of the Commonwealth of Virginia, and a reminder that the work that you're doing is nothing less than noble. Continue to work as you have in the past. I know that new leadership always brings changes, but I'm sure that you're ready for it because we have been talking about change all along. One of those books that we all read together and talked about was about our iceberg melting. Remember to follow the steps that we were talking about in that book, and you will all be okay. Take good care. Thank you all. Thanks to Peter and Jane for including me, and of course Bobby is the superstar of the conference. And thanks to my proctor Bill Isaacs. As I told you earlier, these are the individuals who introduced me to dialogue back in the 1990s in Texas. Bill, thank you for getting me started on this journey, I appreciate it. Thanks to all of you.

Jane:

Thank you, everybody. Bobby is going to put on some music to play us out. The conference centre remains open for a week, so you can still message each other and read anything you like. There are links to the music, and some of the chats are being transposed into the conference centre. So, it is all yours for the next week.

Peter:

Thank you everybody, and until next time!

www.ingramcontent.com/pod-product-compliance
Lightning Source LLC
Chambersburg PA
CBHW041610260326
41914CB00012B/1445